KT-461-298

THE WORLD WAS MY LOBSTER

GEORGE COLE

MY AUTOBIOGRAPHY

THE WORLD WAS MY LOBSTER

GEORGE COLE

MY AUTOBIOGRAPHY

WITH BRIAN HAWKINS

JOHN BLAKE

Published by John Blake Publishing Ltd,
3 Bramber Court, 2 Bramber Road,
London W14 9PB, England

www.johnblakepublishing.co.uk

www.facebook.com/Johnblakepub   facebook

twitter.com/johnblakepub   twitter

This edition published in 2013

ISBN: 978 1 78219 469 9

792.092 |COL

All rights reserved. No part of this publication may be reproduced,
stored in a retrieval system, or in any form or by any means, without
the prior permission in writing of the publisher, nor be otherwise circulated
in any form of binding or cover other than that in which it is published
and without a similar condition including this condition being
imposed on the subsequent publisher.

British Library Cataloguing-in-Publication Data:

A catalogue record for this book is available from the British Library.

Design by www.envydesign.co.uk

Printed and bound in Great Britain by CPI Group (UK) Ltd

1 3 5 7 9 10 8 6 4 2

© Text copyright George Cole and Brian Hawkins

Papers used by John Blake Publishing are natural, recyclable products made
from wood grown in sustainable forests. The manufacturing processes
conform to the environmental regulations of the country of origin.

Every attempt has been made to contact the relevant copyright-holders,
but some were unobtainable. We would be grateful if the
appropriate people could contact us.

To the British Heart Foundation and to heart specialists
Mr Stephen Westaby and Dr Adrian Banning and the
Cardiac Team at the John Radcliffe Hospital, Oxford
without whom I would not have had another ten years
enjoying the world that was my lobster, and to my
wonderful wife Penny and our children Tara and
Toby who helped me through a worrying time.

CONTENTS

FOREWORD

Now that I've surprised myself and finished writing the main text of this book, it seems strange to start writing the words that go right at the front. It makes a lot of sense though because it's only after writing an autobiography that you fully realise who the important people are in your life.

One person of whom there was never any doubt of the importance she has in my life is my wife, Penny Morrell. She has remained steadfastly and lovingly by my side since our marriage in 1967, and she is the mother of our two wonderful children, Tara and Toby, and grandmother to our three delightful grandchildren. She selflessly put her own acting career on hold while our children were growing up to enable me to pursue my career, and that was something for which I can never thank her enough. There was a Mrs Cole before Penny but the marriage ended in a divorce that was heartbreaking for all concerned, especially for the two children that came from it. The circumstances are all very personal and private, and have no place in a book that sets out to chronicle the pride, joy and happiness with which I have been blessed throughout my more than 70 years in the acting profession. This will be the only mention of that marriage in this book.

There is much mention in the book of my good friend and mentor Alastair Sim and his wife Naomi. There is good reason for this. Many autobiographies talk at length about the author's parents and their contribution to the writer's life. In my case, for many years, as I was starting my career, Alastair and Naomi were my surrogate parents and I owe them an enormous debt of gratitude. They were wonderful people and are fully deserving of every kind word I have written about them.

There have been many other people over the years who deserve kind words and I would like to take this opportunity to mention them. I have acted in hundreds of roles throughout my career and have worked with thousands of talented people on stage, television and film, both in the public eye and behind the theatre curtains and cameras. I treasure all those experiences and value each and every contribution those people have made to my career. I offer my sincere thanks to everyone who has been a part of it.

There is another group of people who play a critical part in a performer's life and usually do not even realise it. This is the audience, whether watching a play in a theatre, or a film at their local cinema, or a play or drama series on television. No matter how good an actor's performance may be, it doesn't mean a thing unless there is someone there to watch it, and if people don't watch, the show is a failure. I have been fortunate throughout my career to have had more successes than failures, so I offer my heartfelt thanks to everyone who has watched my performances over the years and has contributed to those successes. Many people have even gone as far as to write to tell me what they think of my work. I always get great pleasure from receiving letters from fans and hearing their comments, and I am genuinely humbled that they have spent the time to contact me to pass on their thoughts. They can never know how much that contact has meant to me and I thank them with utmost sincerity.

I am indebted to Brian Hawkins for prompting me to recall long-forgotten incidents from the past and then helping me record them in a cohesive manner. My first contact with Brian was when he interviewed me in 2002 while he was preparing his amazing book *The Phenomenon That Was* Minder.* We kept in contact afterwards and he suggested to me a few times that we do this book together. I always refused on the grounds that I didn't think I was old enough for an autobiography. I still don't but I am delighted that I eventually gave in because I have enjoyed the process immensely.

I must also thank Henry Holland, Alan Coles, Grant Taylor and Matthew Lee plus their many contacts for so diligently tracking down copies of many of my film and television appearances that I have referred to in the pages that follow. Not only did they do a brilliant job, they are wonderful people as well. They made the writing much easier than it might otherwise have been.

I am grateful to John Blake and his staff at John Blake Publishing for all their help and for having sufficient confidence that I would have a story worth telling. As I write this, they haven't seen the finished manuscript, so I hope they are not disappointed. The title *The World Was My Lobster* is by kind permission of Crispin Cole (John Blake: please note that he has already been paid!).

Finally, I would like to thank everyone who takes the time to read this book – both those who read it from cover to cover and those

---

*Hawkins, B. (2002) Chameleon Press, Hong Kong.

who delve into it looking for an answer to a niggling question about a show I might or might not have been in. I am immensely honoured to be the subject of your interest and I hope to have provided you with some entertainment along the way.

George Cole
Oxfordshire
February 2013

CHAPTER 1

BOY WANTED

Britain in 1925 was slowly recovering from the devastation and heartaches of the First World War, which had ended seven years earlier. London saw the introduction of its first double-decker bus with a covered upper deck, and Scottish inventor John Logie Baird created Britain's first television transmitter in a primitive studio in London's Soho – an invention that would later figure prominently in my life. The first full-length movie film with recorded sound – another invention of great importance to me – would not be released for another two years, when *The Jazz Singer*, featuring Al Jolson, was released in October 1927. For their musical entertainment, people were listening to such classics as *Charleston*, *If You Knew Susie*, *Five Foot Two, Eyes of Blue* and *Yes Sir, That's My Baby* on their wind-up gramophones.

I arrived on 22 April 1925 at a nursing home at 19 Defoe Road in Tooting, a district in south-west London between Wimbledon and Streatham, and was given the names George Edward.

I lived for the first five years of my life in a flat in Coverton Road in Tooting with my parents, Florence and George Cole, a few streets away from Tooting Broadway. When I was five we moved to a council flat a couple of miles away in Morden and this remained the family home until my mother moved to the Midlands many years later after my father died.

I don't have many recollections of my early life. I have only two of Tooting. I can remember my father going out on a bicycle one day and getting the wheels stuck in a tramline and falling off. I also remember being put in a pram with a baby girl who had mumps when I was about four years old. I think the idea at the time was to expose children to infectious diseases as soon as possible and get them out of the way (the diseases, not the children). I can't remember whether I actually caught mumps as a result of the experiment. Somehow, I remember there was a pub just round the corner from the place I was born and, strangely, I went in it for the first time nearly 60 years later when we were shooting an episode of *Minder* there in the 1980s. My first flat was still there as well.

I have one recollection from Morden about a man that used to come round pulling a wheelbarrow asking for old clothes or shoes, and who would give you a toy in exchange. One day I swapped a brand new pair of shoes for a little toy windmill that was probably worth a couple of pennies. My mother came home and was absolutely furious about it. She went out and found him and gave him a right telling-off. She got the shoes back but I can't remember what happened to the windmill.

There were several people like that who used to come round exchanging things for old clothes. I remember one who gave you unmatched china cups and saucers. If you gave him a really big bundle, you might get a dinner plate. He used to ping it with his fingers before he gave it to you to show that it was sound and that there were no hidden cracks. Some of these rag-and-bone men, as they were called, would give you a goldfish in a little bag of water in exchange for the old clothes. We used that idea in a *Minder* episode 40 years later and discovered that, although Terry McCann was a tough hard nut, he could not stand touching fish.

We had another man coming round on a horse and cart selling fresh milk from a churn. You took your milk jug out to him and he would fill it from the churn. I can't imagine what the health-and-safety people would say about that today. Another man on a horse and cart came round on Sunday mornings selling shrimps and winkles by the pint; he would fill up a pint mug with shrimps or winkles and that would be your pint. There were countless mobile hawkers who used to travel around the streets peddling their wares. One was the hokey-cokey man, who sold coloured ice cream, and another was the muffin man, who used to sell small flat disks of yeast-leavened bread, which we still refer to as muffins, and would warm them up and flavour them with butter and jam. They were absolutely delicious. He used to come round with all his paraphernalia balanced on his head. People in his trade were the basis of the old children's song that asks if you have seen the muffin man who lives in Drury Lane. All these hawkers were highly colourful and entertaining characters in their own way and were a special part of London life at the time when I was growing up.

These days it's hard to imagine London without a lot of traffic but in those days there were far fewer motor vehicles on the roads and horses were still a common sight. Apart from the man with the milk churn, we used to have our bottled milk delivered by a man with a horse and cart. There were two main dairies in London: the United Dairy with its distinctive orange carts and the Express Dairy with its mauve carts. There was tremendous professional rivalry between them. As a child I was always fascinated by their beautiful shire horses. They towered above me but were as gentle as lambs. But without a doubt, my favourite sight was the brewers' drays that used to deliver beer barrels from the breweries to the public houses. The drays were flat carts without sides and were normally pulled by two shire horses that were always immaculately turned out, always wearing blinkers and driven by an attendant in a formal dark suit and wearing a bowler hat. The barrels would be carried two-high on the cart and the attendant would effortlessly manoeuvre them down a ramp at the back of the cart onto the pavement. From there they would be rolled down another ramp into the basement of the public house through a trapdoor in the pavement. I never tired of watching these deliveries.

I was an only child and I adored my parents. My father was an epileptic and suffered gas poisoning during the First World War. On top of that, he had a double hernia. He was never a well man after the war. He had several jobs but none of them lasted long because of his health. On one occasion, he was out of work for a long time and was having problems finding the rent, so the council found him a job – pulling a heavy roller. To this day, I am convinced that the physical exertion from pulling the roller contributed in some way to his early death. My mother worked long hours as an office cleaner, so I became independent at an early age. But, despite spending a lot of time on my own, I didn't waste it. My parents instilled in me the value of an education, an opportunity that they never had. I read a lot and always had a healthy thirst for knowledge.

I don't have any memories of my primary school days but I do remember my secondary school. It was the Surrey County Council Secondary School in Morden. I was a fairly good student and was always in the top three in my class, although more often than not I was either second or third – there was a terrific swot in the class who usually took first place. But I managed to win a couple of book prizes that made up for it. I don't think I read either of them.

I had some memorable and helpful teachers. One I have never forgotten was Bob Charman. He was the French teacher but also played the piano and produced all the school plays and shows. I remember one of the shows in particular because it had a clever title: *Columbus in a Merry Key*.

I always had a part in the school plays and I usually did a piece in the end-of-term school concerts but I remember getting into trouble one year when I did George Formby's song *When I'm Cleaning Windows*. He was a popular comedian with a strong Lancastrian accent who used to sing comic songs and accompany himself on the ukulele. These days his lyrics sound relatively tame but in those days they were regarded as quite saucy. I remember being called into the headmaster's study one day and being told in no uncertain terms that such songs were not suitable for a school concert and certainly not what a 13-year-old should be singing.

In my own defence, I have to say that I didn't consciously try to copy George Formby. I heard the song and thought it sounded catchy, so I learned it and thought I would give it a try at the concert. I couldn't believe that people would not like it.

The other teacher I've never forgotten was Mr Halliday, our form master. We especially liked him because he was always perfectly fair towards us. On one occasion, we were doing something about how to calculate areas. At the end of the day I was the first one to take my book out to him to be marked and I'd made a small mistake. He said, 'If it wasn't for the fact that I know your mother is waiting for you outside the school gate, I would make you do it again.'

I said, 'Sorry, Sir. But actually, she isn't.'

'Isn't what?'

'Isn't waiting outside the school gate.'

'Well, in that case you can go back to your place and do it again.'

Of course, because he was a teacher, we all somehow felt that he inhabited a different world from ours. Then one day I saw him on the Tube carrying a baby and that convinced me that he really was a normal human being like us after all.

Some of the teachers were terrible and completely unable to maintain discipline in the class but we had a pretty tough headmaster, Mr W. J. Roberts, who was very free with the cane. He was also very bald and we called him 'Eggy' behind his back, but none of the students would dare step out of line while he was around. Whenever there was any trouble, he would come in and sit at the back of the class and that was certainly very effective.

By now, we had moved to the new council estate in Morden. In their spare time my mother played the piano and my father played the drums, and we used to do comic songs together at British Legion concerts in the local community hall. George Formby having been banished from my repertoire, I had to learn some new material. I remember learning one that I heard from a well-loved Jewish music-hall comedian named Issy Bonn. I think he called it 'Oy, Oy'. The audience loved it and always had a good laugh when I sang it in Issy Bonn's style. I was paid in chocolates! I think that was when I decided I wanted to go on the stage. I don't think I had any particular ambition to become a serious actor; I just wanted to sing comic songs.

I was always something of an inquisitive child and, when I was 13, I became impatient to know what Christmas presents I was going to get. I climbed up to look for them on top of a wardrobe in my mother's bedroom and was shocked to discover an envelope containing a letter saying I had been adopted by the Cole family

6

when I was ten days old, and that arrangements had been made for a certain amount of money to be paid to them once a month. I had no idea. There was no National Adoption Society in 1925. This did not appear until the following year and so the adoption was a private arrangement. It could have been arranged anywhere, even in a pub for all anyone knows, but was perfectly legal.

I've never had a birth certificate. As far as I know, there has never been one and I suspect that my birth was never registered. Many years later, when I needed a passport, I think I had to make some sort of legal declaration that 'George Edward Cole' was the name I always went under, and I used some of my theatre programmes and my RAF demob papers to support it. But I couldn't tell anyone my real surname at birth because I never knew it.

According to that well-known fountain of wisdom Rumour Hassit, I was the result of a liaison between a hotel manager and his youngest employee. I don't know how much credence to attach to that because I never knew them. In later years, I spent a lot of time at Somerset House trying to track down a birth certificate, but I never found one and I'm now pretty convinced that there never was one. Whenever I need to prove who I am these days, I just send a copy of the photo page of my passport.

Naturally, I was curious about my birth parents but the adoption was never an issue. I cried buckets when I first found the letters, but perhaps some of those tears were because I also discovered that I wasn't getting the magic set I was hoping for at Christmas. However, I loved my adoptive parents; they treated me wonderfully and I had a tremendous childhood. As far as I was concerned, they were my parents. I asked my mother about the adoption when I found the letter and she told me the truth. There was no big drama about it but she was anxious that I should not tell anyone else. She never told me why she wanted it kept a secret. Looking back, I was surprised she was not proud of the fact that she had given an unwanted child a home. She simply said, 'Please don't tell anyone you are adopted.' In fact, she asked me to promise that I wouldn't. And I didn't, except for a few close friends, until after she died. What was even more odd was that when I married Penny, my mother said, 'You won't tell Penny you're adopted, will you?' I thought, 'Well, what do I do? Do I say, "Of course I won't," and then tell her anyway?' On the other hand, I think it would have upset my mother if I had said, 'Why not?' So I didn't commit myself either way.

Over the years, I've developed a theory as to why she was so secretive about the adoption. I suspect that she couldn't have children of her own and that she knew her family would have a certain attitude towards adoption. It was probably easy for her to convince her family that she was having a baby. The family lived a long way away and they didn't see each other often. The fact that I was adopted at ten days made it reasonable for her relatives to assume that the baby was hers if they happened to see each other subsequently, but I suspect that somehow the family must have found out about the adoption. Once they knew about it, I think it was firstly because of the adoption and secondly because I was illegitimate that my mother's family didn't want anything to do with me.

The reason I think this is because when I was a young child, I learned that my grandfather lived in Wimbledon and I walked about five miles to his house to see him. When I got there, I knocked on the door and I suppose it would have been my grandmother who answered. She said, 'What do you want?'

I said, 'I've come to see how my grandfather is.'

She replied, 'He's fine,' and shut the door in my face.

But how they found out I was adopted I'll never know.

While I was at school, there was no compulsory education after the age of 14. Those children whose parents could afford it had the option of staying longer at school but, in places like middle-class Morden, most youngsters left school as soon as they reached 14 so they could go out to work and supplement the family income.

In April 1939, I was one of the boys who left school at 14. In fact, I had won a scholarship to go to a private school when I reached 14 so the school fees would not have been that much of a problem for my parents. But, for one thing, I didn't want to go to a posh school where you had to wear a uniform and, even if I did, I doubt if my parents could have afforded to buy one.

On the Friday I left school, all the boys who were leaving that day had to queue up outside the headmaster's study and then go in to meet the man from the Board of Trade. You would tell him what job you wanted to do and he would try to find one that suited you. When it came to my turn, he asked me what I wanted to do. I said, 'Please, Sir, I want to go on the stage.' The headmaster sent me back to the end of the queue. When I got to the front again, the Board of Trade man asked me the same question and I gave him the same answer. He told me to go to Kay's, the butcher by Morden station, the following Monday morning to become a delivery boy.

There weren't a lot of jobs around for 14-year-old boys and most of those lucky enough to find a job earned just a few shillings a week as 'the boy' doing menial jobs like sweeping up, making the tea and running general errands. For me, it seemed that I was destined to become a butcher's delivery boy. At least there was just a chance that I could learn something of the butchery trade along the way.

I used to have a few part-time jobs at the time. I did an early-morning newspaper round, an evening paper round and, at weekends, a milk round. Every weekend, with my earnings, I would buy my mother a big slab of chocolate and my father a packet of ten Player's Weights cigarettes, and I'd save the rest.

In those days, the London evening newspapers were the *Star*, the *Evening News* and the *Evening Standard*, and I always tried to read them from cover to cover. In an amazing stroke of serendipity, I happened to see a small advert in the *Star* on the day I left school saying 'small boy wanted for London musical' and it gave the address of the Helvetia Club just off Shaftesbury Avenue in Soho in the middle of London.

Without having any idea what to expect, I went along to the audition on the Saturday morning. When I arrived, I thought I was in heaven because I was surrounded by all these beautiful and scantily clad chorus girls. I decided there and then that I liked show business. When the person in charge asked me to perform something, the only thing I could think of on the spur of the moment was the famous speech by Mark Antony in *Julius Caesar* that I had learned in school – 'Friends, Romans, countrymen, lend me your ears,' – and I did it in my dreadful cockney accent. I was bad.

I must have done something right though because, although I didn't get the part that I auditioned for, they asked me to be the understudy. It was for the musical comedy *The White Horse Inn*. The only problem was that I had to go to Blackpool immediately that day. I told my parents about the audition before I went but I think it went in one ear and out the other. I had no idea that I would have to go away the same day. The only way I could let them know was to send them a telegram. I wrote, 'Have gone on the stage, will write.' It was nine words for sixpence. I would have made sure that I used up all my words but I can't remember what the other two were. Maybe they were just 'Love George'. That afternoon I was on a train to Blackpool, where the show was starting at the Grand

Theatre. On the way, I bought a toothbrush and two sticks of stage make-up, which I still have, from Woolworth's.

I often hear people say that my parents must have been wonderful to allow me to go off by myself at such a young age. And then I start to think, 'But why didn't they come looking for me? Why didn't they call the police? Perhaps they were bloody terrible parents!' It was six months before I saw them again! In order to be fair to the organisers of the show, they did tell me before I left that the mother of the boy I was understudying would look after me, so I knew I wouldn't be completely on my own.

People sometimes jump to the conclusion that I ran off when I left school because I couldn't stand living at home with my adoptive parents. Nothing could be further from the truth. I loved living in that house and I loved my mother and father very much. I left because I saw an opportunity to do what I wanted to do; to go on the stage. Who could ever believe that that one opportunity would determine the course of the rest of my life?

I suppose my parents were rather hoping I would take the job at the butcher's shop in Morden because it would have been another wage coming in. However, I sent them a five-shilling postal order every week out of my wages and it always came back as a parcel of sweets and cake and things like that, so I think they were fairly happy about it.

The White Horse Inn, the show I was about to join in Blackpool in 1939, originally opened at the London Coliseum in 1931 as its first large-scale musical after years as a variety theatre. The original show was a huge production costing more than £60,000 to stage. This was an enormous amount for a show in those days but the show became extremely successful and ran for 651 performances at the Coliseum. The story is set in an inn in a picturesque region of Austria. The headwaiter at the inn is secretly in love with the inn's owner, a young woman who is herself secretly in love with one of her regular guests.

After its success in London in 1931, the show was revived in 1939 but by that time it was generally believed that the country would soon be at war with Germany. The distribution of gas masks to every man, woman and child in the country in September 1938 to protect against airborne gas attacks by the enemy did little to dispel those beliefs. Because of the strong likelihood of war, the organisers made the decision to take the show on tour rather than stage it in London, as it was thought that the city would be one of the first targets of an enemy attack, and I joined the tour's debut in Blackpool.

When I opened in the show, I felt that I would have been happy to stay in it for the rest of my life. It was a glorious feeling. There was one scene where I had to go across the stage dressed in those traditional Austrian leather shorts called *lederhosen*, accompanied by two goats and six pigeons, and I shared a dressing room with them while I was not on stage. The scene went flawlessly every night, until we were reaching the end of the run. Then one night, one of the goats decided he wanted to become a little more friendly with me. He started nibbling at my leather shorts and finally started to nuzzle his way inside them. I had no idea what to do and finally thought it best to let him make up his own mind. The audience loved it and it brought the house down. When I came off stage, a popular comedian at the time, Jack Barty, who was in the show, was standing in the wings and said, 'Son, you were great. You've just learned the first rule of comedy: "Abandon!"' At the time, the term 'abandon' was popularly used to convey the idea that would be expressed today as 'Go for it!' or 'Don't hold back!'

We took the show to many towns around the country and I loved every minute of it. However, while we were playing in Aberdeen I received the terrible news that my father had died. I was devastated.

I suppose that if I had been older, I might have expected it, but I had no idea that it was even a possibility and it came as a terrible shock. I was told that he died of lung cancer but I have long held the view that his body was just too weak to handle the gruelling physical demands of his work pulling that heavy roller for the local council. I received the news just as we were about to go on stage for a matinee and I just had to soldier on as if nothing had happened. Strangely, I heard about my mother's death just as I was about to start a matinee many years later. In neither case was it easy.

The original plan was for the show to go to London after its tour but, because the outbreak of war was still imminent, it was not considered safe to go there. Instead they made the decision to take it to Dublin and Cork in Ireland. And it was from a wireless set in a boarding house in Dublin that I heard the announcement that war had been declared.

CHAPTER 2

WAR YEARS

B ritain's formal involvement in the Second World War began on 3 September 1939, a time when *The White Horse Inn* was enjoying great success in Ireland. The beauty and romance of the show, set in picturesque Austria, somehow acted as a morale booster for the people who saw it, because Austria had been annexed into Nazi Germany in 1938 and was now under Nazi control. Not many people in Britain believed that the war would be much more than a passing nuisance but, in fact, it was the beginning of what was to become a hugely depressing period in the nation's history.

Strangely, the Second World War had a significant effect on my later career but I can clearly remember the announcement by Prime Minister Neville Chamberlain at 11.15 a.m. that morning, as we sat around the wireless set, that the German government had not responded to the British demand for German troops to withdraw from Poland and that, 'consequently, this country is at war with Germany'. This was shocking news and hard for a 14-year-old to comprehend.

What made it more frightening was that Chamberlain's announcement was made while we were in Dublin, 300 miles from my home in London, staying in a boarding house opposite the Labour Exchange. There was tremendous antipathy among the Irish towards the British at the time. We had eight Tyrolean dancers in the show and whenever they came on, or whenever there was anything in the show that was remotely anti-British, the Irish audiences would applaud wildly. Their political sentiments were not concealed at all. In the theatre it was strangely amusing but, as the announcement came through on the wireless, a rowdy group of marchers came down the street carrying an effigy of Prime Minister Chamberlain and chanting anti-British slogans. They stopped outside the Labour Exchange and noisily set fire to the effigy. I peeped out from behind the boarding-house curtains and had never seen anything like that before. To say that it was frightening would be an understatement.

I think the production company had hoped to get the show back into London after its run in Ireland but the theatres in the West End had all closed down when war broke out. When the tour finished, I was offered one of the strangest roles of my career, playing a hyena in the children's play *Where the Rainbow Ends* at the Holborn Empire for six weeks over the 1939 Christmas season. Jack Watling played St George. However, when nothing much seemed to be happening in the war, the theatres in London gradually started to reopen and in 1940 I returned for the opening of *The White Horse Inn* at the London Coliseum, where it became an enormous success. The show was huge by any standard. The advertising posters announced that it had 'an orchestra and cast totalling over a hundred'. One of its stars was Gretchen Franklin, who became well known to television viewers many years later when she played Ethel Skinner in the BBC's *EastEnders*. She died in 2005, a few days after her 94th birthday, after more than 80 years in show business.

I got 28 shillings and sixpence a week for my wages from *The White Horse Inn*, which is about £1.40 in today's money. My lodgings cost a pound and I sent home 5 shillings (25p), so I had the equivalent of about 15p for myself, but I also had the money I had saved from my newspaper rounds. I could not have been happier. I thought I was the luckiest 15-year-old in the country to have a job like that.

I was still the understudy when *The White Horse Inn* arrived in London and I was still sharing a dressing room with the goats and pigeons. My chaperone was still the mother of the boy I was understudying. One day she said to me, 'I'm taking Charles to audition for a play tomorrow. There might be a few famous people there so, if you promise to keep out of the way, you can come and watch if you like.'

The following day I went along with them to what used to be known as the Strand Theatre. There was no scenery – it was just a bare stage and there were around six young boys of my age sitting on the stage with their legs dangling over the front into the orchestra pit. Not wanting to get in the way, I stood quietly by the swing doors at the back of the stage that led to the dressing rooms. Sitting down in the stalls was a rather gruff man who turned out to be the director, Richard Bird.

He must have had a bad day because he was in a terrible temper. He suddenly started shouting at me, 'Don't just stand there boy, come down here, don't waste my time.' I tried to explain that I wasn't there for the audition but he wouldn't listen. With an impatient, 'Come on, come on,' he thrust a script into my hand and told me to read from it.

The part was that of a cockney evacuee and the accent came naturally to me. To cut a short story shorter, I got the part. The play was called *Cottage to Let* by Geoffrey Kerr. It was billed as the first British spy thriller of the war and was shortly to have its debut at Wyndham's Theatre in London.

Richard Bird told me that I would need to go to Oxford that afternoon for rehearsals. It was like déjà vu. I wasn't expecting to be auditioned and it never occurred to me to tell anyone at the Coliseum that I was going to the audition, let alone that I wouldn't be coming in for the matinee. I've been wondering ever since what happened to the goats and pigeons that day.

It was a Sunday and I arrived in Oxford quite late. I was just a small boy lugging my big suitcase around and I had to find somewhere to stay. I'd never had to worry about accommodation previously; the chaperone had always looked after such things. I walked all round Oxford and even tried the police station but to no avail. Eventually, I made my way to the theatre and was almost in tears by the time I got there.

I found the stage director and managed to blurt out my story. As I was telling him, a handsome young man came in and asked what the problem was. It turned out that he was the juvenile lead. Jerry Clifton, the stage director, explained the problem to him. Between them they worked out that Jerry would go and find somewhere for me to stay and the young man would take me across the road to the Welsh Pony pub for something to eat.

He ordered two mixed grills, tipped them both onto one plate and said, 'Get that inside you.' Remember that wartime food rationing was already in effect and this would have required several of his ration coupons. I didn't see him after that because apparently he had just been called up. Thirty years later I was sitting in the MGM studios at Elstree and a handsome middle-aged man walked across and said, 'Is that the young boy I gave two mixed grills to?' It was Stewart Granger. How he recognised me I'll never know because I was made up as an old man. I can only imagine that someone told him I was there.

Somehow, Jerry managed to find some accommodation for me and the next morning I started work on *Cottage to Let*. It was then, in 1940, that I first had the privilege of meeting someone who was to have an extraordinary influence on my life.

Alastair George Bell Sim was born on 9 October 1900 in Edinburgh to a Scottish tailor of modest means and his wife, a fellow Scot, who was born on the island of Eigg in the Inner Hebrides and could speak only Gaelic when she first arrived in Edinburgh. Alastair did his primary education at Bruntsfield Primary School and later moved to the prestigious James Gillespie's High School in Edinburgh, for which his father had obtained a contract to supply the school uniform and had become a school governor. However, his father made it clear to the headmaster that he did not expect any special treatment for Alastair and that he should be beaten like anyone else if his behaviour deemed it necessary. He left school at the age of 14 and, among other jobs, worked as a messenger boy in his father's shop. He used to tell the story of how his father once instructed him to deliver a suit to one of his influential customers at a specified time. On the way to make the delivery, he saw some of his friends playing cricket and stopped off to join them. When he remembered the package, it was well after the appointed time and he was unable to deliver it. His father was livid at the loss of his valued customer and would frequently declare, 'Mark my words, that boy will end up on the gallows.' That does seem a rather severe punishment for failing to deliver a suit on time, so we can only take wild guesses at what other misdemeanours Alastair may have committed as a boy.

He must have had some further education after leaving school at 14 because by the time he was 18 he was studying to become an analytical chemist at the University of Edinburgh. He was called up for his national service in the Officer Training Corps but detested military life, particularly the discipline, and could not leave fast enough. He had a variety of other jobs after he left but felt that he might be well suited for a career in speech and elocution. This was an ideal direction for him as he was gifted with an extraordinarily mellifluous voice that eventually led him back to the University of Edinburgh, where he was appointed to the post of the Fulton Lectureship in Elocution at New College from 1925 until 1930. Among his many duties, he lectured to groups of parsons, teaching them how not to sound like parsons when they spoke. In later years he was elected to the position of Rector of the University of Edinburgh, a post he held from 1948 to 1951.

It was while he was teaching elocution and drama in Edinburgh that Alastair first met his future wife Naomi Plaskitt, who at that point was just 12 years of age, 14 years junior to his 26. He was playing the part of a priest in an amateur production of the play *The Land of Heart's Desire* by W. B. Yeats and she was one of his co-stars. Naomi recalled many years later that when she first saw him, he looked to her as if he were at least 40 years old. They married when she reached 18.

Alastair was a natural performer but his big ambition was to become a director. He spoke to many people in the profession and soon discovered that the only way to get into directing was to become established on the stage. As a result, he moved to London with Naomi in 1930 and secured a part as the Messenger in a run of *Othello* with Paul Robeson in the title role. His first film appearance was in 1935 in an uncredited part in a murder thriller entitled *The Case of Gabriel Perry*, which was directed by Albert de

Courville. He went on to appear in more than 60 films and 46 West End productions.

As well as being a born actor, he was a natural comic. He soon found that, whatever role he was playing, the audience's attention somehow seemed to become directed towards him because there was something strangely comic about him and the audience somehow expected him to be amusing. Many of his most memorable performances on stage and screen after that were comic roles. He was a big man, standing just under six feet tall, with a larger-than-life personality. He had the most amazing talent for making people laugh without saying anything inherently funny. Perhaps it was a small, almost imperceptible, facial gesture, or a slightly unexpected inflection as he spoke, but he just had this certain air about him. And then he could switch flawlessly to Shakespearean elegance.

The great Tommy Cooper had a similar comic talent 20 years later. He could have an audience in hysterics before he even came on stage by saying into an off-stage microphone something quite unfunny, like, 'Is there anyone outside? It's pitch dark in here.' There was something uniquely humorous about his delivery. But I don't think Tommy ever did any serious Shakespeare.

The first time I ever saw Alastair perform was in 1938 when I was about 13 and he was playing the genie in a film I was watching at the Gaumont cinema in Morden called *Alf's Button Afloat*, featuring the Crazy Gang. I was so fascinated by him that I remember staying to watch the end credits to see what his name was. Never could I have imagined that within a couple of years I would be working with him. When I did, he came across exactly the way I imagined him to be: benign, avuncular and extremely funny.

In *Cottage to Let*, I played a cocky and precocious young teenager named Ronald who has aspirations of becoming another Sherlock

21

Holmes. Alastair's wife wrote about me in her autobiography *Dance and Skylark: Fifty years with Alastair Sim*, saying that, although I was fifteen at the time, I 'could easily have passed for eleven'! I don't remember looking that young but Naomi was probably a better (and less biased) judge than I was. My character Ronald had been evacuated to an estate in the Scottish countryside to avoid the aerial bombing raids in London during the Second World War and was under the care of a rather scatter-brained upper-class woman named Mrs Barrington (played by Gillian Lind). Ronald finds himself living in a cottage on the estate where there is another lodger, a bumbling Scotsman called Charles Dimble (played by Alastair), who irritates everyone with his inquisitive behaviour. Leslie Banks played Mrs Barrington's husband, a brilliant but socially inept inventor who is currently working on a bombsight for the RAF. The bombsight is an important part of the story and leads to a kidnap and the appearance of spies and secret agents and people who are not what they seem at first sight. I was fortunate enough to play the person who uncovers the identity of the villain and it always got a good reaction from the audience.

This was my first professional play and it far exceeded any expectations I may have had of what acting was all about. The idea that, barely a year out of school, I could go on stage, swear, make people laugh and then get paid for it was something I found highly appealing.

The play had a successful run at Wyndham's Theatre in London for nine months to packed houses and then the Blitz came and all the London theatres closed down. It was a crazy time at Wyndham's when the Blitz started. Instead of going into our air-raid shelter during the raids, we all went up on the roof to watch what was happening! But then they closed the theatre and we took the play on the road to the Prince of Wales Theatre in Birmingham, to the

Midlands and Scotland and then around the army camps to entertain the troops during 1940 and 1941.

One of the theatres we played in was the Opera House in Leicester, where we did a one-week run in December 1940. As a sign of how times have changed, they had a full orchestra playing light music during the interval. The programme had a telling announcement on the back page:

In the event of an air raid warning, the electric sign at the side of the Proscenium will show 'Raid Alert' for a minute. When the 'All Clear' is given, this will also be shown. Anyone who desires to leave the theatre may do so but the performance will continue and members are advised to remain in the building. Don't panic – keep calm.

Strangely, the war seemed to have quietened down by the time we finished the tour and the theatres slowly started to reopen. We went back to Wyndham's and the show ran for another nine months.

I remember feeling scared only twice during the war. The first time was while we were doing the play in Cardiff. There was one scene where I had to climb into a blanket box on stage during the interval and stay there until my cue, when I would jump out of the box and surprise everyone. On one particular night, a bomb dropped close to the theatre while I was in the box. My heart started pounding and I had to choose whether to jump out of the box and run for cover or keep my cool like the old trouper I was hoping to become. I stayed in the box.

The other time I felt scared was when the V-bombs started falling. I was home on leave from the RAF and I went down to see my mother, who at that time was living in Streatham in south London. I caught the Tube to Tooting Broadway and started to walk the length of Southcroft Road to my mother's flat, which was right at the end. Suddenly an ARP warden appeared from nowhere shouting, 'Get down, get down!' Before I had a chance to ask why, he threw me down in the middle of the road, face down, and then vanished. I lay there for a moment, listening to the throb of the buzz bomb. Then I listened more closely. I had lived in the area long enough and heard enough buzz bombs to know that this was not the usual sound of a buzz bomb. My heart was racing faster than I had ever known before as I waited for whatever was dropping to hit the ground. I looked up and realised that the sound was the throb of a number 8 tram coming straight towards me with no lights on. I leaped to my feet and ran off. There was no sign of the ARP warden.

When the *Cottage to Let* tour finished in 1941, Anatole de Grunwald and J. O. C. Orton adapted the story into a film version directed by Anthony Asquith. He was a brilliantly astute director. His father, Herbert Henry Asquith, was the British Prime Minister from 1908 to 1916. The film kept the title *Cottage to Let* in Britain and was released as *Bombsight Stolen* in the USA, where it had a highly successful run. Once again, I had the good fortune to be a part of it, along with Alastair and Leslie Banks in their previous roles. Jeanne de Casalis played Mrs Barrington. Jeanne was popular at the time in a variety act in which she portrayed a scatter-brained cleaner named Mrs Feather, and was ideally suited to play the similarly scatty Mrs Barrington in the film. John Mills played a Spitfire pilot who parachutes into a nearby loch and becomes a patient at the newly opened military hospital on the estate where the cottage is located. Michael Wilding played Mr Barrington's assistant.

We shot the film at Gainsborough Studios in Lime Grove, Shepherd's Bush. It was just as mad there as it was at Wyndham's. We all slept in the studios but whenever there was an air raid, we went up to the roof to watch. It was total madness. In those days,

24

you could see right across to the East End of London from the roof of the studio in Shepherd's Bush and it was completely ablaze. There was this eerie orange glow across it and a smell in the air that I've never forgotten.

The experience of working with seasoned professionals such as Alastair, Leslie and Jeanne de Casalis had a profound effect on me, especially the way Alastair could convincingly change his character in a split second from a humorous bumbling Scotsman to a seemingly sinister Nazi.

Curiously, the process of wartime evacuation that took my character Ronald to the cottage to let began to play an important role in my life and in my relationship with Alastair. Before the declaration of war, when hostilities seemed imminent, the government set up an evacuation scheme to move civilians, particularly children, from urban areas at high risk of aerial raids to rural areas where the risk was much lower. Millions of people in Britain were 'evacuated' during the course of the war. It's a strange word, 'evacuate'. I think I first heard it at school in a science lesson. Even today, I still think it sounds as if people were having all the air taken out of them.

Initially, Alastair and his wife Naomi invited me to go and spend a weekend with them at their cottage in the Oxfordshire countryside. I call it *a* cottage but, in fact, it was three cottages joined together, with water coming from a well in the garden. It was all highly enjoyable but it was my first real experience of country life and I found it entirely different from what I had grown up with in Tooting and Morden. Nevertheless, I accepted their offer to spend another weekend with them and then another, and then the war started and I became their formal evacuee.

By then I was a 16-year-old boy with a widowed mother living by herself in Morden just a few miles from central London, definitely at high risk of bombing. Alastair and Naomi also lived in London and when Naomi became pregnant, Alastair arranged for her to be evacuated to the country. They suggested that my mother should also go out to the country and arranged somewhere close to where they lived. Not long afterwards, Naomi gave birth to their only child, a daughter they named Merlith.

Like a lot of adults who were evacuated, my mother couldn't stand the country and missed her friends and the familiarity of life back home so, when the Blitz settled down, she decided to go back to London. This was around the time we were touring the army camps, and Alastair became a sort of father figure for me. He also had this wealth of acting experience and a career as an elocution and drama lecturer behind him. I suppose that, because I admired him so much as an actor, some of that craft must have rubbed off on me without my even knowing about it.

A lot of people ask whether Alastair and Naomi adopted me. The answer is 'no'. I always joke that I adopted them – and they spent the next 50 years trying to get rid of me, a task that was not made any easier by the fact that by then I had built a house next door to theirs! When we had houses next to each other, Naomi would always be dropping in for one reason or another. Eventually, we said, 'Why keep walking out of your front gate into ours? Why don't we have a gate in the adjoining fence?' So we built one and called it 'Naomi's Gate'.

Much of the lighting and heating in Alastair and Naomi's house in the country came from paraffin lamps. One of my tasks while I was living with them was the daily filling, cleaning and wick trimming of all the oil lamps spread throughout the house. This was always a time-consuming process and one that didn't particularly appeal to me, although Naomi recalls in her autobiography that I always did it with good humour. She also recalled that her baby daughter's room was heated by a coal stove and that one of my duties was to fill up the coal scuttle downstairs and carry it up to the bedroom. I would announce my presence outside the door with a shout of 'Cole's coal service', which invariably sounded to her like 'Cowl's cowl service'.

I was fortunate that Alastair took me on as a sort of protégé in the way he did. One thing he did want to change from the outset was my broad cockney accent. It was fine in the play because it suited the character I was playing. But when I moved on to the film, I had to make a determined effort to lighten the accent because the film would also be released in America and the audience over there would have had great difficulty understanding me. I think it would have been Anthony Asquith, the director, who pushed for this.

It was round about this time that I remember telling my mother that people had been commenting on my strong cockney accent. She said in her own inimitable way, 'Bloody cheek! What cockney accent?' In later years, she thought it was rather odd that I was speaking so differently.

Alastair and Naomi couldn't stand the accent at all. They were emphatic that, if I wanted to get on in the acting profession, I would have to lose it. I would try to tell them a funny story but whenever I got to the punch line, they would put their hands over their ears. When I asked them why they were doing it, they said, 'Because we can't stand your vowel sounds.' So it was a question of doing something about the vowel sounds or not getting on as an actor. I managed to lose it but, thankfully, I can bring it back when the part needs it.

I remember that Alastair gave me a speech to learn from George Bernard Shaw's *Caesar and Cleopatra*. He told me to go away and look at it carefully and then, when I thought I was ready, to come back and let him hear it. It starts, 'Hail, Sphinx: salutation from

Julius Caesar.' After a bit of practice I went and started reading it to him. I got about halfway down the page when he stopped me and said, 'You sound as if you're having a quiet pee against the Sphinx, not bringing salutations to it!' But he and Naomi were good in that, although they wouldn't let me off the hook, they weren't hurtful in any way. And they always managed to turn things into a joke.

Another question people often ask is what did Alastair actually teach me. It's difficult to define what you've learned from someone you are that close to over a long period. It's like asking what you learned from your parents. In reality, learning is an ongoing process and you are assimilating things all the time. For some of the time I was living with them, Naomi's mother was also living in the house. I do remember that one thing she instilled in me was the practice of looking something up in a book if I didn't understand it, and she taught me how to go about it. I have been forever grateful to her for that and I have made a point of teaching my own children to do the same.

Another thing I can remember is the way Alastair and Naomi tried to teach me how to think laterally. We were on a walk somewhere, Alastair, Naomi and me, and they told me to go and stand in front of a particular tree. When I got there, they said, 'That's not the front, it's the back.' So I moved and they said, 'It's still not the front.' Eventually, they said, 'You're not too good at trees. Let's try it again when we get back with a golf ball.' We did this and I realised that even a golf ball has a front and a back – depending on which direction you are looking from. The front to one person might easily be the back to another. And that was all they were trying to teach me. I hadn't even thought of that until they pointed it out. At the time, it was enormously frustrating for me but, in retrospect, it was a good way of getting me to think about things and not take everything for granted. He had this tremendous passion for teaching, especially to young people entering the acting profession.

I did around eight films and eight plays with Alastair over the years, more if you count the ones he directed but did not appear in. In addition, we took some of them onto television. He was a tremendous influence on my career. But, contrary to what many people believe, he never formally coached me as an actor in the way a student might be coached at drama school. It was just that, by being so close to him over such a long period, I was able to observe him as he executed his profession and I gradually assimilated what I saw. When we worked together on a scene, he would certainly suggest ways of doing things differently to improve it but this is what experienced actors do all the time when they are working with less experienced people, so I would never describe it as formal coaching. I think one of his great talents was his ability to pass on his wisdom in a subtle, almost imperceptible, way. I never thought that he was preaching and, because of that, I never realised, until much later, that he was teaching me at all. And when I did realise, it became apparent just how much I had picked up from him.

I did another 'evacuation' film in 1942 called *Those Kids from Town*, directed by Lance Comfort. This was another comedy drama made for wartime propaganda purposes, telling the story of a group of children evacuated from London to the country and how they interact with the local community. I played Charlie, one of the evacuees. I was 16 by then and could still just about get away with playing juvenile roles. The talented Harry Fowler played another of the children; this was his first film and he was 15. At some point in the film, there is a reference to the poem *The Burial of Sir John Moore after Corunna* by Charles Wolfe, which contains the line 'the sods with our bayonets turning', referring to the sods of earth. Harry, reflecting his tender years, was fascinated beyond belief that people were allowed to write poems containing the word 'sods'. I can't remember how much I got for the film but Harry wrote somewhere that he was paid £5 a day. Also in the cast was Ronald Shiner, who already had a long catalogue of films to his credit and played in countless more comedies over the next two decades until he died in 1966 aged 63. He had amazing talent.

In 1942, for the first time, I played on stage in a role in which there could be no hint of a cockney accent. I had to work hard at it but eventually managed to sound convincing and was suitably pleased that all the work was beginning to pay off. It was for the tour of a comedy entitled *Old Master* by a Canadian actor named Alexander Knox. The story was of a painter who fakes his death and reappears in disguise so he can attend an exhibition of his own work. Sadly, after much hard work, the play lasted only five weeks.

The next play was considerably more successful. This was Terence Rattigan's play *Flare Path*, which opened at the Apollo Theatre in London on 13 August 1942. My part in the play was relatively minor but was still good experience for a 17-year-old. The play is a weepie set near an RAF Bomber Command airbase and tells of a love triangle between a young pilot, Teddy Graham (played by Jack Watling), his wife (Phyllis Calvert) and a film star (played by Martin Walker) with whom Teddy Graham's wife is secretly in love. The title of the play referred to the high-visibility and often short-lived lights used to mark the edges of aircraft landing strips at night or in poor visibility. Terence Rattigan, the play's writer, based parts of the story on his own experiences as a tail gunner in RAF Coastal Command; he was still serving in the RAF throughout the play's run in London. Because of the RAF connection, the play often attracted some of the military's top brass into the audience, including even Prime Minister Winston Churchill, who dropped in one evening accompanied by a whole party of them. Terence was given special leave to attend the performance. I remember him standing rigidly to attention during the official introductions as a succession of senior RAF officers told him how he should have written it. Interestingly, the play recently had a successful revival at the Theatre Royal, Haymarket to celebrate Terence Rattigan's centenary year in 2011.

Over the end of 1942 and beginning of 1943 I played a child named Percy King in J. B. Priestley's comedy *Good Night Children* at the New Theatre in London (which is now the Noel Coward Theatre). The play was about life in a broadcasting studio and the conflict between performing artists and the bureaucracy imposed by the administrators. This was yet another story involving evacuees.

As a young teenage actor, I was hungry to play in anything that came my way, even if I did not get a credit. One of my uncredited films was a comedy in 1943 called *The Demi-Paradise* (which was known as *Adventure for Two* in America) in which I had a small part as an office boy named Percy. This was my third role as a Percy in two years. Small though the part was, it gave me the opportunity to see the great Laurence Olivier at work. I have to admit that I was greatly in awe of him. He was playing a Russian inventor called Ivan Kouzetsoff who comes to England to find a manufacturer for a new propeller blade he has invented and that he feels could assist the war effort. The film was intended to drum up sympathy for the Soviet Union, which was suffering greatly at the hands of Nazi Germany at the time. Harry Fowler was in that film as well, playing another cockney kid.

I managed to work with Alastair again after that in the comedy *Mr Bolfry* by Scottish dramatist James Bridie at the Playhouse Theatre, London. I played the part of a soldier named Cohen, one of two soldiers who are billeted to a manse in the Scottish highlands owned by a strict Calvinist minister named Mr McCrimmon (played by Alastair). Bored one afternoon, the two soldiers and the minister's niece set out to test some of McCrimmon's religious beliefs, with unexpected and far-reaching results. I was fortunate to get that part. I was a fairly young-looking 18-year-old at the time and the part was written for a soldier rather older than that. This was another situation in which I was grateful to Alastair for having the confidence in me that I would be able to pull it off. The play originally opened at the Westminster Theatre in August 1943 with the part of Cohen, the part I later played, taken by Alfie Bass, who became well known to television viewers more than a decade later in the television series *The Army Game* and *Bootsie and Snudge*. When Alfie was called up for military service, Alastair brought me in to replace him. The play moved to the Playhouse Theatre around the same time.

I did *Mr Bolfry* with Alastair again 12 years later at the Aldwych Theatre in London in August 1956, playing the same part. This time my real age matched the character perfectly. Alastair directed the play and took the title role rather than that of Mr McCrimmon, the part he had played the first time. The show was very successful and ran for just over three months.

Around the time we did *Mr Bolfry* for the first time, Alastair and I appeared together in a wartime public-information message produced by the Ministry of Information, reminding people not to waste fuel. Television was off the air at the time and messages of this sort were often played in cinemas, which were a highly popular way for people to turn their backs on the war for a couple of hours. News theatres were also very popular: they played programmes lasting an hour or so containing a mixture of newsreels, cartoons, one-reel 'shorts', public-information films and wartime propaganda. Although the news was often several days old by the time the newsreels reached the cinemas, the coverage was often more comprehensive than the news broadcasts on BBC radio because the newsreels were less susceptible to enemy interception. In our public-information film, I played a schoolboy in uniform, wearing regulation short trousers (even though I was 18), in a museum studying a statue of the Roman emperor Nero, played by Alastair. Nero recites a poem describing his wrongdoings and I had to say, 'That wasn't just cruel, that was wasting good fuel and that's what I call a real crime.' And then I hit him over the head with his fiddle. The film ended on a close-up of a placard around Alastair's neck saying, 'Don't be like Nero – be a good citizen and SAVE FUEL.'

The government took projects such as this extremely seriously. To write the script, they brought in acclaimed screenwriter Roger MacDougall, who in later years did the screenplay for the Ealing Films comedy *The Man in the White Suit*, for which he received a 1952 Academy Award nomination. We shot the Nero film in a single day at a strange little place called Marylebone Studios. To reach the studio, you had to go through a church, which was rather disconcerting if there was any sort of religious activity going on at the time.

As I approached my 18th birthday, I knew perfectly well that I would soon be called up for wartime military service. The government had now made this compulsory for all able-bodied citizens aged 18 to 41, except for certain exempted categories. People used to joke that along with your birthday cards on your 18th birthday there would be a buff-coloured envelope containing your call-up papers. Mine arrived three or four days afterwards. I eventually joined the Royal Air Force. But a few months would pass before I was helping to protect the realm.

CHAPTER 3

SERVING KING AND COUNTRY

I decided long before my call-up that I wanted to join the RAF but, while I was waiting for that time to come around, I was given the chance to play Jim Hawkins in *Treasure Island*. It was a part I really wanted but I knew there was no way I could play it once I had been called up. But I had a cunning plan to get around the small obstacle of war service. I tried to sign up early so I could apply for a deferment. They called me into a selection board and asked the obvious question, 'Why do you want to join the RAF?' I replied, 'Well, I want to play Jim Hawkins in *Treasure Island* and I've heard that, if you accept me, I'll be able to get a deferment.' What I was supposed to say was, 'I want to fly planes and fight the enemy.' It was almost a repeat of the 'go back to the end of the line' debacle in the headmaster's study four years earlier. They didn't accept me.

As it turned out, I did manage to get my entry deferred. I was given some credit for my work in *Flare Path*, which was considered part of the war effort. I had also been offered the part of the Boy in a film production of *Henry V* that was released in November 1944. Prime Minister Winston Churchill personally requested that the film be produced as a morale booster for troops fighting in the war, and it was partly funded by the British government. The RAF could hardly refuse my application to defer if I were working on a war-related project initiated by the Prime Minister!

Laurence Olivier directed it and played the title role. Leslie Banks, who I worked with in *Cottage to Let*, was also in it, playing the part of Chorus. Several other actors who later became familiar to British film and television audiences also took part, including John Laurie, Jimmy Hanley, Max Adrian and Leo Genn.

Olivier was a wonderful director. I had never encountered direction like that before. He would play everyone's part in rehearsal, but not in a way that said, 'This is how you *should* play it.' It was more like, 'This is how you *could* play it.' He managed to coax the best out of everyone and it was amazing to watch him work.

I had one line in the film that was a forerunner of Arthur Daley. My cue was, 'You'll be famous, Boy, you'll be famous.' As I walked off, I had to reply, 'I'll give all my fame for a pot of ale and safety.' Years later, I thought this was pure Arthur Daley: 'Never mind about fame, show me the pub!'

I had another line that, unfortunately, was cut out by the censor. One of the characters had brought a Frenchman down on his knees and was obviously pretty annoyed with him. He called the Boy to translate for him. He said, 'Tell him I'll ferret him. I'll fur him. I'll ferk him.' I was supposed to say, 'I don't know the French for "ferk",' but the censor decided that it was not a line the audience needed to hear.

Eventually, my deferment ran out and in August 1943 I was

posted to RAF Cardington in Bedfordshire for basic training – which essentially meant square-bashing.

After eight weeks of learning how to march in a straight line and turn round without dropping our rifles, we had a period in which they assessed our aptitude for various branches of the service. It was what the cynics among us described as 'seeing what we are good at so they can get us to do something else'. They initially thought I might be useful as a wireless operator and tried to teach me how to be one. It's funny, I never have problems learning lines but I just could not manage the dots and dashes in Morse code. I didn't do at all well and they eventually gave up and made me ACHGD – 'aircraft hand general duties'.

'General duties' can mean anything in the RAF. One of my first assignments was when they sent me off to Blackpool to clean out the Winter Gardens, which coincidentally was where I had made my stage debut a few years earlier in *The White Horse Inn*. One day I was on parade and the sergeant barked, 'Come out here, Basil Rathbone.' Delighted with his little joke, he waited for a reaction. Naturally, I knew that Basil Rathbone was a highly popular actor but I had no idea who it was that the sergeant wanted to go out there so I stayed fell-in. So did everyone else. Nobody moved. The sergeant realised that his joke had fallen flat and made it clear in no uncertain terms to whom he was talking.

I was told that I had to report to Pinewood Studios to take part in a film about the RAF called *Journey Together*. Not wishing to disobey an order, and hastily in case they changed their minds, I went. The film, written by Terence Rattigan and the first to be directed by John Boulting, was about a group of cadets hoping to become RAF pilots. I had a part as a bomb aimer. The film was made as a tribute to the RAF pilots and crewmembers who served during the war. The opening credits described it as 'A story dedicated to the Few who trained the Many' and stated that it was 'Written, Produced, Directed, Photographed and Acted by members of the Royal Air Force' (capitalisation as on the film).

Among the RAF cast were Richard Attenborough, Jack Watling and David Tomlinson, along with many other serving members of the RAF. To add a little American interest, the RAF flew Edward G. Robinson over from Los Angeles to play a part. He had a great time over here and cleaned out the entire crew playing poker! The film was produced by the Royal Air Force Film Production Unit, which was under the direct command of John Boulting, and was filmed largely at 149 Squadron Station at Methwold in Norfolk. It had its UK release in October 1945 and in the US the following year.

At one point, we were in the tank at Pinewood Studios shooting a scene in which our Lancaster bomber had come down in the sea and the crew were trying to escape. We had to escape from the mock-up plane into a rubber dinghy and paddle to safety. One of the props people had a hidden line attached to the dinghy and slowly winched it away from the plane to give the required effect. We happened to have one of the RAF top brass visiting and watching the shoot. He evidently enjoyed what he saw and said to the director, 'Jolly fine show. Could I have a little go at working that pulley thingy?' We did the scene again with the bigwig in control and he pulled the dinghy straight onto a spike protruding from the scaffolding, puncturing the rubber dinghy and causing it to deflate immediately, scattering the newly rescued airmen in all directions. Nothing could have been more amusing than to see me, supposedly weak from the crash and with stage blood all over my head, swimming like a maniac to be the first to get out of the tank!

Much as I enjoyed the chance to be acting again I didn't feel it was altogether fair that the other actors in the film were able to go home at the end of the day and put their feet up and that I had to go back to Coastal Command to shovel coal and perform whatever general duties had been assigned to me for the day. But at least I was doing my bit for the country and I suppose one consolation was that I was spared any real conflict.

Eventually, they sent me off to Coastal Command Headquarters in Northwood to run a bar. While Prime Minister Winston Churchill was announcing the end of the war on the wireless, I was on sentry duty outside the back gate of Coastal Command Headquarters. They couldn't even put me outside the front entrance where passers-by could stop and thank me for my help in winning the war. That was the extent of my VE Day celebrations! But I must have shown some aptitude for bar work because before long they posted me to Germany to run another one. And that is where I stayed until I finished my national service with the RAF.

CHAPTER 4

BACK TO CIVVY STREET

I know that a lot of young people these days assume that all the service people were released as soon as the war ended to go back to what they were doing previously. In fact, it was not like that at all. There were millions of people in the services and it would have been completely unmanageable if they all left at the same time. The process was performed in phases: the older people and those who joined first were released first and the younger ones, who joined later, were released later.

The process of completing military service and returning to civilian life was officially known as 'demobilisation', which was popularly known as 'demobbed'. Civilian life was known as 'Civvy Street'. I was demobbed in the spring of 1947 after four years in the RAF and, like everyone else when they left the forces, I went home with a new suit and an outfit of clothes paid for by the government. I can't remember if I ever wore it.

I headed straight back to the stage in 1947 after my demob and over the next three years did three plays with Alastair Sim written by the Scottish playwright James Bridie. This was the pen name of a medical doctor in Glasgow named Osborne Henry Mavor, who later became involved in establishing the Edinburgh Festival. He and Alastair had become close friends and Alastair's wife refers to 'Jimmy' with great affection in her autobiography. She tells of her enormous pride that Jimmy and his wife were present at the ceremony in 1949 when Alastair was formally declared Rector of Edinburgh University after his election the previous autumn. Alastair, too, had tremendous respect for James Bridie and I think the knowledge that Bridie was present at his installation made the occasion one of the most significant in his life. The rector is largely a ceremonial appointment but one in which the incumbent is wholly elected by the student body to represent their interests as president of the university court. He or she can appoint a representative to do this, in which case their major official duty is to deliver a rectorial address when they are elected. Alastair chose as his subject 'The Qualified Fool'. Over the years, Alastair received numerous awards and honours from many quarters for his work but I believe this one meant more to him than any of the others because of his being elected to the position of rector by young people – the same young people he set out to nurture and to encourage to obtain the best they possibly could from their lives.

Bridie's plots were usually complex and always meticulously researched. As a doctor, he was perfectly comfortable writing about medical themes: *Dr Angelus*, the first play I did when I left the RAF, was about a general practitioner; *The Anatomist*, the next one I did, was about a doctor who wanted to study more about the structure of the human body. As a proud Scot, Bridie based many of his characters and settings on Scots and Scotland. *Mr Gillie*, which I did in 1950, was about a Scottish minister in the highlands.

Dr Angelus, a comedy thriller set in Glasgow, was based on the true story of a general practitioner named Pritchard who started poisoning members of his family in Glasgow in the 1860s. Bridie adapted the story to make it relevant to 1919, just after the First World War. As well as playing the title role, Alastair produced and directed the play. Thus, he was able to delay the opening until I had been relieved of my pint-pulling duties in Germany for the RAF. We opened in June 1947 in Edinburgh and moved down to the Phoenix Theatre in London at the end of July. We stayed there for six months.

I played Dr Angelus's young and inexperienced partner Dr Johnson in what was my first real adult part, but it posed a few challenges. Firstly, the accent had to change, again. I had been making a conscious effort to improve it before I was called up but I don't think four years in the RAF, particularly working in a bar for the final year, did much to reinforce all the work I had put into improving the accent. This part *demanded* that it change and I had to make sure it did.

The part was not an easy one and I found the rehearsal a little more difficult than I expected. After one of the rehearsals, I happened to overhear Alastair talking about it to his wife Naomi. He told her, 'He hasn't got it yet. I'm going to give him until next Wednesday but if he hasn't got it by then, I'll have to put the understudy on instead. It will be sad but I'll have to.' That must have been the jolt I needed because I improved a lot over the next few days and I managed to do it exactly the way Alastair wanted. I think he was genuinely proud of the performance.

I was even presented to Queen Mary after one of the shows. I had one of the biggest parts in the show and she looked down at me (we had to sit on footstalls while we were being presented) and said, 'And what do you do, young man?'

The central theme of the play was the relationship between Dr Angelus and his assistant. When Dr Johnson first becomes the junior partner of Alastair's character, he is not immediately aware that Dr Angelus is playing an 'angel of death' role and slowly killing off his ailing relatives with poison. I soon cotton on though and much of the play concerns my reluctance to do anything about it out of respect for him as my superior. In the end, I am the one who has to sign the death certificate that will result in my boss receiving a handsome life insurance pay-out, but I know that it is wrong. I am torn between loyalty to Dr Angelus and loyalty to my profession.

The show did well and ran for six months, which was the maximum time Alastair would allow for a run. He felt that an actor needed to do something fresh after six months and always included a stipulation to that effect in his contracts.

He was also innovative in promoting his plays. He began to put A-boards outside the Phoenix Theatre containing all the critiques of the play. The good ones were printed in black and the bad ones in red, so passers-by could immediately compare them.

He never stopped pushing me to improve my performance. While we were doing *Dr Angelus*, Naomi would come up to London one or two nights a week and sit in the front row to take notes. We would always go to a restaurant somewhere in Charlotte Street afterwards and one night she asked me, 'How do you cope with the fact that we are having dinner and you've just done a show and Allie has not stopped giving you notes?'

My answer was immediate, 'Well, that's how you learn, isn't it?'

She observed, 'But you seem not to mind.'

I said, 'No, I don't. Why should I if it's helping me improve?'

It was obviously clear to her that I was being hassled but I was always very aware that it was all in a good cause and it really didn't bother me.

Dr Angelus appeared on BBC Television in 1948 and was one of the first theatrical plays to appear on television following its stage run. This was an effective and economical way of bringing theatre to the masses in those days because the plays could often be transplanted directly from the stage using existing sets and direction and usually with the original actors. Alastair and I both appeared in the television adaptation.

I think this was the time when I bought my first television set, so I could catch up with what was going on in the West End. The BBC had started the practice of televising successful stage plays from Alexandra Palace live on a Sunday evening. In those days, recording material in the studio for subsequent transmission was still something for the future and they would get everyone back the following Thursday to transmit the play live again.

The days of live television were wonderful, in an exciting sort of way. Every so often they would lose the feed to the transmitter somewhere in the telephone system. The screen would go blank and the continuity studio would put up a caption board saying, 'Normal service will be resumed as soon as possible.' The studio staging the production would not know immediately that they were off the air and we would continue acting until the floor manager received a message from the central control room through his headphones. He would stop the action and everyone would take up their positions at a convenient point just before they went off air, waiting for the feed to be restored. Eventually, the floor manager would announce, '30 seconds, studio, stand by,' and would count us down so we could start again as if nothing had happened when he waved his hand. I doubt if many actors today have any idea of how much drama there was behind the television screen in those early years, let alone on it.

In autumn 1948, the year after we did *Dr Angelus* on stage, we had a successful tour in Scotland of Bridie's play *The Anatomist*, followed by a run at the Westminster Theatre in London from 2 to 13 November. The news that Alastair had been elected rector of the University of Edinburgh was announced from the stage before the opening curtain on the first night.

The Anatomist was based on the true story of Scottish anatomist, Dr Robert Knox, who did his research on cadavers obtained by body snatchers Burke and Hare. When the supply of cadavers began to decline, they took it upon themselves to create more. Dr Knox, meanwhile, distances himself from the exact origins of his specimens. Alastair played Dr Knox and I played his assistant Walter Anderson. Also in the cast was the lovely Scottish actress Molly Urquhart playing Mary Paterson, an eventual victim of Burke and Hare's misdeeds. There was one scene where I had to manhandle her a bit. She went to Alastair afterwards and said, 'Could you have a wee word with young Georgie because I've got bruises all the way up and down my arm.' Alastair took me to one side and said, 'Georgie, you've got to learn how to act, not do things.'

Naturally, I went and apologised to her but I was so cross that it had happened that, as I went off stage in one scene, I slammed the door a little too hard behind me and the handle fell off. Alastair was still on stage at the time and had to exit at the end of the scene. He couldn't exit through the door because there was now no handle and so he went over to the window. But then he realised they were supposed to be three storeys up. He went off through the fireplace like a Scottish Father Christmas! But the story doesn't end there. I was getting a real earful from him on the way home while I was driving his car and, in the middle of all that, I went to change gear and the gear lever came off in my hand. This was enough for me. I got out and walked.

The play had a successful run in Scotland but was less successful when it came down to London, probably because Bridie had insisted that it retain the Edinburgh accent and Scottish dialect expressions that would have meant little to audiences south of the border.

Denis Webb later adapted the play for television and it was shown as a film on ITV's *Play of the Week* in 1956, produced and directed by Dennis Vance. Alastair and I performed in it in our original parts.

We finished the run of *The Anatomist* in the winter of 1948 and I was away from the theatre for a year doing film work. My next play after that was *Mr Gillie*, the latest from the pen of James Bridie. Once again, Alastair produced, directed and played the leading role. We took the play to Glasgow first and opened at the Garrick Theatre in London in early March 1950. Four months later, on 25 July, we performed it on BBC Television, produced by Kevin Sheldon.

The Mr Gillie of the title was a schoolmaster in a Scottish mining village who has an undying passion to help his students unearth their hidden talents and go out into the world, even to the extent of taking risks. I played a poor mineworker in the village named Tom Donnelly on whom Mr Gillie works his magic, releasing Tom's hidden talents for poetry and writing. He encourages Tom to marry his girlfriend, doctor's daughter Nellie Watson (played by the celebrated Scottish actress Janet Brown) and to go in search of fame and fortune. Sadly, we find ourselves in bad company and return a year later as a bitter disappointment to him. Alastair was particularly fond of this play, perhaps because it so closely reflected his own passion for bringing out hidden talent in young people. He later adapted the play for television and appeared in the title role in the BBC's *Sunday Night Play* series ten years later in 1960. I was not in that one.

Alastair was demanding as far as work was concerned and, if you were not up to scratch, he would let you know it. I remember an occasion in 1956 when I was working with him and Annette Crosbie in the rerun of Bridie's *Mr Bolfry*. There was one scene in which Annette had to make an entrance carrying a tray. Alastair felt that she was not being funny enough, so he got up and demonstrated how he would do it. But he was Alastair Sim. There was no way that Annette could be expected to do it the way he did. I stood up against him and said, 'Alastair, that is not helpful. She can't do that.' I think he was such a perfectionist that sometimes he just forgot how talented he really was.

I remember another scene in the comedy film *The Green Man* a few years later when he suddenly said to me, 'If you're going to do it like that, I'm going to take it.' I thought, 'What does he mean?' But the next time we did the scene I played it differently and he simply said, 'Good boy!' and I got the message. I think I must have been somehow lacking in energy and he was trying to tell me that if I carried on doing it like that he would have to make himself the focus of the scene instead of me. It ended up as a lovely comedy scene with me going mad trying to dial 999 when I suspect there is a body hidden in a grand piano.

He would put his own money into every play that he directed. He didn't mind rehearsing in a room for three weeks but he insisted that for the fourth week he wanted a theatre, a stage, the set and the props, so by the end of the fourth week we'd have run the play for a week. He could be subtly harsh in his direction occasionally. I remember once he was in the stalls watching and I was on stage with the cast. He called out, 'Georgie, just move a little more to your right – just a little more, that's perfect, now I can't see you at all.' That was enough to let me know that I hadn't been concentrating on my positioning. It always worked. There is absolutely no doubt that all of this interaction with him and his gentle cajoling made me a much better actor than I otherwise would have been.

Much as I loved working on stage with Alastair, I eventually had to say to him, 'No, I'm sorry, I can't work for that money. I can go and do something for television or film instead.' One of the problems was that he would pay me only what he thought I was worth but that was usually starvation wages. That's why I had to make a stand and tell him I couldn't work for the money he was prepared to pay. He was perfectly understanding about it and we still continued to work together after that but not with me being paid directly by Alastair.

One of his biggest successes was a play called *A Clean Kill* by Michael Gilbert. It opened in Bournemouth in October 1959 and at the Criterion Theatre in London on 15 December the same year, where it got wonderful reviews. Alastair produced it and I was the associate director. Some of my money was in that as well as his. Despite the good reviews, the ticket sales dropped below the get-out figure and the company exercised their right to close it. But instead of Al saying, 'We did well, let's forget it,' he moved it to another theatre. Unfortunately, it didn't work out there either but still he didn't want to take it off and he moved it to the Westminster. This was the kiss of death because it was a long way away from the West End, out in Victoria somewhere, which in those days was a place where playgoers tended not to go. So all the money he made from its initial run at the Criterion was finally lost.

Around the time I was doing the Bridie plays in the late 1940s, I also started to get some more experience in the cinema. The first of my post-war films to be released was in 1948 when I co-starred with Jack Warner in the Gainsborough Pictures film *My Brother's Keeper*, written by Maurice Wiltshire, directed by Alfred Roome and with screenplay by Frank Harvey Jr, which we shot on location and at Shepherd's Bush Studios. We played a pair of prisoners on the run, handcuffed together after jumping out of a police car on the way to a remand centre. I played a slightly slow-witted young man, Willie Stannard, who had not been in trouble previously and strongly denies the charge of rape for which he is about to stand trial. Jack, who was in his fifties, played a tough career criminal called George Martin, who had spent most of his adult life in prison.

I think this was one of the first times I received a review for a film in which I played an adult. One critic wrote a review in something like *Picture Show* or *Picturegoer* along the lines of, 'George Cole has a name I wouldn't wish on a house painter and a face that makes Bela Lugosi look pretty.' Bela Lugosi was a Hungarian actor in the early part of the 20th century who was well known for playing roles in horror films, often with minimal make-up. That was when I gave up taking notice of reviews. I know I'm not as ugly as Bela Lugosi and I don't care what house painters think of my name. And if reviewers have to stoop to making irrelevant personal comments, I don't think their reviews can carry that much weight.

One incident that remains in my mind from when we were making that film is when Jack Warner managed to upset Kathleen Harrison. As there was only an hour's break for lunch, we 'stars' were allowed to eat in a private room with waitress service so we didn't have to suffer the hurly burly of the canteen. The wonderful Kathleen Harrison was also there working on one of *The Huggetts* films. One day the lunchtime special was rabbit stew. This was a time when meat was still subject to wartime food rationing. Kathleen remarked how nice the rabbit was. Jack Warner (who was Kathleen's stage husband in *The Huggetts*) announced, 'You know, we wouldn't be having rabbit stew today if the ginger-beer crate hadn't fallen on the cat.' Dear Kathleen was not at all amused and I don't think she ate another mouthful after that.

Jack Warner was a wonderful British actor who remained a close friend of mine until his death in 1981. His best-known television role was that of the avuncular London policeman George Dixon in the BBC's popular television series *Dixon of Dock Green* that ran from 1955 to 1976. By the time the series ended he was 80 years old, way beyond the retirement age of a British police officer in real life, but he was so popular and such a comfort for the audience to have around that nobody seemed to care too much. Besides his television and film career, he had a thorough grounding in music hall and radio. His real surname was Waters and he was the brother of Elsie and Doris Waters, who were extremely popular as the comic duo 'Gert and Daisy' on British radio during the Second World War and into the 1950s.

Jack was a driver during the war and, for a time, worked as a racing driver. On location he had a few tricks with the car that were a young boy's dream. If there was a gravel path, he'd drive along it at great speed, take his hands off the wheel, look absolutely panic-stricken and grab hold of the window frame with both hands until the car skidded to a halt. It was absolutely terrifying to watch, particularly for anyone in the car who was not expecting it. He had a terrible end to his life, with arthritis and a stroke that resulted in his having both legs amputated.

There was another story I recall about Jack Warner. It was when Richard Widmark visited England in the late 1940s after his first film, *Kiss of Death*. The film was an enormous success when it was released in 1947 and is memorable for a scene in which his character kills a wheelchair-bound woman by pushing her down a flight of stairs. He travelled over to England on one of the big liners and, when he arrived at Southampton, he was met by a group of reporters. Asked which British actors he would most like to meet while he was in England, he replied, 'Jack Warner and George Cole: Jack because of his performance in *The Captive Heart* and George because of *The Kite* sequence in Somerset Maugham's *Quartet.*' That compliment made me extremely proud – and honoured to have heard it alongside one directed towards Jack Warner. We saw a lot of Dick Widmark after that and became close friends.

The Kite, directed by Arthur Crabtree, was my second film to be released in 1948. This was one of a four-part anthology of stories by W. Somerset Maugham under the collective title *Quartet*, made by Gainsborough Pictures. This was a deep drama in which I played Herbert Sunbury, a slightly nervy and introverted young man who has had a lifelong passion for kite flying since his parents took him to see the kites at a local park when he was a young boy. His parents support his hobby until he grows up and meets his future wife, played by Susan Shaw, whom his mother feels is beneath his class. Hermione Baddeley, with whom I worked again a couple of years later in *Scrooge*, played my domineering mother, and Mervyn Johns played her henpecked husband. My character Herbert continues to take an interest in kite flying behind his wife's back and, eventually, the marital relationship breaks down.

The film opens with Sunbury in a prison cell being interviewed by a prison visitor who discovers he is there because he refuses to pay maintenance to his wife after she destroyed one of his kites. The prison visitor later talks to the prison governor, who surmises that Sunbury views the kite as a symbolic representation of himself, soaring up into the clouds and escaping from the restrictions of life on earth. But the prison service has nothing to offer to help him resolve his problems. Maugham, in a voice-over, suggests a possible ending to the story. He suggests that the prison visitor went to visit Sunbury's wife after visiting him and persuaded her to take her husband back by taking an interest in kite flying. The film closes with the wife flying a kite on the common and being met by Sunbury on his release from prison.

On the instructions of the British film censors, the ending was very different from the way Maugham intended. In Maugham's original story my character ended up going backwards and forwards to gaol for repeatedly refusing to pay his wife's maintenance. Whatever the motive of the censors, they definitely changed the feel of the original story. The American censors also had their say. I had a line in the film where my wife, from whom I was now separated, tried to get me back after I had gone to live with my parents. The line I had was, 'No thanks. I know when I'm well off. I've had enough of married life to last me a lifetime.' When it went to America, the censors insisted that I replace 'married life' with 'marriage'. Apparently, they felt that 'married life' implied living together but not being married.

One thing I especially liked about this film was that the whole story was told from start to finish in around 30 minutes.

The film's reviews were good and I felt that I was making some progress in the profession but I spent 11 months without any acting work after that. I developed a theory that when you get good reviews, directors get to hear about you but don't call you because they think you're busy. I managed to hold out without taking any other sort of work. There was probably some temptation to do something else because I was sharing a flat with two other actors at the time, Francis Matthews and Richard Mills and, whenever they were without an acting job for six weeks, they would be off doing a completely different sort of work. But in 1949 a romantic drama film, *Gone to Earth*, came along and I was back at work again.

Gone to Earth was based on the 1917 novel of the same name by Mary Webb. The film featured Jennifer Jones as Hazel Woodus, a beautiful, innocent and superstitious country girl of gypsy heritage who likes to escape her domineering father by walking in the countryside, interacting with the animal life that she loves. One night while she is out, the lecherous local squire notices her. He is attracted by her beauty and sets out to conquer her. Tears begin to flow when the squire wants to lead the local hunt in pursuit of the girl's pet fox that she raised. The film was beautifully shot in Technicolor at Shepperton Studios and on location in and around the village of Much Wenlock in Shropshire where the story is set. I played Hazel's cousin Albert, probably her only true friend. I think this was the only time I've played a part that needed a dialect for which I needed to have a dialect coach. Shooting started in autumn 1949. Following its UK release more than a year later, the film was subsequently re-edited for the American market after a disagreement between the director Michael Powell and the producer David O. Selznick, who was dissatisfied with the original version.

Michael Powell could be a difficult person to work with. I never really liked him as a person, although I was a great admirer of his work. He was fine with me but could easily reduce the actresses to tears. I remember him making one particular actress do repeated retakes of a scene that were all completely unnecessary. I can appreciate the fact that he was looking for artistic perfection but he had little regard for the artists involved and I think he lost a lot of respect because of it. The re-edited film was released in the United States in 1952 under the title *The Wild Heart*. I worked for only 4 days on this one but after 11 months without work it was a marvellous feeling to be back.

At that time, I was under contract with the Rank Organisation to do one film a year. I had already done *My Brother's Keeper* and *The Kite* for Gainsborough Pictures, which was under the J. Arthur Rank umbrella, but then they cast me in a film called *Boys in*

Brown, released in 1949, as an intellectually impaired Welsh boy who is sent to borstal.* Jack Warner was in the film playing a judge. He was also under contract to Rank. The film painted a tough picture of borstal and the producers consulted various authorities to see if it was a fair depiction. My character was treated almost like scum by the other characters. One of the reports that came back about my character said that you would never get a boy with such serious intellectual difficulties sent to borstal. So my part suddenly became nothing because he was no longer intellectually impaired and the part was deleted from the film.

Since Rank had a contractual obligation to cast me in one film a year, they gave me a part in *The Spider and the Fly*, a love-triangle film released in December 1949. The film was directed by Robert Hamer and set in Paris just before the start of the First World War. Eric Portman and Guy Rolfe played the two men in the triangle with the stunning Nadia Gray. Eric Portman played a French detective who is intent on catching a suave and notorious burglar played by Guy Rolfe. I played a detective named Marc who was the assistant to Eric Portman's character. When the war breaks out, the spider and the fly become allies. I think I was only put there as a walking stick for Eric Portman's character. Of all my films, I think this is the only one I truly regretted doing. The part just had no substance and I really don't know why I accepted it.

Between 1948 and 1950 I worked on two other films for the Rank Organisation, called *Morning Departure*, released in 1950, and *Lady Godiva Rides Again*, released in 1951, both of which I

---

*'Borstal' was a generic term used for institutions under the British prison service providing strict discipline for young people with serious delinquent behaviour during the first eight decades of the 20th century. The system was abolished in 1982.

describe in the next chapter. But after that, my contract with Rank had finished. By then I had started to get reasonable money in the theatre and I felt that, even if the film work started to slow down in the 1950s, I would probably be able to get along comfortably from my stage work. I didn't know it at the time but I need not have worried too much. The next decade was to prove a highly successful one for me on the cinema screen.

CHAPTER 5

THE FIFTIES

As we went into the 1950s, the country was slowly recovering from the effects of the Second World War. Conditions were still austere and rationing was still in effect for many items. Television broadcasts began again in 1946 after being suspended during the war for security reasons. However, at the start of the 1950s relatively few people could afford a television set. People relied mainly on the wireless and the cinema and maybe their 78-rpm records for their family entertainment. I had not ventured into radio yet: this did not happen until 1953 when *A Life of Bliss* came along. But British cinema was having a boom time at the start of the 1950s.

To protect the British film industry from the influx of Hollywood imports, the government passed the Cinematograph Films Act in 1948 stipulating that British cinemas had to screen a minimum of 45 per cent of British-made first features and 25 per cent as supporting films.

From my point of view, I was 25 years old and still trying to make a name for myself as an adult actor but I was still not clear whether I should be heading for a long-term career as a stage actor or a film actor. I loved to work on the stage and had started to get reasonable money in the theatre. But there was already a lot of excellent talent around as people came back into the acting pool after the war and, to be practical, films tended to pay more.

My first screen appearance in the 1950s was in the submarine drama *Morning Departure*. This was set in the late 1940s, after the war, and was based on the stage play of the same name by Kenneth Woollard. The screenplay was by William Fairchild, who was a naval officer during the war and admirably qualified to write it. We made the film in 1948 but it was not released until February 1950. Roy Baker was the director and I worked with him a lot over the years, particularly some 30 years later when he directed more than a dozen episodes of *Minder* under the professional name Roy Ward Baker. The cast of *Morning Departure* read like a who's who of contemporary British cinema, including such stalwarts as John Mills, Richard Attenborough, Kenneth More, Victor Maddern, Nigel Patrick, James Hayter and many more. Even a youthful Michael Caine made an uncredited appearance as a tea boy. The film told the story of a Royal Navy submarine that becomes trapped on the sea floor during a routine training exercise after it hits a mine left over from the war.

I played a ship's engineer called E. R. A. Marks. The E. R. A. stood for 'Engine Room Artificer', which was a rank for skilled mechanics in the Royal Navy. Dickie Attenborough played another member of the submarine crew with a similar rank to mine. My character was Jewish in the original script and Dickie's character had an intense hatred towards mine as a result. There was no particular bad feeling between us while everything was well with the submarine but as soon as the submarine developed a problem, the conflict began to appear. Who gets the life jacket? The Jew or the non-Jew? Unfortunately, this storyline had to be rewritten because the Jewish businessmen who were funding the film didn't approve of the way my character was treated by the others, particularly by Dickie's. This was a pity because in the final version Dickie's character is not a happy man and feels animosity not just to me but to everyone in the crew and the audience is left wondering why. The original version left plenty of opportunity to develop the relationship between us.

There were some intense dramatic sequences that drew every bit of performance skill from the cast. I remember one scene in particular where there were not enough escape sets and the crew had to draw lots to determine who would get the ones available. They used a pack of cards and were dealt one card each so that the men with the highest-value cards would get the escape sets. It was a long scene but, even today, you can still feel the tension as the crew gradually learn their likely fate. At the end of the scene there is a twist, followed soon after by another. It was direction at its best and a tribute to Roy's artistic vision. The film was released under the name *Operation Disaster* in America the following year and was favourably received there, resulting in Roy Baker being invited to work in Hollywood a couple of years later.

One of my most poignant memories of the film is that in January 1950, just before it was scheduled for release, there was a real-life submarine disaster in Britain with the loss of many lives. The submarine HMS *Truculent* was returning to Sheerness after a refit and collided with an oil tanker in the Thames Estuary and sank. A total of 64 people died as a result of the accident, many from the effects of the freezing weather conditions, but several were trapped under water in the submarine in similar circumstances to those depicted in the film. The producers had serious doubts whether it would be appropriate to release the film under these tragic circumstances and sent the script to the Admiralty for advice. The Admiralty replied that they felt the film should go ahead because it would have an uplifting effect on the audience rather than a depressing one. In accordance with the response from the Admiralty, the opening credits contained a message explaining that the film was completed before the loss of the *Truculent* and that after due consideration it had been decided to release the film as a tribute 'to the officers and men of H. M. Submarines, and to the Royal Navy of which they are a part'. When the film was finally released, the producers received letters from the relatives of some of the victims saying how grateful they were that the film had been made.

A few weeks after the release of *Morning Departure* in 1950, another film I had been in the previous year was released. This was entitled *The Happiest Days of Your Life* and featured the cream of British comedy with such names as Alastair Sim, Margaret Rutherford, Joyce Grenfell, Richard Wattis and George Benson. This was, in many respects, a precursor of the *St. Trinian's* films that began in 1954, although that was not the original intention. I think the idea for a sequel came about as a result of the outstanding success of *Happiest Days* at the box office; it ranked as the fifth most popular film released that year. When *The Belles of St. Trinian's* was made in 1954, the producers used similar sets to those used in *Happiest Days*, retained the Ronald Searle cartoons in the opening credits and used many of the same cast.

The storyline of *Happiest Days* involved an old established boys' school, where Alastair is the headmaster who is forced to have an all-girls school merge with his because of bureaucratic bungling and wartime financial restrictions. Margaret Rutherford played the headmistress of the girls' school. I had a small and uncredited part as a boiler stoker. I wasn't formally cast in the film, I just happened to be visiting someone at the studio. Director Frank Launder saw me there and said, 'Do you feel like playing a stoker?'

I said, 'Fine, why not?' and I worked for half a day on it.

All I had to do was answer the phone and say something like, 'Oh yeah, I understand, I think you'd better have a word with the guv'nor when he comes back. I think he's stoking the boilers.' My pay for that was an Omega wristwatch, which I still have today and which still keeps perfect time.

By 1950, I had known Alastair Sim for around ten years and I was becoming extremely privileged that he was showing such confidence in my ability to go further in the profession. Without a doubt, it was due to his influence that I had already appeared in four major stage plays and two television broadcasts based on the work of the Scottish playwright James Bridie. Now I was about to do a Bridie play on film.

Flesh and Blood, which was released in 1951, was based on Bridie's 1935 play *A Sleeping Clergyman* about three generations of a Scottish clan. It was set in Glasgow during the time of Joseph Lister, the pioneer of antiseptic surgery. One generation of the family includes a medical student who dies from tuberculosis and who leaves behind an illegitimate daughter. Many years later, the daughter becomes pregnant by my character, John Hannah, and subsequently kills him. Despite his troubled childhood, the son who results from the liaison later becomes a successful doctor who gets the chance to save the world from a mysterious infectious disease and reverts the family to the genius and respect it had in his grandfather's generation. The story was adapted for screen and produced by Anatole de Grunwald and the film was directed by Anthony Kimmins. Richard Todd, Glynis Johns, Joan Greenwood and André Morell all had major parts.

I started a contract with Associated British Picture Corporation (ABPC) in 1950 to do one film a year for six years. Before the war, most of their film output was aimed at the domestic market but, after the war, the company went into a partnership with Warner Bros in the United States that effectively opened up the market for Associated British products to America and beyond.

My first film under the ABPC contract was a feel-good comedy romp released in 1951 entitled *Laughter in Paradise*, with Alastair Sim, Fay Compton and Guy Middleton in the cast. This was also the first of four films I did in the 1950s directed by Mario Zampi, all four of which were under my ABPC contract. Mario started out as an actor in Italy in the 1920s and later found his way to Warner Bros in London as an editor. In 1937, he and fellow Italian Filippo Del Giudice founded Two Cities Films, originally planning to produce films in London and Rome, but they subsequently worked extensively in London where they made more than 60 films, including *Henry V*, in which I appeared in 1944. They later became well known for their comedies.

It must have been a major challenge in the early days for someone whose first language was not English to direct comedy films in English but Mario seemed to have the knack of finding the best scriptwriter right at the beginning and taking it from there. Michael Pertwee wrote the scripts for the majority of Mario's films and for all four of the ones I did with him; he collaborated with Jack Davies on three of the four. The scripts were all brilliant and Mario managed to get the best out of all of them. He was a wonderfully easy director to work with.

I have always had a special fondness for *Laughter in Paradise* as it was a fairly big part and one that I could really put myself into. And another thing – I was not playing a Percy. I played the part of Herbert Russell, one of four relatives who are in line for generous inheritances from a deceased relative, provided they perform acts that are completely foreign to their characters. My character had to hold up the bank where he worked with a toy pistol. Alastair had to get himself arrested and jailed for at least 28 days; Fay Compton's character, a tremendous snob, has to work as a domestic servant; and Guy Middleton's caddish character has to marry the first woman he meets. Comedy greats Joyce Grenfell and John Laurie also had major roles. This was classic 1950s comedy from Associated British Pictures and great fun to work on.

Alastair had a fantastic scene. The producers hired the whole ground floor of the London department store Swan & Edgar one Sunday to do a scene in which he had to get himself arrested for shoplifting. He walks around the store trying to steal things and nobody takes any notice of him. Finally, he tries to steal a necklace and put it in his pocket but, as he does so, he discovers that all the necklaces are linked together and he has to try to pocket not one but many necklaces. He did the whole scene in one take and it was absolutely brilliant. There was no dialogue in the scene and Alastair's performance harked back to the days of the black-and-white silent comedy films of the 1920s with the likes of Buster Keaton and Fatty Arbuckle.

The film was one of the earliest professional appearances of Audrey Hepburn, who had a minor role as a cigarette seller. She was listed in the opening credits on a frame saying 'and Introducing Veronica Hurst [and] Audrey Hepburn'. This has naturally led many people over the years to assume that it was Audrey's first film but, in fact, she had already appeared on film three years earlier as an air stewardess in a 1948 film entitled *Dutch in Seven Lessons*, made by Charles van der Linden and Henry Josephson. She also had minor roles in three other films in 1951 that came out around the same time as *Laughter in Paradise*.

Mario Zampi was apparently a regular visitor to Ciro's Club in London on the lookout for new talent and he saw Audrey Hepburn working there in the cabaret. Legend has it that he initially considered her for a major part in *Laughter in Paradise* but, realising that she lacked the necessary experience, offered her the part of the cigarette girl to help her get a foot on the ladder. She did one day's work at Elstree and got plenty of exposure as a result. The film was one of Britain's highest-grossing films of the year.

Another of my films released in 1951 was a thought-inspiring satirical comedy for the Rank Organisation called *Lady Godiva Rides Again*. It was about the beauty pageants that were becoming popular around the country at the time, particularly at seaside resorts. Much of the location work took place in and around the town hall at Folkestone, a seaside resort in Kent on the south-east coast of England.

Frank Launder and Val Valentine wrote the story, Frank Launder also directed, and he and Sidney Gilliat were the producers. There was a sizeable roll call of both established and emerging film talent in the cast. The seasoned pros included Alastair Sim, Stanley Holloway, Kay Kendall, Dora Bryan, and 20-year-old Diana Dors, who was already a cinema veteran with 15 films behind her. Sid James appeared in one of his first film parts as a producer of dubious integrity. In addition, the publicity poster for the film promised us 'dozens of beauty queens and artists models!' Pauline Stroud got an 'and introducing' opening credit. Joan Collins made her uncredited film debut as one of the beauty contestants, along with several others including Dana Wynter and Ruth Ellis, who four years later became the last woman to be executed in the United Kingdom following her conviction for murder. She was four months pregnant when her scenes were shot but managed to conceal the fact from the cameras.

The film was set in 1951, the year in which the British government held a nationwide 'Festival of Britain' to celebrate the continuing recovery of the nation after the Second World War. The festival was conceived as 'a tonic to the nation' and was focused on what was previously a derelict area on the south bank of the Thames between Westminster Bridge and Hungerford Bridge that was specially redeveloped for the occasion. On it was built the Royal Festival Hall and some other exhibition attractions that have long since disappeared.

The story told of Marjorie (played by Pauline Stroud), a dull and naïve waitress in the Midlands who unexpectedly wins a provincial beauty contest for which the prize is a part in a Festival of Britain parade in her hometown as Lady Godiva. I played her boyfriend Johnny, and Stanley Holloway played her father. Marjorie believes she is set for fame and fortune, until her life starts to spiral out of control as she is mercilessly manipulated by the people she works for.

Alastair's cameo, as a film director Marjorie goes to in search of a job, provides a genuinely touching scene as he describes to her how his once-successful business is now over and there is nothing left for him in life. When the lights go out in his office as the last bit of power he can afford runs out, he graciously takes Marjorie by the hand to walk her to the bus stop.

I had a wonderful moment when Marjorie's family were trying to get into her room and I announced, in the style of the best police dramas, 'Stand back. I'll break the door down.' I take a wild and pitifully unsuccessful run at the door and sheepishly explain to the onlookers, 'It's mahogany.' The film was released in America under the title *Bikini Baby*.

It was always fascinating to work with Frank Launder and Sidney Gilliat. They worked as a partnership for many years and formed a production company called Individual Pictures. One would work as director and the other as producer and the roles would change depending on the type of film. Frank tended to direct the comedies and

Sidney the thrillers and dramas. They always employed the best writers available, which ensured that the scripts were always top class, but they never seemed to have a lot of money left to spend on actors. If Alastair was in the film, there was even less because he got most of it.

Frank would always say after a take, 'Lovely, wonderful, let's have another one.' Sidney got so fed up with it one day that he said to Frank, 'Look, why, if you say it's wonderful, do you always say, "Let's have another one"?'

Frank replied simply, 'Well, you never know.' He was very much the practical one. Sidney was more the intellectual.

Halloween night 1951 saw my final film release of the year – one of my all-time favourites. This was *Scrooge*, based on Charles Dickens' *A Christmas Carol*, which was produced and directed by Brian Desmond-Hurst with screenplay by Noel Langley. I played Scrooge as a young man, while he was still a decent chap who had not yet been turned sour by the ugliness in the world around him. Alastair Sim had the major part as Scrooge in his later years. Again, we were privileged to have a brilliant cast, including Kathleen Harrison as Scrooge's charwoman Mrs Dilber, Hermione Baddeley as Mrs Cratchit, together with Mervyn Johns, Clifford Mollison and Jack Warner (by special arrangement with the J. Arthur Rank Organisation to which he was under contract). Patrick Macnee played the young Jacob Marley, and Michael Hordern played the dual role of old Marley and Marley's ghost. The film was released in the United States as *A Christmas Carol* and premiered in New York City on Halloween night 1951. Originally, it was intended to have its American premiere during the Christmas season that year but the distributors felt that the story was more appropriate for Halloween and the film had a successful run there. In recent years the film has become a Christmas classic on American television and enjoys regular reruns. Sadly, though, some of the versions we see these days have been artificially 'colourised' by computer, which completely spoils the atmosphere the film is trying to convey.

I have a special fondness for this film as it gave me the opportunity to perform alongside some of the greats of British cinema in such a wonderfully produced version of this timeless classic. Alastair's performance throughout was outstanding and the final scenes of Scrooge's redemption, when he is given another chance by the people he has wronged, have always remained with me as an example of what is meant by the term 'consummate professional'. To my mind, he set a standard for portraying Scrooge to which I feel that all actors should aspire but I doubt that many can achieve.

In addition to the four films that were released in 1951, I worked on others that were released the following year but I also managed to squeeze in two quality plays between the films. These were *A Phoenix Too Frequent* and *Thor, with Angels*, both by Christopher Fry, at the Lyric Theatre, Hammersmith, alongside such talents as Diana Churchill, Jack Hawkins, Dorothy Tutin, Eric Porter and Jessie Evans. I went for the audition having never met Christopher Fry before. The play I was going for was *A Phoenix Too Frequent*. It is a lovely one-act play where a Roman centurion is guarding several hanged men. Suddenly, a rather fetching woman appears and the centurion finds himself spending the night with her rather than the hanged bodies. When he returns in the morning, he discovers that two of the bodies have disappeared during the night. The centurion was the part I went for. To my amazement, Christopher Fry took me to one side and asked, 'Do you like poetry?' I replied, 'No, not much.'

'Why not?' he asked.

'Well, I like the sort of poems I learned in school, like *The Highwayman*.'

I recited a few lines and Christopher blanched. I think he decided there and then that I needed to be taken in hand and that it was time to enrich my education.

He said, 'I want you to audition for the other play, *Thor, with Angels*.'

Set in sixth-century England, the play was about a Jute warrior who repents his warring ways and becomes a Christian. Its style was very poetic.

So I did the audition and so did John Gregson, along with some other actors – and I got both parts! It's the story of my life, playing parts I didn't set out to play. What I didn't know was that in *Thor, with Angels* I had to be crucified every night.

I had a harness under my clothes with a hook attached and, as they lifted me up onto the cross, a person from behind would put the hook into an eye so I hung there for the rest of the scene. But on the first night everyone was a bundle of nerves and all I could hear from behind was, 'I can't find the f***ing hook. Where is it? Where's the f***ing hook?'

Another voice eventually said, 'We'll have to leave it. He's not going anywhere.'

So I was crucified the first night and was hanging by my wrists without a hook to take the weight. And all you could hear was this ghostly creaking from the leather harness whenever I moved to try to get more comfortable. And there I was for the rest of the scene. It was horrid.

They got it right eventually and my crucifixion each night became more tolerable. But, interestingly, the Lyric Theatre was right above Hammersmith Tube station and every few minutes the theatre would vibrate a little and you would hear the sound of a train passing underneath. Jack Hawkins was also in the play and I would hear him saying under his breath, 'There goes the 9.57.' And when they got me down from the cross, he would say amusing things under his breath like, 'He was one of my best players.' It was hard to keep a straight face. Jack was enormous fun.

In some respects, I prefer the theatre to film and television because you get an immediate reaction from the audience (or sometimes no reaction at all, which can be a little unsettling). I was doing a stage show one Christmas when it was snowing and the theatre staff had to go out and recruit five passing shoppers so we had someone to perform to. I think they liked it though. They seemed to be clapping in the right places but, thinking back, it might just have been so they could keep warm.

1952 was another productive year for film releases and all three in which I appeared were comedies. I never consciously set out to become a comedy actor but somehow those were the parts that were coming my way. First to be released was *The Happy Family* in which I appeared with Stanley Holloway, Kathleen Harrison, Naunton Wayne and Dandy Nichols. The film was produced by Sydney Box and was the first film to be directed by his wife Muriel. It was based on a play of the same name by Michael Clayton Hutton and was another story revolving around the Festival of Britain. The Lord family run a grocery shop in south London that is scheduled to be demolished to make way for a building associated with the Festival of Britain, and the film tells how the family takes on the government to prevent their eviction. I play Cyril, the prospective son-in-law of the family that owns the shop, who strongly encourages the family to put up a fight – a fight that culminates in flour bombs and assorted missiles aimed at the authorities in the best tradition of British comedies of the time. The film received surprisingly good reviews in America, where it was released under the alternative title *Mr. Lord Says No*. Unusually for a British-made film, it was released in the USA around six weeks earlier than it was in Britain.

Next to be released, in June 1952, was *Who Goes There!* (released in America as *The Passionate Sentry*), based on a stage play by John Dighton. The director was Anthony Kimmins, who in a packed career had managed to work as an actor, playwright, director, producer and commentator on the D-Day landings. This was a farce in the best British tradition, with humour, romance, people going away and returning unexpectedly to find others in embarrassing situations, and with happy endings all round. I played Arthur Crisp, a soldier in the Queen's Guard at St James's Palace in London. I think I looked resplendent in my red tunic and bearskin hat but, unfortunately, the film was in black and white and the effect was diluted.

One night, I am on sentry duty at the palace when my girlfriend (beautifully portrayed by Peggy Cummins) comes looking for me. Trying to avoid trouble, I leave my post and hide her away in what I think is an unoccupied room at the palace. When the caddish British diplomat who lives there (played by Nigel Patrick) returns, he discovers the girl and promptly falls in love with her. I have become infatuated with the diplomat's sister (played by Valerie Hobson), but my senior officer (played by Anthony Bushell) is already in love with her. Everything works out well in the end, as it usually does in British farce, and I had plenty of opportunity to reuse the marching and saluting skills the RAF had instilled in me nine years earlier. On top of that, there was some stirring background music from the Band of the Coldstream Guards.

My third film to be released in 1952 was the second one I did that was directed and produced by Mario Zampi. The film was called *Top Secret* and was written by Jack Davies and Michael Pertwee. It was released in America the following year under the title *Mr Potts Goes to Moscow*. The story was of my character, George Potts, a slightly absent-minded plumbing expert in the civil service who goes on holiday and accidentally takes with him the plans for a new secret weapon being developed by the British government, believing them to be the plans of his new plumbing invention (the Potts multi-plunge fast-flow filter) after the two sets of plans become switched. The Russians catch up with him and, thinking him to be a brilliant weapons scientist, offer him a job in the Kremlin doing research (which he, in turn, believes to be on plumbing). Eventually, both sides discover their blunders and Potts, having now fallen in love with a secret agent (played by Nadia Gray), has to come up with a plan to get himself back to safety.

Christopher Lee, who later shot to fame playing Dracula, had a single line in the film as a Russian agent and did not get a credit. Previously, he played the part of a police constable in *My Brother's Keeper*, the film I did with Jack Warner in 1948, but his scenes were deleted from the final cut. I hope that doesn't explain why we never worked together after that.

Another five films in which I appeared were released in 1953. The first, on 19 January, was *Folly to Be Wise*, a comedy from the Frank Launder and Sidney Gilliat team starring Alastair as an army padre who takes over the role of entertainments officer at his camp and attempts to introduce a 'brains trust' to improve the men's minds. I played a small uncredited part as a soldier in the audience who delivers an eloquent appeal from the floor for the brains trust to become a regular part of the entertainment programme after the first one falls into total disarray and unintentionally provides unparalleled entertainment. My part took only a day or so the previous year. Alastair clearly dominated the film and was nominated for Best Actor at the British Academy of Film and Television Arts (BAFTA) awards for his role but lost out to Ralph Richardson for his performance in *The Sound Barrier*. The story of *Folly to Be Wise* was based on the James Bridie play *It Depends What You Mean*. Alastair had previously produced the play at the Westminster Theatre in 1944 and was instrumental in getting it made into this film.

Next, released on 25 August, was *Will Any Gentleman...?* – a hilarious comedy film directed by Michael Anderson and written by Vernon Sylvaine based on his play of the same name. I did this under my contract with Associated British. Coincidentally, the film featured two future Doctor Whos (William Hartnell and Jon Pertwee) and was the first film appearance of Lionel Jeffries. We made it in Technicolor at Elstree Studios. The film also featured Sid James, Joan Sims and Peter Butterworth, all of whom later became mainstays in the *Carry On* films. I played the central character, Henry Sterling, a timid put-upon bank clerk, who unintentionally finds himself transformed into an assertive extrovert by a stage hypnotist, brilliantly played by Alan Badel. I enjoyed playing my part but I remember having some major arguments with the producers about it in the early stages. In the stage play, Robertson Hare played the part I was playing in the film and the producers wanted me to play it the way Robertson Hare did. I think I was a little arrogant at the time because there was no way I was prepared to copy another actor's performance, no matter how much I admired it. But I think we achieved the right balance.

There was one awkward moment while we were shooting it though. In the early part of the film, while I was still a timid introvert, I had a small moustache. As soon as my character underwent his hypnotic transformation he shaved it off and we shot the scene where I first appeared without it. But films are not made in the order the scenes appear on the screen. We continued shooting for the next three days and then someone noticed that I no longer had my moustache. He said, 'George, I think you were supposed to have a moustache in those scenes we've been shooting over the last three days.' The continuity girl checked her notes and confirmed that I should, indeed, have had a moustache. We had to reshoot three days' worth of material, all because of that horrible little moustache. To make matters worse, we were shooting in Technicolor, which was extremely expensive. I don't think the director Michael Anderson was too pleased about it at the time. But he was a wonderful director to work with and he soon mellowed. I did, however, have a falling-out with ABPC over the film.

As part of their pre-publicity, the company had the idea of running a 'sneak preview' of the film at a cinema in, I think, Streatham in south London. This in itself was fine. They could drop a quiet word to the press about it and get some valuable promotion. But then they asked me to go along as well. I said, 'How can I possibly turn up if it is a sneak preview? If it is a sneak preview, it means that nobody knows about it. So if nobody knows about it, how can I go along and keep up the pretence that it is being done behind the company's back?' We had some quite angry words about it and I didn't turn up. And that, I think, was the end of my contract with ABPC.

The Intruder, directed by Guy Hamilton for British Lion Films and released in October 1953, was my first non-comedy film for quite a while. The story involved a retired British army officer, Colonel Wolf Merton (played by Jack Hawkins), who discovers a burglar in his home and is shocked to find that the burglar was a trooper named Ginger Edwards (played by Michael Medwin) in his tank regiment during the war. My character, John Summers, was in the same regiment as Edwards and together we saved the squadron from certain death by running through enemy fire to radio for help from a disabled tank. When Edwards escapes from Merton's home after the burglary, the colonel is unable to reconcile how such a good soldier could resort to petty crime. Rather than informing the police, he begins contacting former members of his squadron to try to discover why Edwards should have targeted him. Based on the novel *Line on Ginger* by Robin Maugham, the film took a sensitive look at some of the readjustments service personnel had to make after returning from the war.

Another rather different film I worked on, released in November 1953, was *The Clue of the Missing Ape* (also known as *Gibraltar Adventure*), written and directed by James Hill for the Children's Film Foundation. This was a non-profit-making organisation set up in 1951 to produce quality films for children and was subsidised, in part, by a tax on cinema-ticket sales known as the Eady Levy. *The Clue of the Missing Ape* was a children's adventure story telling how an alert young sea cadet, Jimmy Sutton, rescues a pilot from a crashed plane and is rewarded with a visit to Gibraltar. There he meets Pilar Ellis, the daughter of a British naval officer stationed on the island, and together the children foil an anti-British plot to kill off the island's ape population and to sabotage the docks where a number of British naval ships are moored. I played a local character named Gobo who procures supplies for the gang and is the person poisoning the apes. I tried to make the character of the animal poisoner as believable as possible for the intended young audience while at the same time maintaining a comic element they could laugh at. The film relied heavily on assistance from all three of the armed forces. We had fun making it and I think we achieved a pleasing end result.

It was back to comedy for the last of my film releases in 1953. *Our Girl Friday*, released on 1 December 1953, was directed by Noel Langley (who also wrote the script) and had a marvellous cast including Joan Collins, Kenneth More, Robertson Hare, Hermione Gingold, Walter Fitzgerald and Hattie Jacques. The story was based on the book *The Cautious Amorist* by Norman Lindsay. This was the sort of book that, in those days, you never wanted to be seen buying. It told the story of rich girl Sadie Patch (played by Joan Collins), who is shipwrecked on a Pacific island along with three men after their cruise ship is involved in a collision with another ship in a fog patch at sea. In her autobiography *Second Act*, Joan Collins describes her part as that of 'a spoiled and sulky rich girl'. Robertson

Hare played a studious professor, Ken More played a stoker and I played Jimmy Carrol, a young journalist with an attitude. The Spanish island of Mallorca played the Pacific island. Originally, I was cast as the stoker and Ken as the journalist but, when we arrived on set, the powers that be decided we should swap roles. The film tells how the three men each set out to conquer Sadie.

Much of the filming was done in a bay near the village of Paguera about 20 kilometres outside of Palma, the capital of Mallorca. The film was shot in Eastmancolor and was an absolute pleasure to work on. It was released in the United States in 1955 under the title *The Adventures of Sadie*.

All the principal cast and production team flew out together and we went to our respective hotels when we arrived. Noel Langley, the director, went upstairs to his room and decided to investigate the view from the balcony. I think he may have had a tincture too many on the flight because he stepped outside the French window and immediately found himself in the garden below. There was no balcony.

There was one scene in which Ken More and I had to swim naked. In those days, the British Board of Film Censors had a category called 'U', which stood for 'Unaccompanied'. This meant that children below the age of 12 were allowed to enter the cinema to see the film without an accompanying adult. The U certificate was very important for this film and the producers were anxious not to lose it. Noel Langley therefore decided that during our 'naked' swim, Ken and I would only be seen from the waist up. He insisted, however, that to maintain authenticity we should shoot the scene without wearing our swimming trunks. Ken More wanted nothing to do with this and protested vehemently and the issue resulted in a major confrontation involving the whole crew, all of whom seemed to have an opinion on the matter. Eventually, I said, 'I'm game,' and Ken had no alternative but to go along with it. We both stripped off our trunks and ran into the water. We did the scene once, shot from behind, and Noel said we needed to do another take because my hosepipe was showing and it would lose us our U certificate. I have to say that I didn't know how to interpret exactly what he meant by that. I hope he wasn't being personal. But over the years, I did three nude scenes and they were all rewarded with U certificates.

Ken More recalls in his autobiography *More or Less* that, after the take, we swam back to the beach and walked back to where the crew were. Joan's stand-in was a local lady who was sitting on the beach knitting. It turned out that she was easily shocked. When she saw these two naked men walking towards her, she fainted!

I don't think Joan Collins was much more than about 18 at the time. She claims that she was the first person to wear a bikini in a cinema film while she was doing this one. I don't have any reason to disbelieve her. She rips up Ken More's shirt at one point in the film and spends most of the rest of the film with the remainder of the shirt carefully folded around her bosom.

Perhaps it was because of the persistent sound of the waves while we were on location but we had to re-dub the entire film when we arrived back in Britain after the shoot and that took an enormous amount of time.

By now I was 28 years old and I felt I was doing well in the profession that I had got into largely by accident. I had worked with many of the greatest names in British stage and film drama and I used every opportunity available to learn their craft. Now, again, almost by chance, I happened to find myself immersed in another medium. Radio was calling, in the form of a new show whose title coincidentally summed up how I viewed my life at the time.

CHAPTER 6

BLISS

A Life of Bliss was a new weekly radio sitcom on the BBC Home Service that had its first airing on Wednesday evening, 29 July 1953. The show was to have David Tomlinson in the starring role as the absent-minded bumbling bachelor David Alexander Bliss, who finds himself in a different awkward situation each week.

David Tomlinson was playing in the comedy play *The Little Hut* in the West End at the time, along with Robert Morley and American actress Joan Tetzel, and the show had enjoyed an impressive run of more than three years. When the show ended its London run, six weeks after *A Life of Bliss* started, Tomlinson was under contract to go on tour with it, which made it impossible for him to do the Sunday recordings of *Bliss*. Producer Leslie Bridgemont had to make the difficult decision of whether to cancel the show or find another David Bliss.

Fortunately for me, my name came up and I was offered the part. I first appeared in the eighth episode on 16 September 1953, playing the title character, and I stayed in the role for 110 episodes. In the early episodes I was joined by Nora Swinburne, who played my character's sister Anne, and Esmond Knight, who played her husband Bob Batten. Their parts were taken over in a later series by Diana Churchill and Colin Gordon. Animal and bird impersonator Percy Edwards also played an important role in the series as the bark of David Bliss's pet dog Psyche.

This was a whole new experience for me. The shows were recorded on Sunday nights at the Playhouse Theatre in the centre of London. The Playhouse was a beautiful theatre rebuilt in 1907, with plush red seats and polished brass and elaborately carved plaster angels set into the proscenium arch. There was always an invited audience (meaning that they did not pay for tickets) who were there to watch the performers stand and read from scripts, and laugh and applaud at the appropriate time. There were signs that lit up to prompt them in case they forgot to laugh and applaud as well as a stage manager who would clap his hands excitedly above his head at the proper time to make sure the audience had fully got the hang of what they were expected to do.

One of the most unusual things about the show was that we often started the recording without knowing how the story was going to end. The writer, Godfrey Harrison, who is sadly no longer with us, did all the writing by himself. He had had a prolific writing career in radio and television and wrote or adapted some of the BBC's earliest children's serials, including *Kaleidoscope* (1951), *The Man in Armour* (1951) and *Emil and the Detectives* (1952). But by the time he came to *Bliss*, he was notoriously disorganised and frequently arrived at the studio with an unfinished script. He would often sit at the back of the stage furiously writing the ending while the cast was recording the beginning. As he finished another page his wife would quietly slip it to the actors so the recording could go ahead without stopping.

It was a real 'backs to the wall' job. Sometimes we would run out of script before Godfrey had finished writing it and the recording would have to stop. Percy Edwards would do some more animal and bird impressions to try to keep the audience warmed up. I swear that some of the bird sounds that he conjured up were figments of his imagination and did not relate to any bird that anybody anywhere has ever encountered or ever will. But occasionally we needed more time than Percy's repertoire could accommodate. Leslie Bridgemont, the producer, would then suggest to the audience that they go out for a drink (there were plenty of pubs nearby) and come back in half an hour. This would always be the last resort because, inevitably, the audience would be a little depleted when they filed back half an hour later, having lost a few who had decided that the pub was a more attractive entertainment option for a Sunday night.

When the radio series first started, Godfrey's rather chaotic approach to scriptwriting was not known about. The BBC had asked for four scripts before they started production. But by the time they reached episode five, he had written only ten pages.

There was one occasion when the recording ended at midnight with about four people left in the audience after the rest had given up and gone home. The sound engineer had to dub in laughter and applause from *Ray's a Laugh* to keep up the atmosphere.

We had one actress who waited until 11 p.m. and then said, 'Well, I can't stay any later, I've got people coming over for supper and I need to leave.' That meant that everything we'd recorded earlier had to be adapted to the fact that she wasn't there anymore.

Godfrey had a small office backstage. I went in to see him on one occasion and while we were talking he casually leaned across the table and picked up an empty water jug in one hand and an empty tumbler in the other. He then poured some imaginary water from the jug into the glass, put the jug back on the table, the glass to his lips, drank the imaginary water and said, 'That's better, now where were we?'

They were marvellous days. I worked with some wonderful people and had a lot of fun. The stories were a great hit with the listeners and I got the chance to work with the lovely young singer Petula Clark, who played one of David Bliss's girlfriends. When she left him at the altar at the end of one series, the BBC was deluged with letters of complaint from listeners around the world.

There was another time when we were recording at the Paris Cinema in Lower Regent Street and we had Pet Clark, Phyl Calvert, Sheila Sweet and someone else on stage at the same time, and they were all pregnant. You could hardly get near the microphones. On another occasion, we were rehearsing before the audience came in and there was a woman sitting in the front row reading the *Evening Standard*. I said to the director, 'Can you do something about that woman in the front row reading the newspaper? It's terribly distracting.' The director replied, 'That's my mother!'

When Godfrey Harrison died a few years later, I went to his funeral with Penny and I remember looking at the plaque on his coffin showing his birth date and exclaiming, 'Look at that! All these years he's been telling people he was five years younger than me and, look, he's actually four years older than me.' But he was a scriptwriter and it was his job to invent stories. He was a lovely man and is sadly missed.

David Bliss was always an innocent bachelor – innocent to the point of nausea – but he remained hugely popular and endeared himself strongly to the audience.

People would occasionally come up to me if I was drinking in a pub with the cast and say things like, 'You know, you ought not to be seen drinking in pubs because David Bliss would never do that.'

That's sometimes the price of success! Despite its long run, the radio show only usually occupied my Sundays, so I was able to continue with my film career. The BBC did 20 episodes of a television version that went out in 1960 and 1961 and, surprisingly, followed this up with three more series on radio. The final radio series went out in the spring of 1969. By that time I was getting a little fed up with the programme's tag line: '25 and still a bachelor'. I was in my forties when the final episode went out and, I have to confess, a little relieved when I heard it was to be the last series! Even David Bliss needed to grow up. But for me, one of the biggest milestones in my life came in 1954, the year after *Bliss* began, when I teamed up with Alastair Sim again in a film that saw the screen debut of one of the characters that people frequently associate with me – Flash Harry.

CHAPTER 7

ST TRINIAN'S

1954 opened for me with some post-production work on my third Mario Zampi comedy film, *Happy Ever After*, which was released on 29 June and featured David Niven, Yvonne De Carlo and Barry Fitzgerald. This was an amusing story of how David Niven's character Jasper takes over the running of a hunting estate in Ireland when his wealthy Irish great uncle (played by A. E. Matthews) dies as a result of a riding accident. Unhappy with Jasper's management and his plans to sell off the estate, the villagers use the occasion of the annual appearance of the estate's ghost to drive him away. I played a slightly dim-witted young worker on the estate named Terence who was chosen by secret ballot to bump off Jasper, unaware that several other people were secretly trying to do the same thing. I was listed in the opening credits as 'guest artist'. The film was released in the United States under the title *Tonight's the Night*.

In the meantime, Sidney Gilliat and Frank Launder were working on a follow-up to their highly successful 1950 film *The Happiest Days of Your Life*. The follow-up was based on the fictitious St Trinian's School for Young Ladies created by cartoonist Ronald Searle. The name 'St Trinian's' came from a real girls school in Edinburgh called St Trinnean's Academy for Young Ladies that had been founded by a minister's daughter in the 1920s. Searle heard the name in 1941 from some students at the school for whom he was doing a casual cartoon, juggled the letters around a bit and came up with the name 'St Trinian's'. Obviously not expecting the enormous exposure it would enjoy, he used the name in his cartoon and submitted the cartoon to the magazine *Lilliput*, where it was published in October 1941. He did some similar cartoons during and after the war and they were published in book form.

The St Trinian's of Searle's creation was a far-from-conventional girls' boarding school. In Searle's imagination, the pupils were more interested in racing form, petty crime and moneymaking schemes than in passing any traditional exams. Less than a decade later his creation evolved into the film *The Belles of St. Trinian's*, which was released on 28 September 1954.

One of the characters in the Ronald Searle cartoons was a spiv named Flash Harry, and I had the tremendous good fortune to be cast in the part in *The Belles of St. Trinian's*. This was certainly one of the most important milestones of my career. In the film, Flash Harry was depicted as previously being a boot boy at the school – a very junior porter – one of whose duties was to clean shoes and run errands. With all this experience he now knows his way around and has no difficulty acting as the bookie for the girls' racing bets and disposing of the bootleg gin they are distilling in the school chemistry laboratory.

Frank Launder, Sidney Gilliat and Val Valentine wrote the screenplay and Frank Launder directed. The film seemed almost

84

Appearing as George Potts in
Mario Zampi's *Top Secret* in 1952.
Courtesy of STUDIOCANAL Films Ltd

Above: My first film role as a wartime evacuee in *Cottage to Let* (1941) directed by Anthony Asquith. Pictured here with Muriel Aked (centre) and Jeanne de Casalis (right).

© *Moviestore Collection/Rex Feature.*

Below Left: As Young Ebenezer Scrooge in *Scrooge* (1951) directed by Brian Desmond-Hurst

© *Renown. Reproduced with kind permission*

Below Right: Peering around the corner as Flash Harry in *The Belles of St. Trinian's* in 1954.

Courtesy of STUDIOCANAL Films Ltd

The Belles of St. Trinian's (1954) was very successful. Here I am as Flash Harry (*above*)
pointing something out to Richard Wattis and (*below*) with Alastair Sim.

Courtesy of STUDIOCANAL Films Ltd

Here I am during filming of
A Prize of Gold (1955) with
(*above*) an amused Richard
Widmark and (*right*) Nigel
Patrick offering some help
on *The Time*s crossword

© *Getty Images*

Above: Pictured in costume with Robert Taylor in *Quentin Durwald* in 1956. © *Getty Images*

Below: *The Green Man* in 1956 with Alastair Sim has always been one of my favourites.

Courtesy of STUDIOCANAL Films Ltd

Above: As defence counsel in the surreal comedy film *One Way Pendulum* (1964) directed by Peter Yates.

© *Woodfall Productions*

Below: Mady the dog played my character's best friend Psyche in *A Life of Bliss* on BBC television in 1960.

© *BBC*

Above: Appearing in the *Armchair Theatre* episode 'The Wedding' in 1959.

© *Fremantle Media Enterprises*

Below: As Major-General Stanley alongside Pamela Stephenson in *The Pirates of Penzance* at the Theatre Royal, Drury Lane in 1982.

© *James Gray/Associated Newspapers/ Rex Features*

I did two films with Elizabeth Taylor: *Cleopatra* in Rome in 1963 and *The Blue Bird* in Russia in 1976. 'Super Dog' refers to my part in *The Blue Bird* as 'Tylo the Dog'.

tailor-made for Alastair Sim in the dual roles as the school's headmistress Millicent Fritton and her brother Clarence, who is secretly aiding and abetting the girls in their nefarious activities. Alastair was initially asked to play the secondary role of Clarence Fritton while Frank and Sidney looked for a strong female lead. Eventually, when the search seemed to be going nowhere, Alastair suggested, 'Why don't I play both parts?' It was quite an innovative suggestion at the time but after a preliminary investigation into whether the existing technology could handle it, Frank and Sidney decided to go with the idea.

The highly talented comic actress Joyce Grenfell played a local police sergeant, Ruby Gates, who has been assigned to work undercover as the school's new games mistress to investigate the criminal activity known to be rampant there. Joyce was an absolutely wonderful person to work with. She had an amazing sense of humour and a huge wealth of general knowledge. She could finish *The Times* crossword in half an hour, while I was still struggling with two across. Richard Wattis, who was a mainstay of comedy support roles in films of that era, played a hapless official from the Ministry of Education who has to inspect the school after the previous two inspectors have failed to return.

The film has always been one of my favourites. I've done a great many films throughout my career but, for the sheer pleasure it gave, I think *The Belles of St. Trinian's* may well have been the best of all. It showcased the talents of some highly prominent actresses known for their comedic skills, including Hermione Baddeley, Beryl Reid, Irene Handl and Joan Sims.

The plot centres on the fact that the school is heavily in debt and in danger of being closed down. Then its luck seems to change with the arrival of a new student, Princess Fatima of the fictitious country of Makyad, whose rich father intends to race his horse in an upcoming Gold Cup meeting. When Headmistress Fritton discovers that the girls are betting heavily on the horse to win the race, she reluctantly bets the school's remaining funds on the same horse. Her brother Clarence, however, is betting heavily on another horse and becomes involved in a plot by the sixth-form girls to kidnap the competing horse. When the fourth-form girls discover the plot they set out to recover the horse. It was good family entertainment and great fun to work on. As a sign of the times, Lorna Henderson, the 12-year-old actress playing Fatima, needed to have black make-up applied for the part because they wanted someone of vaguely middle-eastern appearance. I think it is fair to say that the make-up made her look slightly unusual but the film was still banned in South Africa because it had someone dark skinned in the cast.

I was paid £750 for that film. Today it doesn't sound much but in those days it was a lot of money, especially for someone of my age. I felt that I was beginning to make it in the cinema.

My character Flash Harry was an archetypal spiv of the type that could often be seen on street corners in those days taking bets and flogging nylons, liquor and lots of other things that were difficult to get hold of. They were also common outside theatres selling tickets to latecomers when there were no tickets left at the box office. What they were doing was usually illegal, in a petty sort of way, and they would have an air of being constantly in a hurry and on the lookout for possible trouble from the authorities.

What we now regard as a spiv seems to have evolved out of wartime austerity. The term came into prominence during the Second World War for a particular type of low-level criminal with a distinctive type of flashy clothing who was able to provide goods that were hard to come by during the difficult period of rationing. The goods they supplied were usually black market, stolen or fake, and frequently all three.

As soon as I was offered the part of Flash Harry, I realised that it was going to become a highly significant part, not only for the film but also for my career. Someone came up to me afterwards and told me that a famous comedy actor was claiming that I had pinched the character of Flash Harry from him. I met the actor some time later and said to him, 'I understand that you think I pinched the character of Flash Harry from you.' He said, 'That's right.' I replied, 'Well you're wrong. I pinched it from Sid Field!'

That was true; I did get the feel of Flash Harry from Sid Field. He was a brilliant stage performer in the 1930s and 1940s and played a huge range of comedy characters in his act, including a cockney spiv named Slasher Green who he introduced in the film *London Town* in 1946. Four years later the great British stand-up comedian Arthur English played a similar character called 'Tosh the Spiv' at the Windmill Theatre in 1950. But, in all honesty, Flash Harry's character was created by the artist Ronald Searle in the cartoons for the St Trinian's books. In the books, Flash Harry is shown leaning around a corner at an impossible 45-degree angle, complete with the moustache and hat. Everything was already there. Ronald Searle had made it all for us.

Were it not for the fact that there were so many characters of this kind around, Flash Harry could well have been the inspiration behind a string of similar characters that popped up in films and television in later years, such as Private Walker who was played admirably by James Beck in *Dad's Army*. He was an archetypal spiv but he did have some charm about him. I've met a few spivs in my time and usually they don't have that much charm.

I did another three *St. Trinian's* films after that: *Blue Murder at St. Trinian's* in 1957, *The Pure Hell of St. Trinian's* in 1960 and *The Great St. Trinian's Train Robbery* in 1966. Alastair Sim appeared only briefly in *Blue Murder*, reprising his role as Miss Fritton the headmistress (whose first name was changed for some reason from Millicent in the first film to Amelia in this one). By now she had found herself in prison and Alastair was seen in a cameo role in a five-second head-and-shoulders shot through the bars of a prison cell at the beginning of the film, and then for less than a minute as Miss Fritton welcoming the girls back to school at the end. He did not appear in the other two films.

Contrary to what many people believe, the first *St. Trinian's* film and his brief appearance in the second were the only occasions in his career that Alastair performed in drag but he looked quite amazing. He looked just like his mother! I think those images were so striking that many people who saw them at the time have such a solid recollection that they believe he played many other female roles.

In the totally implausible plot of *Blue Murder at St. Trinian's*, the army has been drafted in to maintain order at the school and Flash Harry is now running the St Trinian's marriage bureau. A rich playboy in Italy wants to select one of the St Trinian's girls as his wife and, in order to get the girls to Italy so he can make his choice, the school has to win an international essay competition. Lionel Jeffries played an excellent part as a diamond thief who is the father of one of the girls and hides out at the school after a diamond robbery. When the police arrive, he has to pose as the headmistress while the real one is hidden away in the belfry.

Lionel had to perform in drag for this part and was quite embarrassed about it. It was still early in his film career and in those days most actors did not look with relish upon appearing in drag, except for the occasional outing with *Charley's Aunt*, which was generally considered acceptable. He told fellow cast member Terry-Thomas that the only reason he agreed was because his wife Eileen had talked him into it. But he was absolutely brilliant and appeared in a woman's Harris Tweed outfit. Even more hilarious was the fact that he did not wear a wig and so the bogus headmistress was completely bald.

Also among the cast were Joyce Grenfell, again as Sergeant Ruby Gates, Richard Wattis, again as the Education Ministry official, and comic actor Terry Scott in his first film role playing a police sergeant.

Shapely actress and model Sabrina, who had recently come onto the entertainment scene, had a non-speaking 'glamour' role as a sixth-former named Virginia. She was listed in the credits as a 'guest artiste'. Her only role was to lie on a bed reading a book and keeping abreast of the times while the other action took place around her. She featured prominently in some of the posters for the film so I assume she helped sell a few tickets.

Three years later, in 1960, I did *The Pure Hell of St. Trinian's*. Like the previous two, it was written by Frank Launder and Sidney Gilliat, and directed by Launder. The story takes place after the pupils have burned down the original St Trinian's school. An Old Bailey judge places the girls under the care of a dubious Professor Canford (played by Cecil Parker) of the fictitious University of Bagdad (*sic*), who claims he can rehabilitate them with the help of an equally dubious headmistress (played by Irene Handl). The professor's motive, far from being altruistic, was to take the sixth-form girls away on a bogus cultural tour of the Greek islands and force them to marry the sons of an Arab sheik. Again, the principal cast were highly experienced comedy actors, including Eric Barker, Joyce Grenfell, Irene Handl and Thorley Walters, all of whom could milk every bit of humour from whatever the situation. My role as Flash Harry continued as the unofficial marriage agent for the school, who saw the safety and security of his girls as his prime responsibility.

1966 saw the release of *The Great St. Trinian's Train Robbery*, written and directed by the same team as the previous three and the first to be made in colour. This was released three years after a genuine great train robbery had taken place in Britain and the topic was still fresh in everyone's minds. Only Eric Barker, Richard Wattis and I remained from the previous two but we had great support this time from Reg Varney, Frankie Howerd and Dora Bryan.

Frankie Howerd plays a hairdresser named Alphonse who leads a gang of crooks to steal mailbags containing £2.5 million from a train (the same amount as in the actual train robbery three years earlier) and store the loot in a derelict mansion in the country. In a stroke of clever casting, the robbery was coordinated by a character known as the Governor, played by Stratford Johns, who was well known at the time for playing a senior police officer in the BBC Television crime shows *Z-Cars* and *Softly, Softly*. Only his voice was heard in the film but he was immediately recognisable. The idea of having an unseen voice giving the instructions was a parody of the Ernst Stavro Blofeld super-villain character in the James Bond films *From Russia with Love* and *Thunderball*, in which his voice is heard but only his hands and the back of his head are seen. There was also a definite James Bond connection in the use of gadgets, such as a converted hairdryer and a specially adapted television set in Alphonse's hairdressing salon that were used to communicate with the Governor.

While the gang waited for the dust to settle after the raid, the mansion was converted into new accommodation to replace the old St Trinian's school that was burned down. By the time the gang attempts to retrieve the loot, the mansion is occupied by rebellious schoolgirls and drunken teachers. In order to access the proceeds, Frankie's character arranges for his two wayward daughters to join the school. The gang's attempts to recover the loot end in a memorable train chase in the true spirit of British film comedies of that era. The train chase was filmed at Longmoor Military Camp in Hampshire, where there was a private railway track for military purposes.

In 1980, after a 14-year break, writer and director Frank Launder made a fifth film in the St Trinian's saga, *The Wildcats of St. Trinian's*. I was offered a part in the film but I was already contracted elsewhere. The character Flash Harry remained, however, and was played by Joe Melia.

Apart from location work, the majority of the first four films were shot in and around Shepperton Studios in Twickenham, Middlesex, about 10 miles from the centre of London. The medium distance exterior views of the St Trinian's school building and much of the interior of the school were shot at a 17th-century house on the Shepperton Studios site, officially named Littleton House but generally known simply as 'the Old House'. The house has featured in hundreds of films and television shows over the years and still remains in frequent use for film locations and functions. It also houses studio production offices.

The external long shots of the school, looking from the entrance to the drive, were done at a real educational college in Easneye in Hertfordshire and not, as many sources suggest, at Oakley Court in Windsor. The fifth film, *Wildcats*, was made at Bray Studios, which is next door to Oakley and they used Oakley Court for the exterior shots of that film but not for the first four. The two buildings have similar architectural features but it is easy to spot which is which: Oakley has a tower and Easneye does not.

The scriptwriters and designers went to great lengths to create what at first sight appears to be a respectable school, even to the extent of having a school motto on the wall of the reception hall near the imposing staircase. The motto was *in flagrante delicto*, a Latin term used by lawyers to indicate that someone was 'caught in the act' of committing an offence. The term literally means 'in burning offence' and is often used in divorce cases in Britain to refer to being caught in a situation in which respectable young schoolgirls would not normally be expected to be involved.

St Trinian's had another reincarnation in 2007, this time from producers and co-directors Barnaby Thompson and Oliver Parker, in a film called simply *St. Trinian's*. This had its premiere in December that year. The film had a sizeable cast of both emerging and established talent. Colin Firth played the Education Minister, Rupert Everett played the dual roles of headmistress Miss Fritton and her brother, and Russell Brand played Flash Harry. Stephen Fry played himself. Everyone involved seemed to have put a lot of effort into it but, in all honesty, I didn't think much of it. I really didn't see any need for an update. The original belonged to a particular time in history when society was very different. We could laugh at unruly behaviour in a school in those days because, for the most part, it was a rarity. Today you see it all around you – on trains, in shopping centres and definitely in the schools. To me, it is not something to laugh about anymore, unless you do it in the context of a point in time when it was not common. That's why I still laugh at the original. One thing I did appreciate, though, was that the schoolgirls in the remake were not seen smoking. That was a highly laudable message for the makers to put across.

CHAPTER 8

BACK TO
THE FIFTIES

M any of the films we made in Britain during the 1950s had one
or two American actors in the cast. Some rather cynical
British actors at the time (of whom I was definitely not one)
resented this and referred disparagingly to the 'token Americans'
but the reality was that many of our films could only be
distributed in America if they included an American actor,
preferably one of star quality. The British distributors would sell
films to their American counterparts as a package consisting of a
major feature and a shorter 'B' film that was usually made on a
lower budget and not intended as a primary audience attraction.
Distribution in this way ensured that British actors who tended to
appear more often in 'B' films stood a reasonable chance of getting
some exposure in America.

One of my first film releases after *The Belles of St. Trinian's* was
one that had an American lead – a lead we were extremely

privileged to have working with us. *A Prize of Gold* was released in February 1955. It was directed by Mark Robson and starred American actor Richard Widmark. The film was set in Berlin soon after the end of the Second World War. Dick Widmark played a master sergeant in the US Air Force Police stationed in the British Sector and I played a Military Police sergeant. For some reason my character was Scottish and I needed to use a Scottish accent. Nigel Patrick played an ex-RAF pilot.

Most of the film was shot in Berlin. When construction workers discover a buried cache of gold bars during land preparation for the city's redevelopment, Dick's character and mine are assigned to arrange for it to be flown to England for disposal. In the meantime, Dick has become romantically interested in a young refugee (played by Mai Zetterling) who is caring for a group of German war orphans and yearns for the chance to move them to Brazil, where she hopes to set up an orphanage and give them a new life. Why Brazil, we never find out. Dick comes up with a plan to hijack the plane transporting the bullion to England and use the proceeds to fund the orphanage. The hijack goes smoothly but, once it is over, Dick and I begin to have second thoughts about what to do with the proceeds. It is not all bad and we seriously consider giving it back.

Dick and I became close friends after we did this film and, whenever he came over to England for any long period after that, he would ask me to find a cottage out in the country where he could stay during his visit.

There were large numbers of British army personnel in Berlin when we did the film and they asked if the cast of the film could do some sort of entertainment for them. Nigel Patrick suggested that we get hold of a copy of *The Green Eye of the Little Yellow God* by J. Milton Hayes. It is a serious poem but I was introduced as 'Queen Victoria's Favourite Monologist' and I did the monologue while

Nigel sat in the audience shouting interruptions throughout. It was a very funny double act.

I did the monologue again in 1979 when Penny produced a charity concert in Henley, just outside London, to save a historic well not far from where we live. The well was originally paid for by the Maharaja of Benares in India during a terrible drought in the Henley area in the middle of the 19th century. The Maharaja donated the money to sink a 300-feet-deep borehole to provide a water supply to the local farming community. This was in recognition of the work and dedication of a civil servant named Edward Anderdon Reade, who was born not far from Henley and had spent many years in Benares helping to find water for the people there.

The well was officially opened in 1864. When it needed extensive renovation a few years ago, Penny and Roy Hudd's then wife Ann, who lived nearby, went around canvassing people to make sure they would come to the concert. One of the people they approached was an ex-Beatle, the late George Harrison, who also lived in the area. He wasn't too interested in attending the concert but said he would have a look at the well and, if he liked it, would buy it and shift it onto his property. They had to tactfully explain that that was not the object of the exercise but thanks all the same. The concert finally raised enough money to completely renovate the well and restore it to full working order.

In May 1955, three months after the release of *A Prize of Gold*, another of my comedy films was released. *The Constant Husband* was an amusing and critically well-received comedy from Frank Launder and Sidney Gilliat. Sidney directed and wrote the screenplay with Val Valentine and they were jointly nominated for a Best Screenplay award for the film at the 1956 BAFTA awards. This was undoubtedly Rex Harrison's film as he appeared in practically every scene. His character wakes up in a hotel room in Wales with no knowledge of who he is or what he is doing there. With the help of a memory specialist (played by Cecil Parker), he gradually discovers to his horror that he has several wives in different parts of the country and begins to contact them one by one to help piece together his forgotten past. Finally, he is arrested for bigamy and is defended by a glamorous female lawyer played by Margaret Leighton. I had a lovely part as a character named Luigi Sopranelli, who is a relative of one of Rex's wives. The part was enormous fun but I can't think what came over me to accept it. I had to use a thick Italian accent. Fortunately, it was a comedy film and so I doubt if many people were too concerned about its authenticity.

The film had its American premiere on NBC television under the title *Marriage a la Mode* six months after its British release. It needed to have more than 20 minutes edited out to fit into a 90-minute television timeslot and was one of the first British films to go straight to American television before its theatrical release. The full-length version did not appear in American cinemas until more than two years after its UK release.

Next to be released was *The Adventures of Quentin Durward*, an ambitious costume drama produced by MGM that had its British premiere on 1 March 1956, four months after its release in America. The film starred Robert Taylor in the title role as Quentin Durward, a 15th-century Scottish knight who is sent to France to evaluate the beautiful Countess Isabelle of Marcroy (Kay Kendall) as a suitable wife for his elderly uncle Lord Crawford (Ernest Thesiger). The film was adapted from the novel *Quentin Durward* by Sir Walter Scott, which was first published in 1823. The countess has no interest in the proposed marriage and goes to King Louis XI of France (Robert Morley) seeking his protection. Durward pursues her and along the way encounters a gypsy named Hayraddin (the role I played) with whom he later collaborates to rescue the countess from a plot by the king to marry her off for his own political gain. By now Durward is himself in love with the countess but cannot court her because of the oath he took to his uncle. The film tells of his adventures leading up to the time he becomes free to follow his destiny.

The film was made at MGM's British studios in Elstree, just outside London, and on location in the spectacular chateau region of France.

The role of Hayraddin was originally played by Austrian actor Charles Goldner. Sadly, Charles died unexpectedly while the film was being made and the studio had to cast another Hayraddin. Leonard Samson, who is a great friend of mine, was a publicity man for Warner Bros at the time and was involved in the discussions. Apparently, the camera operator said, 'There's only one person who could take that part – it's George Cole.' They all said, 'He's much too young.' Len said, 'Give him a wig and he'll be perfect.' He asked me if I wanted to do it and, before I knew what was happening, I was being made up like a very old man.

Much as I enjoyed playing the part, it was a rather eerie feeling for the first few days knowing that I was only in it because the original actor had died. It wasn't made any easier being asked by someone I knew well what it was like to be acting in a dead man's shoes. I could have done without that; even though he was a friend, I thought it was something that didn't need to be said.

Robert Morley had a wonderful part as King Louis XI, and the beautiful Kay Kendall played the heroine. Tragically, she died of leukaemia three years later at the age of 32 while she was married to Rex Harrison. We lost a superb artiste.

My part in *Quentin Durward* eventually led to my first appearance in a television commercial. Five years after we made *Quentin*

Durward, the film was shown on British television one Sunday afternoon. Joy Jameson, my agent, rang me the next day and said, 'We've had a request for you to appear in a television commercial.'

I replied, 'Well, I'm sorry. I can't do it because I'm working at the Hampstead Theatre.' I was getting £27 a week. Joy said, 'Well, it's too good for you to turn down. I'll get back to them.'

The advertising agency asked her when I would be finishing at the Hampstead and when she told them, they replied, 'Don't worry – we'll do it the week after he finishes.'

The commercial turned out to be for Hamlet small cigars. The script was one of the best I've ever seen. It was set on a bridge across the Bosphorus River in Istanbul. When I saw the script, I thought, 'There's no way they'll do it in Turkey. They'll probably do it somewhere like Bushy Park near Hampton Court.' But Penny, my wife, who has done lots of commercials, said, 'Oh yes, they will!' – and they did.

When they told us we would be doing it on location in Istanbul, I assumed they would at least give us a business-class flight and a nice hotel but all they could manage was a package holiday. But what they saved on the travel they made up for in the commercial.

The set was spectacular. I was on the bridge dressed in a white suit and a white panama hat and with a red carnation in my buttonhole. Another person with a red carnation appears and I offer him a cigar. Appearing surprised, he takes one but, to my horror, he takes a real cigar and leaves behind what I expected him to take, which is really the rolled-up plans for a bomb. I frantically indicate to him that he should take the rolled-up plans, so he takes them, sets light to them in a nearby brazier, lights the cigar with them and walks away. At that moment, someone else appears dressed exactly the same way as I am. Without a word being spoken we know immediately that the newcomer is the person who should have been offered the cigar. It was absolutely brilliant the way they were able to convey a fairly complex story with no dialogue in the 60 seconds available. The advertising agency Collett Dickenson Pearce won all sorts of industry awards with it, including the inaugural Test of Time trophy at the 1989 International Advertising Festival in Cannes for ads more than 15 years old. The strange thing is that I just could not warm to the director. He simply didn't seem to be fully into it.

Back in August 1956 my next film to be released was the musical comedy *It's a Wonderful World*, directed by Val Guest. The story is about a pair of struggling music composers (played by Terence Morgan and myself) who discover an attractive young French singer (played by Mylène Demongeot and credited as Mylene Nicole) living in an adjacent flat. Hoping to become better acquainted with her, they offer her one of their songs to get an audition with bandleader Ted Heath (who plays himself). The singer has a successful audition with Ted but the two composers continue to struggle to come up with new material. By chance, they find they can create new music by playing existing music backwards and passing it off as original work from a reclusive and totally fictitious avant-garde composer in Europe. The new music is absolutely terrible but, not wishing to appear out of touch, the public starts to accept it and it starts to become popular. The French singer, however, unintentionally becomes wise to what the pair are doing and it starts to look as if they will suffer serious consequences.

The film contained some impressive production numbers with the Ted Heath Band, including a high-spirited version of *Hawaiian War Chant* featuring drummer Ronnie Verrell filmed on location at the Hammersmith Palais. My good friend Kathleen Harrison also appeared, as did Richard Wattis and Reginald Beckwith. This was a real 'feel good' film that had a good storyline and was fun from start to finish. One thing I particularly liked was the surprise twist at the end of the film, which I won't reveal in case anyone reading this is moved to get the DVD from the movie library. I worked again with Mylène Demongeot, who played the singer, nearly 40 years later when she appeared in a *Minder* episode as a French woman who mistakes Arthur Daley for an old flame when he gets stranded in France on a liquor-buying visit for the Winchester Club.

The Green Man, released on 18 September 1956, has always been one of my favourite films with Alastair Sim because it was terribly funny. Frank Launder and Sidney Gilliat, who produced and adapted the film version, based the story on their stage play *Meet a Body* and received a Best Screenplay nomination for the film at the 1957 BAFTA awards. I went to see the play and thought it would make a marvellous film, so I bought a copy and showed it to Alastair and he thought the same. He took it to Frank and Sidney and said we would like to make it into a film. They agreed that it was a good idea but then said they wanted to give the part I liked to Ken More. I thought, 'No, you can't do that! I'm the one who brought it to you,' and I think Alastair put his foot down because I got the part.

We made it at Shepperton Studios, just outside London. From the outset Alastair made it clear to Launder and Gilliat that he would like to direct the film. However, it soon transpired that he would not be able to because he did not have trade-union accreditation as a film director. Eventually, they were able to negotiate an agreement with the union under which he was permitted to have a directing role but only under the supervision of an accredited director. That role was accepted by a well-qualified camera operator named Robert Day. In the event, Alastair more or less directed it but under Robert Day's nominal 'supervision' and Robert was credited as director.

The film stars Alastair as Hawkins, a quiet watchmaker who is also a professional assassin in his spare time. The story is set just after the Second World War when Alastair's character is contracted to eliminate Sir Gregory Upshott, a pompous government official (played by Raymond Huntley), at the Green Man Hotel on the south coast of England. His plans go awry when my character, William Blake, a hapless vacuum-cleaner salesman, interrupts him and discovers the plot. When no one believes Blake's story, he goes to the Green Man Hotel to try to save Sir Gregory, who is targeted to meet his end through a bomb placed in a radio in the hotel lounge. There is some confusion when I arrive at the hotel and mistake another guest – a caddish member of parliament (played hilariously by Terry-Thomas) – for Sir Gregory but I finally manage to find the right person.

My favourite scene was when I go to the house where Alastair's character lives to ask him to call the police because I think there is a body hidden in the piano in the house where I am demonstrating a vacuum cleaner. I don't know at that stage that he was involved in the crime. It is a fast-paced scene combining my panic at having discovered a body and Alastair's panic at trying to hide the fact that he was an accomplice. That sort of scene would be extremely difficult to script. We rehearsed it a few times and he eventually told me, 'Forget about the lines, just act.' On the final take we were both completely ad-libbing but it worked well and turned out to be a highly amusing scene.

After the gentle comedy of *The Green Man*, my next film, released a week or so later, was a tense and disturbing black-and-white thriller entitled *The Weapon* (directed by Val Guest). This was primarily intended for the American market and was written by American screenwriter Fred Freiberger, starred American actors Steve Cochran and Lizabeth Scott and was produced by American producer Hal E. Chester. It had a distinct film noir feel about it with its background of the wartime bomb damage in shadowy east London.

I was cast in a role that was entirely different from the ones I was usually associated with throughout my career and one that I was a little uncomfortable taking on. It required that I convey a deceitful character who was not averse to manhandling an eight-year-old boy and getting involved in a fistfight with a policeman to get what he wanted.

The story told of a young boy, played by Jon Whiteley, who finds a German pistol in the ruins of a building destroyed in the Blitz and accidentally shoots a friend with it in a struggle over who owns it. The police discover that the gun was used in an unsolved murder of a US army officer 10 years earlier. An officer in the US army's Criminal Investigation Division, played by Steve Cochran, along with a Scotland Yard officer, attempt to locate the boy who fired the weapon after he flees following the accident.

My character, Joshua Henry, the killer of the American soldier, also goes in pursuit of the boy and ingratiates himself with the boy's mother (played by Lizabeth Scott) in order to get information on his possible whereabouts.

The film is well made and maintains a continuous level of suspense throughout, leading up to a somewhat predictable ending. However, I found the storyline a little disturbing and it isn't one of the films I would like to be remembered for.

During all this film work I still managed to tread the boards in the theatre. *Misery Me!* was a so-called 'comedy of woe' by playwright Denis Cannan that opened at the Duchess Theatre in March 1955 following a four-week tour. Directed by Alastair, the play was a satire of the Cold War. It was set in a mountain hotel to which I had been sent by two men to commit two murders. What neither of the two contractors knew was that in each case the person I was supposed to murder had contracted me to bump off the other one. What I didn't know was that there was also a suicidal woman (played by Yvonne Mitchell) staying at the hotel who proves to be a distraction from my assignment and whom I eventually fall for. Unfortunately, the play ran for only about three weeks because there was a newspaper strike at the time and there were hardly any reviews, so not many people got to hear about it. It's strange how a strike like that can have totally unrelated knock-on effects.

1957 saw my first and only visit to America, where I did an episode entitled 'Rainy Day' in Alfred Hitchcock's television series *Suspicion*. I did the play three times on television, once for the BBC, once for ITV and once in America for Hitchcock. The original episode went out on American television on 2 December 1957.

The story involved two English expatriate managers on an African cocoa plantation who share their quarters on the estate. Nigel, played by Robert Flemyng, was something of a high flyer back in England and always receives lots of letters. The other, George Willis, who I played, is rather pure and simple-minded and has no experience of life. He has no friends or family and never receives or writes any letters of his own. Nigel is always boasting to George about his letters and revealing little snippets of what they contain. This makes my character desperately anxious to have a letter of his own and he eventually persuades Nigel to sell him an unopened letter so he can experience what it is like to have one.

A few days later, Nigel asks me whom the letter was from. I reply, 'I can't tell you that. It's my letter now. It's private. I bought it from you.'

He says, 'Don't be silly! It was my letter to start with. It was addressed to me.'

But I am firm that I will not share it with him. The rest is pure Hitchcock, expertly directed by James Nielson.

The tension gradually builds up between them over the letter and Nigel starts to lose control. On New Year's Eve, at the peak of all this tension, George arranges a small celebration for the two of them at which he plans to reveal the contents of the letter. Nigel, however, has no idea what the celebration is for and the situation begins to get ugly as he continues to press for details. Eventually, he threateningly picks up a champagne bottle. The bottle was a real one and the idea was that the props people would crawl up from underneath and replace the real bottle with a plastic one. I suddenly saw out of the corner of my eye that the props man was trying to wrestle the real bottle out of his hand. I spent what seemed like an eternity trying to stay in character, hoping that Nigel would let go of the real bottle before he hit me with it. Happily, they managed to do the swap and no harm came to me. My character, however, never woke up. The final shot was of the contents of the letter. It was an advertising flyer for a raincoat that began, 'Be prepared for a rainy day!' The story was based on one written by W. Somerset Maugham and was adapted for the screen by Michael Pertwee.

I flew to Los Angeles to do the Hitchcock shoot in Hollywood and returned first class on one of the big Cunard liners out of New York. On the first night aboard I happened to bump into Tommy Cooper, who was also on his way back to England. He wasn't there officially as an entertainer; he was a regular passenger, the same as I was. But he spent his time entertaining himself going up to random groups of passengers and saying, 'Have you ever seen an Eskimo having a pee?' Of course, they would always say no and he would open his flies and all these fake ice cubes would fall out. And for the rest of the voyage, you would keep hearing the clonking of the ice cubes as they dropped out and you'd think, 'There goes Tom. He's working well!'

I stayed in New York for a few days before I sailed back. Dick Widmark, who lived not far away in Connecticut, showed me around and took me to some nice restaurants. The first night we went to a lovely restaurant but I wondered why there was no wine list. What I didn't know was that he had a bad stomach ulcer and couldn't drink alcohol – so he took me to his favourite temperance restaurant. When I got back home and told people I had been out to dinner in New York with Dick Widmark, they all said how wonderful it must have been. I said, 'Yes, it was delightful but I would have loved a drink!' In every restaurant we went to, Dick would say, 'They do the most fantastic chocolate cake here.'

In 1958 I did a play with Alastair called *The Brass Butterfly* in which I played a character named Phanocles. This was a comedy set in Greco-Roman times based on William Golding's short story *Envoy Extraordinary*. We opened in Oxford, did a provincial tour and then ran for a month at the Strand Theatre in London in April 1958. The story was of a Roman emperor of advancing years (played, naturally, by Alastair) who lives on an island retreat and is visited by an inventor (me) who wants the emperor to offer some patronage. One of my inventions is a steam engine, which I try to encourage the emperor to use to make his ships go faster, but the emperor becomes hopelessly confused over how to make use of the time he would save. I also invent a cannon but, again, the emperor is not overly supportive because his military adviser is worried about the changes to warfare that would result. Confirmation of the likely consequences comes when the cannon is unexpectedly fired and brings about equally unexpected results. My next invention is a pressure cooker, which excites the emperor immensely as he is a keen gourmet, and he stops work on the steamship and cannon but rewards me for the pressure cooker. In the end, he appoints me Envoy Extraordinary to China. It was all unashamedly played for laughs and of all the plays we did together it was one of our favourites, tempered only perhaps by Alastair's disappointment that it did not stay longer in the West End.

When James Bridie died in 1951, Alastair lost his favourite playwright and a great friend. It affected him tremendously and he spent a long time mourning the loss. After that, Alastair would often write to a novelist whose work he admired and invite him or her to write a play for him or allow an existing story to be adapted as a stage play. William Golding's *Envoy Extraordinary* was an example of this. Alastair read the short story and wrote to Bill Golding saying he would like to do it as a play, to which Golding wrote back and said he thought it was a wonderful idea. But the path to the stage was not a smooth one. At the first dress rehearsal the play ran for over four hours because nobody had bothered to time it. In fact, it was Alastair's fault because he was the director but the stage manager got the blame.

In those days, Alastair's wife Naomi would always prepare a sumptuous dinner on a Sunday night and they would usually invite a guest – invariably someone Alastair was currently working with or hoped to work with, or someone he had worked with in the past. On one occasion, immediately after the four-hour dress rehearsal, Bill Golding was the guest and they spent a lot of time discussing how to shorten the play. Bill wanted to take one of the characters out completely but Alastair didn't agree. This generated some friction and finally led to a blazing row. By that time I had built my house right next door to Alastair and Naomi and I was often a Sunday dinner guest. On that occasion I rather foolishly took Golding's side, which made life difficult for me because, whenever I went out, I had to go past their house and there was always some unpleasantness. I found myself having to take an alternative road to avoid them. This went on for a while and I thought it was all rather silly, so I finally went along and made the peace.

To say that Alastair was unconventional would be an understatement. While I was living with him and Naomi (with my bed on an upstairs landing), Alastair would use these Sunday dinners to iron out minor problems with the people he was working with. Whenever there was an actor who Alastair wanted to have a go at, his method was to take it out on me by giving me a dressing-down for some trivial reason in front of the guest. Everyone would think 'poor Georgie' and start feeling sorry for me. Then he would start to have a go at the actor he was trying to get through to, who by now knew exactly what Alastair was like when he got wound up and wouldn't dare make any serious attempt to defend himself. After the first time, I got the message that he was not really having a go at me but that he was preparing to have a go at someone else later at dinner. I think the first time it shook me up a bit but it didn't really bother me after that.

He had another unfortunate way of getting his opinions of people across to them. At one Sunday dinner, after a particularly rough rehearsal with the dinner guest, he patiently laid out his suggestions on how the actor might be able to improve his performance. As he was leaving after dinner, the guest said, 'Well, thank you very much for that advice. I'll go away and think about it.' As Alastair was closing the door after him, he said within the guest's hearing, 'For goodness sake, don't do that. You're not bloody capable of it.' But it worked, unfortunately.

Another of Alastair's quirks was that he was an appalling golfer and he kept buying new sets of clubs because he felt they would make a big difference to his game. Naomi described his drive as starting out like a peach and ending up like a banana, which made him extremely cross indeed. I think he considered himself reasonably proficient.

One day he was playing with another actor at Huntercombe Golf Club near where he lived and he had just bought himself a set of expensive Henry Cotton clubs that he firmly believed would bring about a drastic improvement. I was caddying for him. He did one of his dreadful drives and was so angry with the result that he just threw the club right into the wood and told me to go in and get it.

The Huntercombe green was thickly wooded and, as I went in to retrieve the offending golf club, I suddenly came across a section of an RAF training plane that had obviously crashed there sometime earlier. I quickly put the golf club in amongst the wreckage and went rushing back to Alastair, shouting, 'Come quick and see what you've done now, Allie.' He came into the wood and found the wreckage with a Henry Cotton golf club wedged into the tailplane. For some reason, he didn't seem to enjoy the joke that much.

He took his golf painstakingly seriously, even though he wasn't particularly good at it, and I think that because he didn't have a lot of skill, he became defensive. You couldn't make a joke about it because he would jump back at you. But golfing aside, most of the time he was absolutely charming.

Too Many Crooks, which was released on 8 March 1959, was the last of the four comedies I did directed by Mario Zampi. Michael Pertwee did the screenplay based on a story by Christiane Rochefort and Jean Nery. The film was shot in black and white in 1958 when the expense of colour film was still a major disincentive for producers to make their films in colour. This was a comedy in which I played Fingers, the leader of a gang of incompetent crooks that includes Sid James, Bernard Bresslaw and Joe Melia. Bernard had recently started to become instantly recognisable through his appearances in the Granada Television series *The Army Game* about a group of misfits undergoing their National Service, and he went on to play major parts in many of the *Carry On* comedy films. In this film he plays an ex-wrestler, a carbon copy of his *Army Game* character, a gormless, loveable buffoon who spends much of his time reading comics. The brains of the gang – what little there are – are with Sid James, who impatiently stays part of it because of the anticipated proceeds of its activities.

The gang bumbles its way through one botched job after another until they come up with the idea of robbing a wealthy tax dodger, cad and shady businessman named Billy Gordon (played by Terry-Thomas) who does not believe in banks and hides his money at home. For years he has tricked his wife into believing he is penniless while, behind her back, lavishing expensive gifts upon his secretary. When the attempt to rob him fails, the gang attempts to kidnap his daughter but instead discover they have kidnapped his wife (played by Brenda de Banzie). The gang attempts to extract a huge ransom for her return but her husband refuses to pay, as he enjoys having her out of the way. When his wife overhears a conversation between Terry-Thomas and me in which he actively encourages me to carry out my threat to cut her into pieces and spread them along the Great North Road, she retaliates by helping the gang steal her husband's cash. John Le Mesurier played a delightfully bemused judge and Joe Melia had an 'and introducing' opening credit. It was riotous comedy from start to finish and has become something of a cult classic, particularly the legendary kidnapping sequence involving a hearse and a coffin.

Much of the credit for the film's success must go to the brilliantly funny Terry-Thomas. He was a wonderful comic actor and was always a joy to work with. He had impeccable comic timing and was as amusing off screen as he was on it. But the end of his life was far from amusing. He developed Parkinson's disease in 1971 and gradually withdrew from public and professional life, spending long periods at his home on the Spanish island of Ibiza. Few of his friends and colleagues knew he was unwell until the *Daily Mirror* ran a story on its front page on 9 December 1988 saying that he had become handicapped, both financially and physically, because of his condition. As a result of the publicity, actor Jack Douglas and broadcaster Richard Hope-Hawkins organised a benefit concert that raised more than £75,000 for Terry and the British charity Parkinson's UK. He died just over a year later on 8 January 1990. It was a sad loss but his memory lives on in the more than 70 films he left behind.

Don't Panic Chaps was a black-and-white film released in November 1959, directed by George Pollock and produced jointly by Hammer Film Productions and the Association of Cinema Technicians. It was an amusing war comedy scripted by Jack Davies, based on a radio play by Ronald Holroyd and Michael Corston. The film should have been successful at the box office but, unfortunately, was not. I played one of a group of four British soldiers (along with Thorley Walters, Percy Herbert and Harry Fowler) who are landed by submarine on a Mediterranean island close to Sicily during the Second World War to set up an observation and reconnaissance post. For some reason the navy forgets to pick us up at the end of the mission and, while we are waiting for them, we find, quite by accident, that there is a group of German soldiers on the other side of the island who have also been left behind after a mission. As time progresses the two groups learn to live peacefully together, until an attractive woman (played by Serbian actress Nadja Regin) swims ashore. This was another film in which I had to do a nude scene – and was rewarded with a U certificate. I remember being a little surprised that when the young lady did her nude swim, she was wearing a body stocking but when I did mine, I had nothing on except a tin helmet! There was a very funny scene towards the end of the film when the soldiers organised a bacchanalian festival for the lady to substitute for one she should have been attending at home, and the English and German soldiers find themselves dancing with each other to Scottish music dressed in togas. It was excellent entertainment for the whole family.

In the middle of 1959 BBC Television asked me to reprise my old radio show *A Life of Bliss* as a television series. The radio show was still enormously popular and the opportunity to put it on television was not one to be missed. We started work on it towards the end of the year and my first professional appearance of the 1960s was on television as David Bliss.

CHAPTER 9

THE SIXTIES

The first television series of *A Life of Bliss* began on 21 January 1960 and ran over 10 30-minute episodes. Once again, I played David Bliss, and I was still a shy and rather gullible young bachelor who was always putting his foot in it and saying the wrong things. In the first series I was still living in my bachelor flat with my dog Psyche. Isabel Dean played my sister Anne and Colin Gordon played her husband Tony Fellows. Sheila Sweet played my girlfriend Zoe Hunter. Animal impersonator Percy Edwards came with us from the radio show to provide the bark of my pet dog Psyche, who was played by Mady, a wire-haired fox terrier whose real name according to her registration papers was 'Maid for Music'. Graeme Muir produced the first series and Godfrey Harrison produced the second. Godfrey Harrison wrote both.

In the second series of 10 episodes, which began in February 1961, David Bliss had moved out of his bachelor flat to the fictitious coastal resort town of Havenville and was now living with another sister, Pam Batten (played by Frances Bennett) and her husband Bob (played by Hugh Sinclair). According to the storyline, Havenville was once small and exclusive and the original inhabitants show some resentment at the influx of newcomers, of whom the Battens and now David Bliss are some. This resentment formed the basis for some of the episodes.

While we were making one of the shows, I had the great honour of meeting the Queen Mother while she was touring the BBC Television Centre. I have a feeling she was a fan of the show because she showed a strong interest in what we were doing. It was a wonderful experience meeting her; she was a lovely lady to talk to.

I was sorry when the second series came to an end and the BBC made the decision not to do another. It was a lovely series to work on and was still good clean entertainment that the whole family could watch together. I suspect that one of the reasons was Godfrey's problem with getting the scripts ready in time. Everything went out live on television in those days and sometimes we would be an hour away from transmission and there would still be six pages left to write. You can't afford that level of uncertainty in live television. It isn't just the actors who need to know their lines. Camera operators and sound operators need to know who is delivering the next line and how long for. They need to know where other equipment is on the studio floor so they don't collide with each other as they move around. At the best of times live television was stressful but without a proper rehearsal it was a nightmare. Even when we were properly rehearsed, we often had to run from one side of the studio to the other to get from one set to another and, by the end of the show, we would be totally exhausted!

My film work in the 1960s started with *The Pure Hell of St. Trinian's*, which we made in 1960 and which I have already talked about. By the time *Pure Hell* was released in December 1960 I was at the Theatre Royal in Bath in Michael Gilbert's crime comedy *The Bargain*, playing a rather disreputable character named Morgan. We later opened at St Martin's Theatre, London on 19 January 1961. Alastair Sim played a successful solicitor with a crush on his secretary. This was also my first foray into production and I co-produced the play with Alastair. Actually, I think he only asked me to be there to stop him from smoking – he had begun to realise by then that he was smoking much too much. Alastair's daughter Merlith was also on hand as an assistant stage manager for the production. The following year I did two plays by Keith Waterhouse and Willis Hall at the Royal Court Theatre in London: *Squat Betty* and *The Sponge Room*. But most of the early years of the 1960s were occupied with film work.

One of the early ones I did was a swashbuckling Technicolor adventure for children, originally called *'Disneyland': The Scarecrow of Romney Marsh*, which was produced by the Walt Disney Company and directed by James Neilson. Robert Westerby wrote the screenplay based on the book *Christopher Syn* by Russell Thorndike and William Buchanan. The story was about a country vicar named Dr Syn (played by Patrick McGoohan, who was well known at the time from the *Danger Man* and *The Prisoner* television series) who is an accomplished seaman, swordsman and academic. He is also a Robin Hood-type character who runs a smuggling ring he set up to relieve the local community from the ruinous taxation imposed by the king. In his smuggling role, he conceals his identity behind a scarecrow mask made from sackcloth in the manner of such characters as Zorro and the Lone Ranger. My character, Mr Mipps, was Syn's close friend and church sexton who supports him during his adventures using the name Hellspite. Michael Hordern, Geoffrey Keen, Eric Pohlmann and Patrick Wymark also had major roles in the film.

The film was originally conceived as a three-part mini-series for Disney for the American television market. It was then re-edited for theatrical release in Britain and ran in British cinemas over the 1963 Christmas season as *Dr. Syn, Alias the Scarecrow*. The mini-series premiered in America a few months later under its original title *'Disneyland': The Scarecrow of Romney Marsh*. The name 'Romney Marsh' refers to a large and mainly uninhabited wetland area covering parts of Kent and East Sussex in south-east England that was well known for its smuggling activities in the 17th to 19th centuries.

However, the film that put my life on hold for 18 months began production in 1961 when I was given the opportunity to work in the mega-budget epic *Cleopatra* alongside mega-stars Elizabeth Taylor, Richard Burton and Rex Harrison. Directed by Joseph L. Mankiewicz for Twentieth Century-Fox, this was one of the most expensive films, if not *the* most expensive, ever made (adjusted for inflation). It took an astonishing 18 months to complete and was finally released in 1963. It won Academy Awards for cinematography, art direction, costume design, and visual effects and was nominated for five more. Despite its critical acclaim and the fact that it was the highest-grossing film of the year (bringing in US$26 million net), it still made an overall loss for the company because of its enormous production cost of US$44 million.

Rex Harrison played Julius Caesar and I played his barber Flavius, who was a deaf mute. Flavius had a full beard and I had to go into make-up every morning at around five o'clock to have the beard applied. After about three months I asked the make-up man, 'Why do you go to so much trouble? Why don't you just have a removable beard made up for me?' He replied with his hands and all his body, the way people on the Continent often do, 'Ah, but you actors. You like-a the face to move when you speak.' I said, 'That's very thoughtful of you but I'm playing a deaf mute!' But the handcrafted beard remained. The funny part was that, when we went into postproduction the following year back in England, some of the scenes had to be redone and the make-up people used a removable beard. Nobody noticed the difference.

All of my scenes were with Rex Harrison, who I sometimes found a bit prickly to deal with. On one occasion I had to follow him as he made a majestic entrance in front of a huge crowd of extras and I had to carry a bowl for him to symbolically wash his hands. As he made his entrance, I accidentally trod on his train. I can't repeat what he said. I just wished the floor would open up so I could disappear into it. I had worked with him on other films previously and he had seen me on set every day but he reacted as if he had never seen me before. He kept referring to me as 'this little man with the beard and the tin tray'. It is not my favourite memory of *Cleopatra*.

I wasn't the only person to find Rex rather snooty. In his autobiography *Terry-Thomas Tells Tales*, Terry describes how Rex steadfastly avoided making eye contact with him for the entire duration of a flight from London to Florence when they were both in the first-class section of the plane, despite all Terry's attempts to make him smile.

We were on location in Rome for 18 months doing *Cleopatra*. When I first started, I managed to get back home to England every weekend. But then Rex Harrison got held up in the fog in London when he was supposed to be the central character in a sequence involving 3,000 extras and from then on we were not allowed to leave the environment. Rome is a fairly small place and it was difficult to go to a restaurant or have a quiet weekend without bumping into someone from the crew. Sometimes, after a long day, you just wanted to get away from the picture.

This was the time when Elizabeth and Richard had just started their much-publicised romance. As long as it was all going well with them, the film would also go well but, if it were not, one or the other would not show up on set. Elizabeth filmed all her scenes without Richard between September 1961 and January 1962. They did their first work together in front of the camera on 22 January 1962. That was when the sparks first started flying. We were put on permanent standby and had to be ready to shoot at a moment's notice. We were already barred from leaving the area and now we called it 'house arrest'. I had no lines to learn, which was hardly surprising since I was playing a deaf mute and, no matter how beautiful Rome undoubtedly is, you can get bored very quickly there.

I worked with Elizabeth again 13 years later when we were both in George Cukor's film *The Blue Bird*. When she saw me, she said, 'George, I thought you really were a deaf mute when we did *Cleopatra*.' She had never heard me speak!

Strange as it may seem for a professional actor, I haven't done much Shakespeare. I learned a few passages while I was at school and then played the Boy in the film *Henry V* in 1944. And then there was Flavius. But I remember an occasion in the 1950s when Richard Widmark came to dinner one night. The telephone rang and I excused myself and I came back to the table to say, 'I've just been invited to play Othello.' Richard nearly choked on his ravioli and said, 'Where, for Christ's sake?' I replied, 'Ludlow' – a small market town near the border of England and Wales. We couldn't stop laughing.

A few years later, I was working on a film set and a director from the Royal Shakespeare Company came up to me and asked if I would be interested in playing the Duke in *Measure for Measure* and Prospero in *The Tempest*. Not knowing much about the director, I asked another actor who was working on the same film what he knew about him. 'Funny you should mention him,' he said. 'He's just asked me to be the Duke and Prospero for the RSC.'

I arrived back in London in 1963 after *Cleopatra* and went on tour to recover at the Theatre Royal in Windsor in a comedy called *Meet Me on the Fence* by Leonard Samson. We opened in August for a two-week season in which I played opposite Charles Heslop. Two months later I was at the Grand Theatre in Leeds doing the same play, the title of which had now become *The Yes-Yes-Yes Man*. Strangely, I did the play a third time three years later in London under yet another title – as *The Waiting Game*.

In October 1963, I received an urgent phone call one evening from BBC producer Michael Mills. He was somewhere in the north of England, telling me he had a script he wanted me to see and asking if he could send it down on the overnight train to Reading so I could collect it first thing in the morning and let him know straight away whether I wanted to do it. Thus, there came another addition to my list of parts I played because someone else had dropped out, dropped dead, or was otherwise unable to play it. By now the list included the radio series *A Life of Bliss* and *Quentin Durwald*. *The Blue Bird* would be added later. On this occasion Terry-Thomas had been lined up to play in an episode of BBC Television's *Comedy Playhouse* called 'Nicked at the Bottle', written by Marty Feldman and about a crooked lawyer named Mossy. For reasons I have never understood, Terry pulled out on the second day of rehearsals and naturally the producers wanted someone to step in as soon as possible. Whatever Terry's reasons, he provided me with a few weeks' work at the BBC studios and another entry on my list of someone else's parts. Interestingly, Charles Heslop, with whom I had worked on stage a couple of weeks earlier in *The Yes-Yes-Yes Man*, was also in the episode. I never found out if he was the one who put in a good word for me.

I was back on stage in February 1964 with a departure from comedy when I did Henrik Ibsen's intellectual 1890 play *Hedda Gabler* at St Martin's Theatre in London. I played the pedantic academic George (Jörgen) Tesman. Joan Greenwood played my aristocratic new wife Hedda and Minos Volonakis was the director. But I was soon back in front of the film cameras.

One of the most bizarre films I ever worked on was in 1964 when I did *One Way Pendulum*, written by N. F. Simpson and directed by Peter Yates. The film was adapted from a stage play of the same name by Simpson and was made by an independent production company named Woodfall Film Productions. The company was originally set up to make *Look Back in Anger* in 1959 and went on to make many flagship British films of the 1960s, such as *The Loneliness of the Long Distance Runner* and *The Charge of the Light Brigade*.

To simply say that my role in *One Way Pendulum* was that of a defence lawyer would understate the whole surrealistic premise of the film. The story told of a Mr Groomkirby (played by Eric Sykes) who works as a clerk. Away from the office he lives in a suburban terraced house with his family, who could not be more dysfunctional. In his spare time he is constructing a full-scale replica of an Old Bailey courtroom in his house, which has required him to knock a hole in the ceiling to accommodate the statue of Lady Justice. His son Kirby (played by Jonathan Miller, who has no dialogue) spends his life in the attic, where he has modified and trained dozens of Speak Your Weight machines to sing musical works such as the *Hallelujah Chorus* under his direction. Groomkirby's daughter (played by Julia Foster) spends so much time watching the apes at the zoo that she believes her arms are too short. Aunt Mildred (Mona Washbourne) believes that she boarded the wrong train at St Pancras 25 years ago and that she is now in a railway waiting room in the Outer Hebrides. Mrs Groomkirby (Alison Leggatt) buys food and cooks it compulsively and pays a neighbour (Peggy Mount) to finish off the leftovers.

When Mr Groomkirby finishes his Old Bailey replica, he orchestrates a mock trial inside his head in which his son Kirby is accused of murder. The major players in court are people with whom he has recently been in contact. The judge is a maintenance man in his office, the clerk of the court is the assistant in the dry cleaner's shop and I, his defence counsel, am his friend Fred who gives him a lift to work on his motor scooter. Mr and Mrs Groomkirby are the main witnesses.

Before we started shooting the film, the director asked if I would mind going to the Old Bailey to sit through a few trials to get the feel of the courtroom. I did and it was uncanny that, in one of the trials I watched, there was a judge who was totally dismissive towards the young and inexperienced defence lawyer and would not let the poor fellow make his case. It was exactly the situation I was portraying in the film.

Humour that far from the mainstream was not common at the time. The film predated *Monty Python's Flying Circus* by five years. The stage play was reasonably successful but, unfortunately, the film version did poorly at the box office.

I appeared in another Walt Disney film, *The Legend of Young Dick Turpin*, which was released in Britain in 1964. This was also conceived as a television mini-series primarily directed towards the American market. The theme of the story was similar to that of *Dr. Syn*. It told of a farmer in the 1700s who became one of England's most famous highway robbers to avenge the greed he found surrounding him. David Weston played Dick Turpin and I played a character named William Evans. The film premiered in the USA in February 1966 as a two-part mini-series, *'Disneyland': The Legend of Young Dick Turpin*, and in the UK as a full-length feature film with the abbreviated title.

Towards the end of summer 1964 I did a particularly disturbing episode of the police series *Gideon's Way* at the ATV studios in Elstree. This was produced by ITC Entertainment and starred John Gregson as a Scotland Yard police commander named George Gideon, and was based on the novels by John Creasey. My episode was entitled 'The Firebug' and I played a man named Bishop whose wife and young daughter had recently died in a fire in a derelict house. Soon after the tragedy, he starts setting fires in unoccupied derelict houses to draw attention to the dangers of fire and to spur the authorities to quickly demolish condemned properties. But then he unknowingly sets fire to a property that is occupied and burns the four occupants to death and kills a police constable who attempts to rescue them. Initially distraught at the outcome, he begins to justify it as being necessary to get the authorities to act. When Bishop is identified as the person who stole four sticks of dynamite, Commander Gideon has to act quickly to prevent further loss of life. The fact that the story was so totally credible and believable made it especially worrying. David Chantler wrote the screenplay and Roy Baker was the director. The series was released in America under the name *Gideon CID*.

I did my last play with Alastair over the end of 1964 and the beginning of 1965 when we worked together in George Bernard Shaw's 1930s comedy *Too True to be Good*. We played it first at the Garrick Theatre and then at the Strand Theatre. June Ritchie, James Bolam, Dora Bryan and Kenneth Haigh were in the other leading parts. Liz Fraser and T. P. McKenna took over from Dora and Kenneth midway through the run. The story was of a rich and bored young woman who finds two burglars in her bedroom. Instead of handing them over to the police, she runs off with them to live on the proceeds of the burglary. When that does not relieve the problems in her life, she turns to religion. I played an army sergeant named Fielding.

A few months after *Too True* finished, I was performing in *A Public Mischief* at St Martin's Theatre. This was the last play by playwright Kenneth Horne to run in the West End. It was a comedy about a married woman who runs off with her lover and arranges for her disappearance to look like a boating accident. Her husband, who disappears while out looking for her, is then suspected of murdering her. I played the lover, Mark. Kenneth Horne's scripts were always carefully crafted to let the humour come naturally without being forced. He insisted that, in order to work properly, comedy should always be played straight. This play was extremely funny but somehow got poor reviews. The cast were faced with either taking the play off or taking a pay cut. I had no alternative but to accept a fee of £15 a week. And then I happened to see an advert somewhere asking people to become postmen and get £25 a week. It was a sobering observation.

The following year, 1966, I was holding auditions for a play called *The Waiting Game* by Leonard Samson at what was then known as the New Arts Theatre in London. This was when I first met a young actress named Penny Morrell, who came in to audition. I thought she was absolutely right for the part. Still more, however, I'm pretty sure it was love at first sight. I think I knew there and then that I would marry her. Penny's version is that she saw me and thought I looked as if I needed looking after and she found the notion quite appealing.

If you push Penny (it doesn't need to be especially hard), she'll go into the details of how it all came about. She recalls that there were two female parts that needed to be cast and there were a few hopefuls waiting to audition. I was terribly late getting to the theatre. Eventually, the director Hugh Goldie told them, 'I'm really sorry but Mr Cole has been delayed. It seems that he has jammed a teaspoon in the dishwasher door and his kitchen is flooded.' This was probably the first thing that made Penny prick her ears up. Apparently, I was profusely apologetic when I arrived and I read through the parts with all the hopefuls. Penny brought a little blue wig box along with her in case we wanted her to do the part as a blonde. She was so fired up with adrenaline after the audition that she left her wig box on the number 52 bus on the way home and had to claim it back from the bus depot. She got the part in the play as the girl who didn't get the man.

But in real life it was very different. She did get him. But I think she worked pretty hard to achieve it. I never used to have lunch in those days and Penny claims that I looked rather thin and pale when she first saw me. She decided to give up lunch as well and came and joined me during lunchtimes to chat and perk me up a bit. I had tickets for a show somewhere and during the course of one of these lunchtime chats I asked her to come and see the show with me.

We went to the show and our hands somehow became entwined over the programme. Not long after that I took her to dinner at the Grand Hotel in Eastbourne and ordered lobster followed by rice pudding. I think that was probably the point when she finally thought, 'That's my man!' She seemed to think that, if I had the nerve to order rice pudding in such a posh restaurant, I would be prepared to take on anything.

She had a flat in London at the time and would drive over to my place in the country whenever she could in her little two-seater MG sports car. But everything remained proper and she would always drive back to London at night. She would never stay overnight. I still had my first two children living with me and we both felt it would not have been appropriate. After a while, when I thought the time was right, I said, 'You know, if we were married, you wouldn't need to do all this driving. What about it?' I don't think even my character David Bliss could have made a less romantic proposal. Penny looked stunned and, without saying a word, suddenly ran out to her car parked in the drive and roared off at high speed.

I thought, 'What could I possibly have said to upset her? I only asked her to marry me.'

An hour later I heard her car pull up outside. She came in and said simply, 'Yes.'

The only thing I could think to say was, 'Yes, what?'

She answered, 'I needed some time to think.'

We were married on 26 May 1967 at Henley Registry Office. It was just a small affair; the guests were Naomi Sim, Penny's father Roy and my first two children. Afterwards we had a small celebration at the Olde Belle Inn at Hurley in Berkshire.

As for the play Penny auditioned for, it lasted only three weeks and the writer, Len Samson, was inconsolable.

In 1968 I started work on a 13-part ITV series that I found strangely reflective of my own life. *A Man of Our Times*, written by Julian Bond, provided me with an opportunity to play a character I was able to identify with on a personal level. I was playing a man of just over 40 named Max Osborne, and I was just around that age myself. Most of my parts up until then had been of much younger characters and I found myself having to make a conscious effort to play this one as a middle-aged man. Max had two children and had recently separated from his wife. In real life, so had I, and I was able to empathise closely with him. Max had just lost his job in a furniture factory and had taken a new job at a lower salary. His mistress Muriel (played by Jennifer Wilson), who was his first love, tries to encourage him to accept an offer of a job in Australia rather than accept a demotion, and promises to go with him provided he divorces his wife (played by Jean Harvey) so that he and Muriel can get married. He basically has to choose between demotion or emigration and between his wife and his mistress.

One of the fascinating aspects of the series was that it was set in real time and was mirroring what was happening in real life. My character Max was made redundant at a time when the concept of workplace redundancy was not well known. Previously, people tended to stay in their jobs until they retired or chose to leave, not because their employer considered that the employee's position was no longer necessary. I think a lot of people heard the word 'redundancy' for the first time in that series. It was a time when the trade unions were becoming more militant than they had been for years and there were many more strikes then than previously. The characters in the series were also dealing with strikes and this was another reflection of real life. We were even affected by this new trend ourselves while we were making one of the episodes. We were shooting the episode on tape and were suddenly told one day that we would not be able to return after lunch until four o'clock because one of the unions had called a meeting to discuss redundancy. It was uncanny that we were becoming affected by one of the issues being depicted in the show. I think Julian Bond, who created the series, was a wonderful writer and he did an excellent job in making it not only entertaining but relevant to society at the same time.

Wilfred Pickles, the famous BBC radio announcer and host of the long-running radio show *Have A Go*, appeared in two episodes as my father, in probably one of my last appearances on a show with an artist from a previous generation to my own. Wilfred was the first BBC radio newsreader to speak with a regional accent – his was strongly Yorkshire – in a deliberate attempt to make it difficult for Nazis to impersonate BBC accents during the Second World War.

He was lovely to work with but had an annoying habit during rehearsals of going off the set when he finished and coming back a few seconds later while everyone else was carrying on with the scene and saying, 'Was that alright?' It became a nightmare! It drove everyone potty.

Stella Richman and Richard Bates produced the 13-part series for Associated-Rediffusion and it had a one-hour timeslot. The episodes were recorded on tape on a Wednesday and were transmitted from tape the following Monday. On one occasion, a taped episode that was due to go out on the Monday was accidentally erased before it had been transmitted. Stella managed to get all the sets up again, all the cast back again on the Sunday, and we did the whole thing again on the Sunday ready to go out the following day. There was one extra who had to come into the set of a hotel bar where I was, look in the door and then go out again. He came up to me afterwards and said in all seriousness, 'Do you ever have that feeling that you've been somewhere before?' He had no idea that we were re-recording the episode we did a few days earlier.

There was one particular side of that incident that I found particularly heart-warming. The whole process of re-recording the episode must have cost Associated-Rediffusion tens of thousands of pounds, and the technician responsible was on the point of being sacked by the company – until the matter reached the desk of the late Sir John Spencer Wills, the chairman of Associated-Rediffusion at the time, who promptly stopped it. I found that to be an outstanding act of kindness on his part. Sir John was an administrator who I'm sure seldom ventured onto the studio floor, let alone the back rooms of the recording suite, but he had absolute trust in his staff to accept that, occasionally, even in television, people make mistakes. What better boss could anyone hope for?

A few years after we did *A Man of Our Times* I played a rather unkind trick on its writer Julian Bond. Richard Widmark was over here at the time working on an episode of a series called *Madigan* for American television in which each episode was shot in a different capital city, and he was filming one based in London. I had a small part playing a London bobby (a colloquial term for a British police constable).

We were using a hotel just off Jermyn Street in London's West End as our base for wardrobe and make-up, etc. and as I emerged from the hotel, fully attired in my bobby costume, I saw my chance to test it out. Standing on the corner by Fortnum & Mason's was Julian Bond chatting to someone. He was carrying a large Marks & Spencer carrier bag. I tapped him on the shoulder and asked in my best policeman's voice, 'Excuse me, sir, but may I enquire what is contained in that large carrier bag?'

A little taken aback, Julian replied, 'Oh, er, yes, I, er, just under-pants.'

''Ow many pairs would that be then, sir?' I continued.

'Well, er, six.'

'Six, eh, sir? I 'ope you haven't been shoplifting, sir.'

'No, no!' said Julian as he started to panic and rummage through his pockets. 'I've got the receipt here somewhere.'

'Only if you had, sir, I'd have to take you in,' I continued, pointedly ignoring Julian's reply.

'No, no, it's here somewhere,' bleated Julian.

'But since I've already taken you in, I bid you a good day, Mr Bond. The name is Cole, George Cole.' I turned to take my leave. The expletive I heard as I started to walk away cannot be published. But we still remained the closest of friends afterwards.

I had some more fun with the uniform a little while later but this time unintentionally. The main unit was at Notting Hill Gate and those not involved, including some of the cast but mostly extras (of which I was one), were somewhere else having a mid-morning break. We were just lolling about, drinking coffee, doing crosswords and reading newspapers, as actors spend a long time doing while out on location. My policeman's tunic was undone and my helmet was on the floor. I was drinking coffee and had a sausage roll in my hand. Suddenly, a police car drove up with its siren blaring. A man in a senior police officer's uniform stormed out of the car, ignored everyone else and came straight up to me while the assembled company gave him a big round of applause.

'What's going on?' he demanded.

I assumed he was one of the cast 'putting on the dog' a bit in his costume and wanting to engage in some harmless improvisation.

'We're shooting an episode for an American television film called *Madigan*,' I told him, careful to give him all the facts.

'Who's in charge?' he snapped.

'Well, the production manager is but he is out on location,' I responded, giving him more information than he actually asked for.

'Get him here immediately,' he said, looking convincingly angry, 'and button up your tunic, put your helmet on and stand up when you speak to me!'

'What, all at once?' I asked. The rest of the company were enjoying the exchange immensely and by now were laughing and applauding wildly. This did not please him at all and only seemed to make his anger appear more convincing. He started to shout something but, whatever the tirade was about, it was interrupted when Tommy the runner appeared.

'What's up?' Tommy asked.

'Call Barry and ask him to come over, will you?' I told him. 'We've got a problem.' And then, turning back to the new arrival, I politely asked, 'Would you like a sausage roll?'

'Certainly not!' he bellowed. 'I'm on duty. And so are you!'

Still holding the sausage roll, I realised I didn't have enough hands to button up my tunic. I waved the roll in his general direction and asked him, 'Would you mind holding this for a second?'

By now he was well into the part and was showing seething anger. He looked as if he was ready to assault me. 'Absolutely not!' he screamed and went back to his car. Only then, when he started to call on the radio for backup, did it begin to dawn on me that he really was a Chief Inspector. We could all hear his conversation with the radio operator clearly over the loudspeaker.

The operator replied that there was nobody available to come down. The inspector's 'Why the hell not?' could probably have been heard by the operator at his base without the aid of his radio.

The radio operator patiently explained to him that everyone was on duty at Notting Hill Gate directing traffic for a film unit making an episode of an American television film. The poor man was apoplectic and close to tears. At that very minute, Tommy the runner reappeared, went up to the car and asked him, 'Would you like a cup of coffee and a sausage roll?'

The inspector replied meekly, 'Go away!' The assembled company broke into a spontaneous round of applause. This was the best morning's entertainment they had had in months.

As it stopped, the production manager drove up outside, mystified as to the presence of the police car and such an unusually happy bunch of extras. He took over from there. But I have never had so much fun with a costume as I did with that one. And I don't think we ever found out why the policeman was there in the first place!

At times, Richard Widmark could have something of a short fuse. He would explode at the slightest provocation. While we were shooting the *Madigan* episode, he made it clear to everyone on the crew that he had known me for a long time and that we were good friends. Sometimes I would be sitting around waiting for someone else's scene to finish and the assistant director would come over and say something like, 'Could you come on the set for a minute or two?' The first time it happened I was a little confused and said, 'Why? I'm not in this scene.' The AD said, 'That's OK but could you come anyway?' And I discovered that he didn't want me to say anything or do anything related to the scene, he just wanted me to be around Richard to keep him occupied and stop him from going mad over minor irritations. It was nice to know that I had a calming presence. Perhaps it was because he felt more secure having someone in a policeman's uniform sitting next to him.

I did a short film in 1968 called *The Green Shoes* for an independent company named Isleworth Productions. Ivor Jay wrote the story and Ian Brims directed.

I played a shoe-shop manager named Braine who had been seen following a girl wearing green shoes, who is subsequently found murdered in a park. When the police ask the person who was following her to come forward, I voluntarily contact them. The film opens in a police station where Detective Sergeant Mackie (played by Donald Webster) is questioning me and pressuring me to admit to the murder. My character strongly protests his innocence but Mackie is clever at his job and slowly begins to generate some doubt.

The 28-minute film is not particularly well known although it has appeared on television a few times in recent years. I think it would have received more exposure if it had been made as a television play.

I also managed to do some varied work on stage between the television and screen work towards the end of the 1960s. In 1967 I played the part of Andrei Prozorov (Andrey) in a revival of Anton Chekhov's 1901 play *The Three Sisters* at the Royal Court Theatre.

The sisters were played by Glenda Jackson as Masha, Avril Elgar as Olga and Marianne Faithfull (in her professional stage debut) as Irina. Marianne was romantically involved with Rolling Stones singer Mick Jagger at the time and he came to the first night. It was impossible to get anywhere near the stage door! William Gaskell was the director and Edward Bond did the translation.

The following July I was at the Hampstead Theatre Club playing in a double bill written by Christopher Guinee and directed by Philip Grout called *Doubtful Haunts*; this comprised *The Ghost* and *No Principals*. Annette Crosbie and Raymond Platt were also in the cast.

In 1969 I did a brief run in a bedroom farce called *The Passionate Husband* at the Bristol Hippodrome and later that year worked in a lovely show called *There Was an Old Woman* at the newly opened Thorndike Theatre in Leatherhead opposite Dame Sybil Thorndike in what would be her last stage role at the age of 87.

But one of the most exciting moments of the decade was when Penny presented me with our delightful daughter Tara on 6 May 1969 at the Royal Berkshire Hospital in Reading.

CHAPTER 10

THE SEVENTIES

The 1970s proved to be a momentous decade for the family, as baby Tara, who was just seven months old at the start of the decade, was joined by a little brother, Toby, in May 1971. We were still living in the house in our secluded part of Oxfordshire at the time and Penny and I have lived there ever since.

I count myself as being highly fortunate with the huge and varied amount of work that came my way in the 1970s as I found myself agreeably busy with numerous roles on stage, on television and in the cinema.

During the 1970s I was in a few film roles that were – how shall I put it? – rather different from what I had done before. I started the decade in 1970 with a real horror of a film called *The Vampire Lovers*. Shooting began in January 1970 at Associated British studios at Elstree and the film was released that October. The story was adapted from the novel *Carmilla* by J. Sheridan Le Fanu in a screenplay by Tudor Gates. The film was originally given an X certificate in the UK and later changed to a 15. It had an R certificate in America, I think primarily because of the vampire bites on the women's bosoms! The film starred Peter Cushing as an Austrian count. You know it is going to be bloody when Peter is in it. A head was cut off within the first six minutes, before even the opening credits had started to roll. I played Roger Morton, the father of one of the vampire's victims. The film was very daring for 1970. Roy Ward Baker, the director, with whom I was closely associated a few years later in *Minder*, cleverly managed to incorporate some of the explicit lesbianism in the original story and added some mild eroticism to the horror with a number of breast shots. Ingrid Pitt, who played the vampire, achieved some recognition for her performance and went on to play several more vampires in the years that followed. The film was produced by Hammer Films for American International.

As soon as my part was completed at Elstree Studios, I was back into various television studios to shoot three television episodes that went out that year.

First to go out was a comedy in ITV's *Armchair Theatre* series entitled *A Room in Town* by Donald Churchill. It aired on 15 September 1970. I play Ted Nugent. He has rented a small flat in London to entertain his mistress who, when she is not staying at the flat, lives next door to Ted and his wife (played by Pauline Yates). Although Ted has gone to extraordinary lengths to conceal the existence of the flat, his wife happens to discover a receipt for some building work there and confronts the mistress. And then the fun starts.

The Right Prospectus by John Osborne and directed by Alan Cooke was the second episode of the BBC's *Play for Today* series and went out on 22 October 1970. I played a prosperous and self-made man in early middle age; a Mr Newbold who, together with his wife (played by Elvi Hale), enrols in a public school in an attempt to improve their level of general education and elevate themselves to a higher social class than the lower-middle one they currently inhabit. In the play, they have no difficulty getting themselves accepted by a school or by their fellow pupils. Assigned to different houses, they find themselves immersed in the rituals of public-school life with its rugby, cold showers, chapel and inter-house rivalry. Mrs Newbold takes to it with great relish, I with considerably less. In reality, it was difficult for the producers to find a school prepared to accept the disruption that would inevitably result from the extensive location work necessary. I think there were also some concerns from the schools that the finished product might project a less-than-favourable view of present-day public-school life. Their concerns were unfounded, however, and the end result was generally well received and provided an amusing look at class values in the early 1970s.

Killing Time by Hugh Whitemore was an episode in the BBC's long-running *Menace* series that was transmitted on 10 November 1970. Each of the 75-minute stories in the series looked at a different facet of 'menace'. My story was extremely dark and disturbing. I played an introverted and boring accounts manager in a plastics company who is driven to the brink by the tedium of his existence; the irrelevant urgency of his office work, his isolation in the room he rents, the trivial concerns of his house-proud landlady, the slothfulness of her husband and the lechery of her son. A chance comment by his rather plain secretary, who is probably just as lonely as he is (and is splendidly portrayed by Annette Crosbie), unlocks a horrific incident repressed from his childhood and spurs him on to take drastic steps to improve his current life. When his secretary discovers what he has done, she unexpectedly finds herself alone with him in a situation that could soon turn nasty. From the ticking clock as the play opens, to the footsteps in the corridor as it closes, director Anthea Browne-Wilkinson kept the tension running high throughout. It was a wonderful play to be a part of.

Not long afterwards I started a two-year run of Christopher Hampton's play *The Philanthropist* at the Mayfair Theatre in London, playing an academic named Philip. Robert Kidd was the director and Edward de Souza played another academic. I genuinely feel that it is one of the best plays to have been written during my lifetime. That being said, I do think it was a mistake for me to stay in it for so long because, at the end, it started to become something of a nightmare. I would drive up to London every night and find myself going into London Airport for no good reason other than the fact that I didn't want to go to the theatre. You would expect that the longer you do something, the more you are able to concentrate on it but it was completely the reverse. The concentration was paper-thin.

At the Mayfair Theatre there is no stage door and the cast have to go out through the front of house. One night I came out after the show and found a group of people searching for something in the auditorium. I asked what they were looking for and they told me and I said, 'I think you'll find it four rows closer to the front.' They said, 'How do you know?' I replied, 'I heard it roll down.' My concentration was so weak that it had been diverted by the sound of something dropped in the auditorium during the performance.

There was a sad incident one night. There is an incredible *coup de théâtre* at the beginning of the play when a young student writer is sitting down talking with the two academics played by Ted de Souza and myself. The young writer says, 'I'm not mad about the idea.' I keep saying, 'I like it. I like it very much.'

This isn't what the writer wants to hear at all and he keeps telling me to shut up. Finally, the young writer says, 'Well, it's fairly dramatic.' Then he takes out a pistol, puts it in his mouth, pulls the trigger and blows his brains out on stage and they splatter over the wall behind him. Then the curtain comes down. The effect on the audience was stunning. Every night there was a collective gasp from the audience and then stunned silence until the curtain went up almost immediately. There was a hidden gun mounted at the back of the writer's chair full of pasta and tomato sauce and, as he fires the trigger, the gun on the chair discharges the mixture towards the wall. There was a removable panel on the wall behind the chair so it could be removed as soon as the curtain came down, removing all evidence of the mess when the curtain went back up. One poor man in the audience was so upset by the scene that he had to be taken to hospital by ambulance.

I probably wouldn't have stayed in it so long were it not for the producer Michael Codron offering me a generous salary increase at the end of the first year if I agreed to sign on for a second year. But there was one night when I think he might have regretted making that offer.

It was in November and a heavy fog had been forecast and had started to roll in as we arrived at the theatre. All of us in the company were worried about getting home and, I'm ashamed to say, we cut four minutes off the running time. As soon as the curtain came down, we were all out of the theatre in a flash. What we didn't know was that Michael Codron was in the front of house. I suppose he was in the company manager's office because by the time he reached backstage, we had all gone. He sent messages to all of us to come in early the following night. Michael is usually the most mild-mannered man you could ever wish to meet but that night he was very cross and gave us all a severe dressing-down. Strangely, throughout all this his gaze seemed to keep landing on me as if I were the ringleader, the leader of the pack, who should have known better. He asked if we had anything to say for ourselves and I couldn't bring myself to tell him that I was in such a hurry to get home the previous night that I got stopped for speeding before I had even reached the motorway. Or that the police breathalysed me and found I was 100% clear. Or that one of the policemen was still not satisfied and kept muttering, 'But I can still smell alcohol.' And that I didn't have the heart to tell the policeman that I was an actor in a hurry to get home to avoid the fog and had used liquid paraffin to take off my make-up before I left the theatre. It was no wonder I smelled of alcohol!

On another occasion at the Mayfair I was the last person on stage at the final curtain. I took my call and exited, expecting to find the rest of the cast waiting in the wings to take their call, as they usually were. But as I went off, there was not a soul in sight. The curtain came down and the house lights came on and the company manager went on stage to ask the audience to leave as quickly as possible using all the exits. Apparently, the restaurant was on fire. I asked him why he hadn't got the audience *and me* out earlier. He replied, 'Well, there was only half a page left to go, so I decided to take a chance!'

Back in 1970, when I started on *The Philanthropist*, I began a pattern adopted by many actors of doing film and television work by day and stage plays at night. The stage plays are fairly consistent and, apart from the occasional matinee, only need your attention at night. This slots in nicely with the demands of television and film work, which normally only requires your presence in the studio during the day, and then only for occasional days here and there unless it is a regular part in an ongoing series.

With *The Philanthropist* still running at night, I started 1971 with an interesting thriller for Thames Television in their *Shadows of Fear* series entitled *Return of Favours*, written by Jeremy Paul. This was transmitted on 9 February 1971. I played an auctioneer named

Gordon Marsh, who we first see clearing out women's clothes in a bedroom cupboard and packing them into suitcases. Shortly afterwards, a young couple, Judith and Roger, played by Jennie Linden and Robin Ellis, enter the flat with a key and, unaware that anyone else is there, go to a bedroom and start making love. In the meantime, I potter around in the kitchen, boiling water and making tea, and I have no dialogue for the first 11 minutes of the play. When the couple discovers I am there, it transpires that they are having an affair and that my wife has lent them a spare key so they can use the flat one afternoon a week while she and I are at work to give them somewhere to meet and some privacy for their tryst. Instead of throwing them out immediately, I invite them to join me for afternoon tea and engage them in conversation. When they eventually leave, Judith becomes convinced that I have killed my wife. Roger later discovers the truth but is unable to reveal it.

It was an excellent story and the tension never lets up throughout the one-hour play. This was another situation where the tension was generated by the acting and direction without the aid of background music. Kim Mills did a sterling job as director and producer. Caroline Blakiston, who played my wife, was the only other person in the cast.

Later that year I worked on another crime/horror thriller film written by Tudor Gates called *Fright*, which was directed by Peter Collinson and produced by Fantale Films for Allied Artists. The film was released in November 1971. This was a severe frightener about a babysitter (played by Susan George) who has a number of terrifying experiences while she is alone in an isolated country house with the small boy she is looking after. With the parents out of the way, the babysitter's boyfriend unexpectedly comes to visit her at the house, hoping to get what she is not prepared to give him, and he soon finds himself brutally attacked by the child's biological father, who has recently escaped from a nearby psychiatric institution. Honor Blackman played the child's mother and I played her husband. We had a lot of fun with Honor 15 years later when she was a guest artist in *Minder on the Orient Express*.

Years later, Dennis Waterman and I were in a car somewhere while we were making *Minder*. Dennis was in the front seat and I was in the back, and we started talking about the films we had been in. Dennis happened to mention that he had been in *Fright* back in the early 1970s. I said, 'You weren't in that. I was.' Dennis said, 'Leave it out. I was.' Neither of us could remember the other one being in it. It turned out that by the time Dennis made his entrance, I had already gone out for the evening with Honor Blackman, leaving the babysitter in charge, and by the time I got back, Dennis was lying face down on the floor as a corpse. Then we remembered each other!

In 1973 I had an interesting role in Cliff Richard's last feature film *Take Me High* (also known as *Hot Property*). Cliff appears in the unlikely role of a merchant banker who is expecting a glamorous posting to New York but discovers he is being posted to Birmingham. The lovely Debbie Watling provides Cliff's love interest in the film as the owner of a struggling restaurant who Cliff works with to rebrand and introduce a local burger called a 'Brumburger'. I played an opinionated socialist named Bert Jackson who first appears in the film on a television screen ranting about his political ideals and irritates Cliff's boss so much that he demolishes the television in a hail of machine-gun fire. It was a totally implausible scene but one that probably got a good laugh in the cinemas. Later I show my human side and help Cliff and Debbie set up their new business. Christopher Penfold wrote the story, and the film was directed by David Askey (the son of celebrated comedian Arthur Askey) and produced by Kenneth Harper.

There are two films from the 1970s that I often get credited for but which I had nothing to do with. Both are high-octane, high-speed, car-chase films: *Gone in 60 Seconds* in 1974 (not the Nicolas Cage remake in 2000) and *Double Nickels* in 1977. Both have an actor named George Cole in the cast and many people assume that it was me. But it is easy to spot that it was not. The George Cole in those films is an African American! But it is still nice to get letters from fans saying how much they enjoyed them.

At the end of 1974 and for the first part of 1975 I starred alongside Sheila Hancock in what was billed as 'a review of revues' entitled *Déjà Revue* at the New London Theatre in Drury Lane. The show was written by Alan Melville and directed by Victor Spinetti and was essentially a potpourri of old revue numbers, mainly consisting of material from the 1940s and 1950s. Tim Barrett and Anna Dawson also had major roles. Joan Savage took over Anna's place when she left. The New London Theatre was just two years old when we did the show. It is a beautiful theatre with amazing technical facilities and is extraordinarily comfortable for the audience. The only problem was that it was perhaps a little too spacious for the 'intimate revue' we set out to stage. That criticism aside, I got the feeling that most of the audience left the theatre with their spirits suitably uplifted.

Lloyd George Knew My Father was a comedy I did for Anglia Television transmitted on 19 August 1975. It was based on a successful stage play of the same name by William Douglas-Home about an upper-class landowner, Lady Sheila Boothroyd (played by Celia Johnson), who threatens to commit suicide at the exact time when the bulldozers start a project to route a bypass through her ancestral property. The play tells of the way her threat affects the lives of the people around her. I played one of her in-laws, a member of parliament named Hubert Boothroyd. Although it was essentially a comedy, it handled some serious contemporary issues, such as conservation, ageing and attitude differences between generations. I particularly remember a highly amusing scene in which I was complaining at my daughter for wearing ridiculous clothes while I was standing there in hunting pink!

I am not that much a fan of travelling but sometimes the work requires it. In 1975, I began work on the first Soviet–American film co-production, a fantasy film called *The Blue Bird* directed by George Cukor and produced by Twentieth Century-Fox, based on the classic children's story *L'Oiseau Bleu* by the 1911 Nobel Laureate Maurice Maeterlinck. We were shooting in Russia from February to August 1975 and the film was released in the United States in 1976. Maeterlinck's original play was released in 1908 and there were four film adaptations before ours: two silent films (1910 and 1918), a 1940 version with Shirley Temple and an animated version in 1970. Twentieth Century-Fox made the 1940 version in direct competition with MGM's *The Wizard of Oz* starring Judy Garland.

The story involves two peasant children who are taken on a search for the Blue Bird of Happiness (played by Russian actress Nadezhda Pavlova) by the Queen of Light (Elizabeth Taylor). Along the way they are accompanied by human personifications of various entities. Jane Fonda played The Night, Ava Gardner played Luxury, Cicely Tyson played Tylette and Robert Morley played Father Time. I played a dog named Tylo and I looked ridiculous. Richard Pearson looked even more ridiculous. He was playing a loaf of bread! The film is often referred to by the name *Sinyaya Ptitsa*, which I am told is the phonetic translation of the Russian words for 'Bluebird' but, personally, I cannot understand how anyone could possibly pronounce it without hurting themselves.

Unfortunately, the film was not a success at the box office but there are a few interesting stories about it. My part in the 1976 version was originally played by another actor (James Coco) but he had to be taken off the film because of a medical problem apparently brought about by his inability to tolerate the local diet, which resulted in his attempting to survive on bread and butter. Elizabeth Taylor also suffered health problems, beginning with influenza followed closely by amoebic dysentery, which delayed the shoot. I developed a kidney stone while I was there but, fortunately, it cleared up quickly and I was all right. But in Russia you have to go to an outpatient hospital called a *poliklinik* to be followed up. I didn't want to go because I felt fine but the company insisted and I finally agreed.

I went along to the clinic and saw two beautiful blonde female doctors. The interpreter said something to them in Russian and one of them walked across to me and, without a word, unzipped my fly and stuck her hand inside. She said something back to the interpreter and he said to me, 'She wants to know if that hurts.' I said, 'No, it doesn't,' and she took her hand out. But before I had a chance to zip up, the other one came across and stuck her hand inside. By now I had a big smile on my face. I said to the interpreter, 'Can you tell me the names of the doctors?' He said, 'Why?' I said, 'Because you can't allow people to do that to you without knowing them properly.' He told them and they looked a little embarrassed. One of them said, 'Can you come back in a fortnight for another check-up?' The other one looked terribly disappointed and said, 'But I'll be away on holiday then.' It was one of those sweet little experiences in life that you tend to remember.

When you go on location, there is always someone on the crew who absolutely hates it and starts pointing out all the bad things. On this trip someone said we should be careful of the KGB detector vans. I said, 'Well, how can you spot them?' He said, 'They are easy to spot. They have these two big brass circular aerials coming out from the top of the van.' Well, I went out sightseeing by myself and happened to spot one. I thought, 'What *can* they be detecting? Everyone can easily spot them.' When I got back, I took one of the Russian actors to one side and asked him what it was that the KGB detector vans were detecting. He said, 'Which KGB detector vans?' I told him, 'The ones with the big brass rings on top.' I've never seen anyone laugh so much. He said, 'They are nothing to do with the KGB. They are the vans you hire when you get married and the rings on top are supposed to represent wedding rings!'

When I first flew out to Russia, the film company gave me a first-class ticket. I had an enjoyable first-class flight to Helsinki and then had to take a Russian airline from Helsinki to Leningrad (as it was then called). When we arrived in Helsinki, we were given boarding passes for the Leningrad flight. Mine was red and the other passengers were given green ones. Then the staff called for all the passengers with green passes to start boarding. Eventually, I was the only one left, clutching a red boarding pass. I went up to the counter and said, 'When do I get on?'

The woman looked surprised and said, 'Why?'

I showed her the boarding pass and said, 'Because I've got a red pass. I'm first class.'

She studied it carefully and said, 'Oh no, not in Russia. We don't have first class. In Russia, everyone travels in the same class.'

I said, 'Well, why did you give me a red boarding pass and everyone else a green one?'

She said, 'The colour doesn't make any difference. There's no first class, so it doesn't matter what colour pass you get.' There was no way I could argue with her. If there was no first class, there was no point in pursuing the matter.

When I eventually got on board, all the best seats were taken and I enjoyed the same in-flight service as everyone else: a boiled sweet.

It reminded me so much of a Tommy Cooper story in which he tells how he was on a plane and the stewardess offers him a boiled sweet. He asks her, 'What's this for?' The stewardess replies, 'It's to stop your ears from popping as we land.' He replies, 'So can I have another one for the other side?' And that was my trip to Russia.

At the beginning of 1976 I was working with Honor Blackman and Ian Hendry at the Yvonne Arnaud Theatre in Guildford in a murder mystery called *Motive* by Larry Cohen when I received the news that my mother had died. She was in her seventies at the time. By then she had remarried and was living in the Midlands.

I was doing a matinee when I heard she had died. Coincidentally, I also heard about my father's death just before I went on stage for a matinee. My mother had always smoked heavily and had had the lung disease emphysema for some time. I think her husband Len contacted us to say she was seriously ill and shortly afterwards he told us she had passed away.

We went up for the funeral. She never left a will and, because I wasn't officially adopted, I was not automatically entitled to any part of her estate.

She did have blood relatives but I think there was some sort of family problem years ago and she had little contact with them – until she died, and then Aunt Daisy soon reappeared on the scene. Aunt Daisy had two boys and there was some suggestion that my mum had tried to adopt one of them years ago. This was something else that made me wonder if she had had a medical problem that prevented her from having children of her own and caused her to go along the adoption path. The adoption and the fact that I was illegitimate could easily have caused the rift between the sisters. Some people in those days would have had great problems handling a situation like that.

Fortunately, I knew which people she wanted to have certain things when she died and I was able to let Aunt Daisy know. As far as I could see, she followed what I told her, so I was pleased that my mother's wishes were fulfilled.

Later in 1976 I appeared in Ben Travers' delightful farce *Banana Ridge* with Robert Morley at London's Savoy Theatre. The play was directed by Val May and was set on a rubber plantation in Malaya in the 1930s. Robert played Mr Pound, a wealthy and respected plantation manager, and I played his friend and assistant Willoughby Pink. The unexpected arrival of one of Pound's old flames claiming that he is the father of her illegitimate son threatens to damage the relationship between Pound and his wife. I try to help out and nearly wreck my own marriage in the process. Joan Sanderson, Jan Holden and Vivienne Martin were also in the cast.

It was always a pleasure to work with Robert. He was always so relaxed and always extremely funny. I have one bizarre recollection of him while we were doing this play. One matinee day he said to me, 'Georgie, are you going out after the show?'

I said, 'Yes, I'll probably go out and get some fresh air.'

He said, 'Well, if you are going out, darling, would you mind posting a few letters for me?'

I said, 'Yes, no problem, what are they?'

Robert replied, 'They are requests to the local casinos to stop me from going in.'

Whether they really were I'll never know. But he was an inveterate gambler and loved the casinos. He made an enormous amount of money from the plays he wrote and there were stories about him going round on matinee days to the theatres where his plays were running, asking for some of the takings, then popping round to the casino.

Both he and his good friend, fellow actor Wilfred Hyde-White, owned racehorses. On one occasion Robert put something like £5,000 to win on Wilfred's two-year-old. But when it was time to start moving, the horse just stood where it was and looked around for inspiration. It refused to run. Robert took it stoically.

He always had a portable television set in his dressing room and many is the time he would miss an entrance during Saturday matinees when there was horse racing on television. Sometimes, when I went on after him, he would say, 'Well, did it win, darling? What was the price?' – all totally irrelevant to the dialogue. But he would only do this on Saturday matinees.

He messed about an awful lot on stage. There was a young man in the cast who had to say to Robert, 'Well, sir, there's something I've been wanting to say for a long time.' Robert was meant to interrupt him but in one show he didn't. He just sat down, made himself comfortable and said, 'Well, come along dear, what is it? What have you wanted to say all this time?' The actor was totally flummoxed and went scarlet. He hadn't done the homework. One of the first rules of the theatre is 'always be prepared to finish a sentence'. Robert was also a master of foreign languages, having been groomed from an early age to join the diplomatic service. Sometimes in a matinee he would start playing it in French.

Another recollection is the night I was driving into London to do *Banana Ridge* when a petrol tanker overturned on one of the motorways. There was ice everywhere and the conditions were absolutely treacherous. The police had to stop everything on the road. You couldn't move. So by the time I got to the Savoy, it was in the middle of the first act and the understudy was on stage. I said to Robert, 'Don't worry, I'll get changed and made up and I'll be ready for the second act.' He said, 'No, no, darling, don't be silly. He's got his auntie in the front row, there's his mother and his uncle's over there. Don't worry, go home early. Leave the boy alone to enjoy it.' So I did.

The previous year I was on location with him in Russia when we were doing the *Blue Bird* film. He was exceedingly generous and one day took a group of his friends to see the Russian ballet. When he got to the theatre, the staff told him the house was full. Entirely unfazed, he said, 'No, don't be silly, darling. Look, the tsar's box is completely empty. Come along, dears, we'll use that.' So he just took his party to the tsar's box and nobody dared stop him. He was well recognised everywhere he went and I suppose the officials were so surprised that they didn't have time to think. By the time they got around to thinking, he was up in the box and had probably received a round of applause from the audience.

Another thing was that he never stopped talking. I asked him once, 'Why do you gabble on like that all the time?' He said, 'Darling, it's just to stop you from talking to me because I'm very deaf.' And I believed him because Dick Widmark had the same problem. He was deaf in one ear from a perforated eardrum. I suppose it's an effective line of defence for someone in that situation to keep talking. But in Dick's case, he talked like a scriptwriter. He had a rhythm to his conversation and it rolled along smoothly. Robert just talked and talked but whatever he said was extremely entertaining.

I played at the Yvonne Arnaud Theatre again the following year, this time as Inspector Fathom in *The Case of the Oily Levantine* by Anthony Shaffer. There is one scene in the play where the curtain comes down as I am having my head chopped off. But the first time we did it, my head went rolling down into the footlights. Luckily, they were able to retrieve it before it went bouncing into the audience like a beach ball at a holiday camp and managed to make it look more convincing after that.

The wonderful actress Virginia McKenna came to see the show one night and dropped by my dressing room beforehand to wish me luck. She asked where I was going with the play when it finished and I said I didn't think there were any plans to take it anywhere else. She said, 'Oh, I'm so sorry,' and left. A few minutes later she came back in and said, 'Well, if you're not going anywhere, how about coming to Hong Kong with me? There's a nice part for some sort of janitor.'

I said, 'I'd love to but I'd have to take the whole family.'

She said, 'I don't think that would be a problem,' and I went downstairs to do my part.

A few weeks later – by then it was 1978 – Penny, the two children and I arrived in Hong Kong, where I would be appearing in *Something's Afoot* at the Hilton Hotel in the Central district on Hong Kong Island. We had no idea what we might be letting ourselves in for; a strange new country where everyone spoke Chinese and we had no idea if the people there would be able to understand a word we said.

But when we arrived at the hotel, we couldn't believe it. Everyone spoke excellent English. We had a huge suite for the four of us overlooking Victoria Harbour, which separates Hong Kong Island from Kowloon on the mainland. And in the children's room by the beds there was the most enormous gingerbread castle. So from then on we stopped worrying. We stayed about a month and were treated exceptionally well by the hotel staff. The children had a wonderful time, crossing Victoria Harbour on the Star Ferry, travelling up to the top of the mountain behind the hotel on the Peak Tram, watching the planes take off and land along the narrow runway built out into the harbour, and going from one end of Hong Kong Island to the other on one of the rickety old electric trams for less than 10p. I think the children would have moved there permanently if they had had the chance.

The show was one of the hotel's 'dinner theatre' series. It was all terribly colonial and was originally intended to ensure that the predominantly British expatriates working in Hong Kong at the time had access to the theatre culture they were supposedly missing from back home. The hotel would provide a delightful dinner for the audience, after which the diners would adjourn to the ballroom to watch the show. Sadly, the hotel has since been demolished in the name of progress.

I was playing the janitor part and I had a song called *I've Got a Lovely Little Dinghy*. I had to put my janitor costume on in the room every night and then go down in the lift to do the show carrying my little toolbox. And every night, without fail, someone in the lift would say something like, 'We've got a leaky tap in our bathroom in 619. Could you drop in and fix it when you've got a few minutes?' It was all good fun.

This was the most wonderful of tours. I had to keep quiet in the years immediately afterwards because the company kept inviting us back to do other shows. I had to keep saying no because I always had something else happening but, if the children had ever found out, they would have disowned us because they loved Hong Kong so much.

Looking back, I realise how fortunate I was to have done some of the excellent stage plays I worked on during the 1970s. My last play of the decade was a hugely demanding one. It was Dennis Potter's *Brimstone and Treacle* in 1979 at the Open Space Theatre in London, in which I played a character whose daughter has been severely injured in a hit-and-run accident. It was extremely harsh. I used to get ready to go out in the evening and say to Penny, 'Well, I'm off to London now to spend two hours arguing with my wife.' It really was extremely harrowing. The theme of the play was depressing as it involved the rape of the handicapped daughter by a

August 1976 at the age of 75. He died of throat cancer. It was a tremendous loss to his family, his profession and his fans. I felt it personally because of the enormous influence he had had on my life. He was certainly my mentor and very much a father figure. For an actor, it's not just a matter of memorising a part, you need to think about what you are doing and to maintain a certain stillness, and that was one of the great things he taught me. On top of that, he was one of my greatest friends. Over the years, we performed in 11 films and at least 9 stage plays together. He had a big, awesome personality and was so wonderful to work with – and always terribly funny. Of all the stage performances of my career, it is the ones I did with Alastair that I seem to look back on now with the greatest fondness. The two that stand out most for me are *Dr Angelus* and *Mr Bolfry*. I think my performances in those were among the best of my career and I owe that entirely to Alastair. And if it wasn't for him, I might still have my cockney accent!

But despite his on-stage and on-screen persona, he was a private, almost shy person. He was a meticulous craftsman and took his work very seriously indeed but he was uncomfortable with the fame that came from it. He was appointed Commander of the British Empire (CBE) in 1953 but, like his father, he refused to accept a knighthood later in his career. He wouldn't sign autographs for fans because he didn't believe in it but he refused in a pleasant, almost humble way that would not give offence. I think he just felt that collecting autographs is pointless. He rarely gave interviews but, in one that he was persuaded to give to the magazine *Focus on Film*, he said, 'I stand or fall in my profession by the public's judgement of my performances. No amount of publicity can dampen a good one or gloss over a bad one.'

Fans can be highly supportive at times. Soon after Alastair's death, Naomi, his widow, received a lovely letter from a fan saying how much they admired him and offering condolences. The letter was addressed to Alastair and at the top was written 'please forward'. Naomi found the unintended joke quite comforting as she tried to work out how to forward it to Alastair.

CHAPTER 11

MINDER

Without a doubt, the biggest role of my career, and the one that many people remember me for, was that of Arthur Daley in *Minder*. The show started in 1979 and went on until 1994. I originally planned to arrange the chapters of this book according to the decades in which I did things. But since *Minder* spans three decades, I think it deserves a chapter of its own. So here it is.

For me, *Minder* happened completely without warning. I had already become successful in my profession and would have been perfectly content to continue with my stage work and the occasional film and television part if *Minder* had not come along. Little did I know that the show would survive for 106 episodes and 2 feature films spread over 15 years.

I didn't know anything about the show until I was invited to talk to the production company about it. Then I discovered that it was intended primarily as a vehicle for Dennis Waterman to follow up on his success in *The Sweeney* with John Thaw. This, in turn, was closely related to a change in the way television action drama was being produced in Britain.

When the British commercial television service began operating in 1955, the Independent Television Authority (ITA) divided Great Britain and Northern Ireland into various regions to form an Independent Television (ITV) network. ITV programming in each region was provided by a different company that operated under a licence (generally referred to as its franchise) from the ITA to supply commercial television content to that region. Each franchise holder produced programmes for the entire network but had the option of whether or not to show content produced by other companies.

In 1971 Thames Television, which held the Independent Television franchise for weekday programming in the London area, established a subsidiary company called Euston Films under the direction of three executives from the company – George Taylor, Brian Tesler and Lloyd Shirley – to produce quality television programmes on film.

The idea of making a television series on film was a novel one at that time. Usually television shows were shot in a studio, with excellent sound and lighting and at least three cameras. Shooting outdoors, except for sporting events and the like, had a whole range of technical problems. You can see this sometimes in programmes made around the 1970s when a character walks from an indoor scene that was shot in a studio to an outdoor scene, like a busy street with traffic, that cannot be set up in the studio and had to be shot on film. The difference in picture quality between the inside and outside shots is often quite jarring and reminds the viewer that he is watching something that is not real. This is something you don't want in a television show.

One of the earliest productions of the new company, Euston

Films, was the third series of a police drama starring George Sewell in 1973 called *Special Branch*, the first and second series of which had been produced conventionally in the studio. The success of *Special Branch* led the company to follow it up with a new police series called *The Sweeney*, which was a tough action series based in London and starring John Thaw as a detective inspector and Dennis Waterman as his sergeant in Scotland Yard's Flying Squad ('Sweeney Todd' = 'Flying Squad' in cockney rhyming slang).

The Sweeney enormously extended production boundaries and took television drama to a new level. Fast car chases and location shots that could only be dreamed about using a traditional television camera had now become a reality. Shot entirely on film rather than videotape, the series broke new ground in British television with its fast-action depiction of criminal violence and, indeed, police brutality.

When *The Sweeney* came to an end, Euston set about finding a replacement. Whenever a scriptwriter has an idea for a new television series, he or she will prepare for the script executives an outline, which we call in the business a 'treatment', describing the main characters, their backgrounds and how they relate to each other. Coincidentally, around the time *The Sweeney* was coming to an end, veteran scriptwriter Leon Griffiths had sent Thames Television a treatment for a series called *Minder* about a small-time second-hand car dealer and wheeler-dealer called Arthur Daley and his streetwise minder named Terry McCann. At that time, the word 'minder' was not well known outside London, but in London it was often used for a bodyguard for someone whose well-being or security were at risk because of their fame or profession.

Leon was well known in the television and film industry for his prolific output of plays and film scripts, particularly in the crime-thriller genre, in which he had established a reputation for his shrewd, witty and frequently humorous plots and characterisations.

In television he became known for three episodes he wrote for the 1959 ITV series *The Four Just Men* based on the Edgar Wallace stories. He wrote an episode entitled 'Horses for Courses' for a Yorkshire Television series a decade later called *The Racing Game* about horse-race fixing, based on the stories by Dick Francis. Fast forward another decade and in 1978 he wrote a play for the BBC One series *Play for Today* entitled *Dinner at the Sporting Club* about a small-time boxing promoter (played by John Thaw) who has to decide whether he is prepared to match an unsuitable boxer against a clearly superior opponent in order to gain the prestige that would result from the ensuing corporate sponsorship. A similar theme of corruption in the boxing world appeared in a *Minder* episode that Griffiths wrote a few years later. Crime stories with a tinge of humour became his forte and he was excellent at them.

When Euston saw Leon's treatment of *Minder*, they invited him to send some full scripts and immediately realised that they were an ideal basis for a follow-up series for Dennis. He could play the role of Terry McCann as the minder, and so they offered him the part.

Dennis thought that Denholm Elliott would be the perfect person to play opposite him as the Arthur Daley character. He had worked with Denholm back in 1972 in the BBC series *The Sextet*, which consisted of eight episodes using the same cast but telling different stories with a sexual theme. They had also worked together a year or so before *Minder* started in the second film adaptation of *The Sweeney*, called simply *Sweeney 2*.

Denholm was a graduate of the Royal Academy of Dramatic Art and had had an enormously productive career on stage and television. The people at Euston Films, however, didn't think he was exactly right for the Arthur Daley character and, for some reason, their production executive, Verity Lambert, thought that I was more the character they were looking for. That view wasn't unanimous by any means and, apparently, there were heated arguments about it. The general view was that I might be perceived as too middle class for the part but Verity reminded them of my spiv background as Flash Harry and eventually persuaded her colleagues that I might be their Arthur Daley.

I was playing in *Brimstone and Treacle* at the time at the Open Space Theatre in London and my agent asked me to go and meet some people from Thames Television on my way to the theatre because they wanted to talk to me about a new show. I said, 'No, I've already worked for Thames Television in *Armchair Theatre*, so they know my work and what I can do.' Three days later they called again and said, 'Just come in on the way to the theatre tonight and have a quick chat with us.' I agreed, reluctantly, not having any idea what sort of show it was.

I stopped off at the New Cavendish Hotel on the way and talked to them. Lloyd Shirley, one of the production executives at Euston Films, was there along with Linda Agran, their story editor, who had worked previously in the London office of Warner Bros. They showed me the outline of *Minder* and it appealed to me immediately. It said that Daley was right behind the Home Secretary as far as law and order were concerned, his favourite film was *The Godfather* and he dressed like a dodgy member of the Citizens' Advice Bureau. It also said he was the same age as some good-looking American film star. Paul Newman was born on 26 January 1925 and I was born exactly three months later. Arthur Daley often mentioned that he was the same age as Paul Newman.

Lloyd Shirley said, 'Well, that's the outline of the character. It's going to be a thirteen-week series. Do you think you'll have the stamina for that, Mr Cole?' I couldn't stop laughing. The part just came straight off the page at me. I said, 'Yes, I think so. I want to do it.' Three weeks later we were shooting the opening and closing credits.

Many years later Linda Agran talked about our meeting at the New Cavendish Hotel in a BBC One documentary series in 2005 entitled *Drama Connections*. She said, 'I thought George would be ideal. I'll never ever forget the moment he walked into that bar. It *was* Arthur Daley. And I remember sitting there; I could barely talk. I was so excited at the physical manifestation of Arthur Daley.'

The first episode, written by Leon Griffiths, was called 'Gunfight at the O.K. Laundrette' and went out on Monday, 29 October 1979, at 9 p.m. Its appearance was delayed by nearly two months because of a nationwide strike by television technicians that blacked out the whole ITV network following a dispute about overtime. When it did finally go out, there was practically no pre-publicity because of a strike within the printing industry. This was a major blow to the way the show was received by the audience.

Because of the printing strike, viewers had little idea what they would find when they turned on their television sets. Even Thames Television had little advance notice of when the show would go out because nobody knew exactly when the television strike would end. Normally, a production company would set up a huge publicity campaign spread over several weeks for a new series like this, so that viewers would have some feeling of what to expect. *Minder* did not have this luxury. As a result, viewers who were used to seeing Dennis in *The Sweeney* in a controlling role as a police officer saw him being knocked about and held hostage in a laundrette. To make matters worse, there was this strange man on the outside making light of the situation and trying to make money out of it. This rather took the audience by surprise. The response to the first episode was lukewarm to say the least and it took the audience quite a time to work out what was going on. Without the television strike and printing strike, the response would probably have been entirely different.

The title of the first episode began the practice used throughout the series of having a title that was a parody of a well-known show-business title, phrase or saying. This one referred to the 1957 film *Gunfight at the O.K. Corral* starring Burt Lancaster and Kirk Douglas. The *Minder* story was based on a real-life siege a few years earlier at a Spaghetti House in Knightsbridge.

Co-starring in the first episode was the talented Dave King playing Alfie, the proprietor of a laundrette business. Arthur Daley had loaned his minder Terry to Alfie that day to protect Alfie as he emptied the cash machines in his shops while his usual minder was away getting married. Dave King was a well-known face on British television in the 1950s with his own comedy variety show. He was an able crooner with a voice that many likened to Perry Como and Bing Crosby. Following his success on British television and a few hit records, he moved to the United States in 1959, where he also did well. When he returned to Britain in the 1960s, he discovered that musical styles were changing and he switched careers to become a straight actor.

In the *Minder* story, Terry and Alfie walk unexpectedly into an armed hold-up as they enter one of Alfie's laundrettes. They become hostages along with an elderly woman customer who was in the shop doing her washing. Alfie gets shot and loses a lot of blood after the gun goes off accidentally in a scuffle. After a night spent as a hostage in the laundrette, Terry eventually manages to negotiate with the hostage-takers and talk them into surrendering to the police. Unfortunately, Terry's prison record is discovered while he is held inside the shop and the police suspect him of being an accomplice. When he leaves the shop at the end of the siege, the police treat him as a member of the gang instead of recognising him as the hero that he is.

On one level, the story could easily have been used in a regular drama series like *Play of the Week*. On another level, Arthur Daley added a comic element when he tried to exploit the situation by concocting a story about Terry that he could sell to the press. For the first few episodes the audience had a struggle to decide whether the show was intended to be a crime comedy or a serious drama with a bit of comedy added on. One of their problems was that there was no studio audience to laugh when something was intended to be funny and they had to make up their own minds whether or not humour was intended. It definitely took a few episodes for them to decide.

Glynn Edwards, who had had a long career as a straight actor, had a small part as a barman in the first episode and went on to appear in 94 of the 108 episodes. Patrick Malahide had a small part as an inept policeman, Detective Constable Albert ('Charlie') Chisholm, and appeared as an equally ineffective detective sergeant in another 23 episodes until the end of the sixth series.

Lloyd Shirley and George Taylor (*The Sweeney* team) were the producers and Verity Lambert was the executive producer. Born and raised in Canada and never having lost his Canadian accent, Lloyd was the creative brain, with a wealth of experience drawn from working in a range of areas of television – including acting, which is where he started his career. He was the one who dealt with the directors and the technical people. George was the financial wizard and well-organised administrator with a string of executive-producer credits behind him; he could be relied upon to get the job done on time, on budget and with the minimum of hassle. The three of them continued in these roles for the first three series and were able to create a professional working environment that was conducive to making good television.

Tom Clegg was originally invited to direct the first two episodes. He had already done a fair amount of directing for Euston in *The*

Sweeney and its predecessor *Special Branch*. But when he saw the script for the first episode, he began to have some doubts and declined. He felt that it was rather strange to have the two main characters separated for the majority of the pilot episode. Most of Dennis's time on screen was while he was held hostage in the laundrette, while I was outside trying to cash in on the situation. I think Tom would have preferred to have us establish our characters in one-on-one situations. There was no animosity about it and he later directed four other episodes of the show over the first three series. In one of them in the second series, Arthur had to go and meet someone who was refereeing a school rugby game. The only way I could attract his attention was to run onto the field and pinch the ball. What I didn't know was that Tom had primed the boys before the take to chase after me when I ran off with the ball. I think my genuine shock of being pursued by all the youngsters intent on getting their ball back came across perfectly in the shot and helped make it a wonderful scene.

The first episode was eventually directed by Peter Sasdy, a charming Hungarian director who went on to direct two other episodes in the first series. Some of his ideas played a big part in moulding aspects of Arthur's character that remained throughout the show's whole run.

Peter and I felt that Arthur Daley should be a snappy dresser. On this premise, Peter sent me off to Savile Row to have two suits made. I was just finishing a play for Yorkshire Television at the time and I asked the wardrobe lady there who she recommended. She suggested a tailor who started out in Savile Row but was now working somewhere in the City. When I got back with my two suits and told the producers they cost £400 each, they were not at all happy as there was no budget for fancy suits.

In one of the early episodes, we were doing a scene in which I was supposed to get involved in a fight. I said to the director, 'We can't do that. Do you know how much this suit cost? If we so much as get even a mark on it, the producers will go mad.' He said, 'Well, how do you think we should handle it then?' I thought about it and said, 'How about if I nip round the corner when I see him and let Terry sort it out?' And I never did a fight scene after that. Whenever it looked like trouble, Arthur would run the other way. Dennis always used to joke that whenever there was a fight scene, I would always get two days off. At least, I think he was joking!

I had worked with Dennis three years earlier on a *Sweeney* episode entitled 'Tomorrow Man' but we didn't know each other particularly well. I think he was a little surprised when he heard that I was playing Arthur Daley. He was still expecting it would be Denholm Elliott. I first met him on *Minder* during one of the pre-production meetings about three weeks after my meeting with the Thames Television executives. We circled around each other for three or four days but after that we were the best of friends. I loved every minute of it. Today, more than 30 years later, I count him as one of my closest friends.

When we first started, we were given an old single-decker Green Line bus that acted as a communal dressing room for all the cast plus make-up and wardrobe. When we started the second series, Dennis and I asked for a Winnebago each (what the Americans call their 'trailer'). I think that lasted about two weeks. We both thought, 'This is silly. We are both in and out of each other's trailer all the time discussing the script and trying out new things. Why don't we just have one trailer between us?' So we did and it worked out perfectly. Dennis had the front and I had the back.

Dennis and I are actually complete opposites. Dennis is definitely a social animal. He is never happier than being out with the crowd, having a few drinks and generally enjoying himself in the company of other people. Whatever might show up in the characters I play, I am not usually an outgoing person. I am more home-based. If I am not working, I like to be at home, doing *The Times* crossword, tidying up the garden, catching up on some reading and generally keeping myself to myself. I think it was our differences that brought out the best in the two characters we played in *Minder*. Something definitely clicked between us. We used to meet around seven o'clock every morning in make-up and go over any changes we had made in the script overnight. Invariably, if one of us had marked a change, the other one would have marked the same change. That showed just how well attuned we were to each other's characters.

Every series would have a production base somewhere in London where we would have production offices, hold meetings and keep the set for the Winchester Club dressed permanently. For the first episode, we did the Winchester scene on location in a pub just off Shaftesbury Avenue in London. Then we used Leon Griffiths' drinking club in Chalk Farm for a few episodes but then we made up our own set and used that from then on. This was the only permanent set we ever used; everything else was shot on location. If we changed the location of the production base, the Winchester set would be dismantled and reassembled at the next production base.

Leon's drinking club in Chalk Farm was unbelievable. The extras were real members of the club (those who were prepared to allow their faces to be seen). If you got into conversation with them and asked what line of business they were in, they tended to look around furtively and whisper behind their hand, 'Removals.'

The first base we had was at the old National Savings Building in Blythe Road, Hammersmith, just behind the Olympia exhibition centre. This was just a few streets away from the location we used for Arthur Daley's original car lot. The next base was by the side of

Putney Bridge and the one after that was in Scrubs Lane behind Wormwood Scrubs prison.

Even Arthur's lock-up changed location whenever we changed bases. We always found a location for the lock-up as close as possible to the base because our time was so tight. Any time spent travelling to a location was time that came off our shooting schedule. For this reason, some of the police-station internal sets were also constructed at the base. This is why the policemen's offices often remained fairly constant throughout a series but changed from one series to another. Terry's flat also moved from one place to another for the same reason.

We would have two weeks to complete one episode and would try as far as possible not to film during the weekend so everyone could get a bit of rest, although this wasn't always possible.

A large part of the first episode was filmed in Danebury Avenue, SW15, in Roehampton near Putney* and involved two tiring overnight shoots. After that we usually managed to finish any night scenes in a single night.

In the third episode, I used the term ''er indoors' for the first time to refer to Arthur Daley's wife and it became a catchphrase. It stayed as a regular part of the show for the entire series and was used in most of the episodes. By 1997 it had even found its way into the *Oxford English Dictionary* as a colloquial term to mean a person's wife or girlfriend or 'any woman occupying a position of authority who is regarded as domineering'. Writer Leon Griffiths, who came up with the term, got a mention for it in the *OED*. But back in episode three it was used in a piece of clever scripting

---

*At the time of publication of this book, many of the locations used in *Minder* over the years are described in detail on the unofficial fans of *Minder* website at www.minder.org.

intended purely to get a laugh. Arthur and Terry see an attractive girl at the bar of a pub and I say to Dennis, quite unrelated to the main story, 'See, that's what 'er indoors don't understand. A young bird like that hanging round keeps yer feeling young.' Dennis replies, 'I thought it was Phyllosan and Grecian 2000.' Phyllosan was a proprietary vitamin tonic, advertised as 'Phyllosan fortifies the over-forties', and Grecian 2000 was a hair dye.

People all over the country started to call their other half ''er indoors' (or ''im indoors') and the expression became hugely popular. Dennis used it as the basis for a Christmas novelty song he wrote in 1983 called *What Are We Gonna Get 'Er Indoors*. The record spent five weeks in the UK pop record charts and reached the number-21 position. Dennis and I even went on the BBC's flagship pop-music show *Top of the Pops* to perform it.

That was a terrifying experience for me. I saw all those youngsters in the studio with their strange hairstyles and strange clothes, dancing to pop records I had never heard, and I was wearing Arthur Daley's overcoat and trilby hat. I said to Dennis, 'I can't go in there,' and he almost had to drag me on. The song wasn't the sort of material that could be lip-synched and we had to do it live. I think it was the only song performed live in the whole show. To make matters worse it started with some spoken patter between the two of us and I had to sing the first line, 'What are we gonna get for 'er indoors', unaccompanied. Fortunately, I sang it in the right key and the audience seemed to enjoy it. Dennis was in his element in a pop-music environment but, for me, I think the best description would be that it was an interesting learning experience.

The funny thing about that record is that, after Dennis had got the record company interested in the song, he casually mentioned to me, 'Oh, by the way, they want a B-side next week.'

I said, 'Fine. What are you going to write?'

Dennis laughed and said, 'I'm not going to write it. You are.'

'But I've never written a bloody song in my life. I wouldn't know how to start.'

'Well, I'm not going to do it. I've written my side.'

I was like a young child learning to tie his shoelaces but I managed to cobble together an idea about Dennis falling in love with a lady police officer. I called it *Girl in Blue*. But the funny thing is that the A-side – the one Dennis wrote – starts off with a Christmas carol written by Gustav Holst and what nobody realised at the time was that it was not out of copyright. So Dennis's royalty payments for the record have a deduction towards Gustav Holst's estate but my song was totally original and I got the full whack.

Leon Griffiths said later that he didn't invent the term ''er indoors' but had heard it used by a minicab driver in his London drinking club. The driver apparently said that he couldn't stay for another drink because he had to get back to 'er indoors. When Leon mentioned it again to the driver some time later, he denied ever saying it, which probably did him out of a big tip!

I think it must have been in the character outline but I recall that it specified somewhere that Arthur Daley was terrified of 'er indoors. I think he had been in prison many years earlier and she had been a prison visitor. When he came out, he sold her a car that turned out to be a dud and he'd been paying for it ever since.

We did 11 episodes in the first series, 6 of which were written by Leon. The scripts were brilliant. There was always a bit of humour, often some violence, and Dennis's character establishes a reputation for climbing into bed with the women at the first opportunity. 11 is an unusual number of episodes for a television series; they usually make 12 or 13. Unfortunately, it was so long ago and I can't remember if we made more episodes and held some over to the next series, or whether the shooting schedule was affected by the strike of television technicians and we only made 11 – or if it was 11 for some other reason.

Whatever the reason, by the end of that first series the show had started to attract something of a cult audience. But the ratings were not brilliant, with a maximum viewing figure around the 9 million mark, and there had been some talk of ending it there and not doing a second series. We had a contract for the first series and that was that. The show wouldn't actually be cancelled. There was nothing to cancel. This was the way it was for the entire run of the show. We never had a contract for more than one series and at the end of each series we had a 'wrap' party. If we were lucky, we would get asked back a few months later, although we all knew there was a chance that we wouldn't.

But as we approached the end of the first series it was all down to the Director of Programming at Thames Television, Bryan Cowgill, to make the final decision whether or not to go forward. The problem with commercial television is that programming decisions are controlled by how much money a programme can pull in from advertising. If advertisers feel that a programme is unsuccessful, they will show their advertisements during another one. I think it was executive producer Verity Lambert's personal plea to Bryan Cowgill that allowed the second series of *Minder* to see the light of day. Unusually for *Minder*, we knew before we finished the first series that we would be back for a second. We started shooting the second series at the beginning of 1980.

Sadly, our good friend and principal scriptwriter Leon Griffiths had just suffered a major stroke and was unable to write. With his typical humour, he managed to say that he was too weak to write a suicide note, let alone a *Minder* script.

We seriously wondered whether anyone would be able to

recreate the magic that Leon was able to put into his scripts but script executive Linda Agran brought in a number of new writers in the hope that it might be possible. One of them was Tony Hoare. He had already written an episode in the first series called 'Come in T-64, Your Time is Ticking Away', about the minicab business. That title came from the practice of boat owners who would hire out rowing boats and pedal boats on park lakes or at the seaside and, at the end of the half-hour rental period or whatever it was, would call out through a loudhailer, 'Come in, number seven, your time is up.'

Tony Hoare had a long history of writing for television crime shows, including *Z-Cars*, *Softly Softly* and *The Bill*. You could not find anyone who knew more about London. On top of this he had served a prison sentence in the 1960s for bank robbery. He was eminently qualified to write for *Minder* and, over the course of the series, he wrote a total of 20 episodes. His writing was crisp and witty and he came up with plenty of good ideas. He wrote four episodes in the second series.

The first episode of the second series was 'National Pelmet', written by Willis Hall, in which Terry has to mind a racehorse. The title was a parody of *National Velvet*, a 1944 film about a racehorse starring Elizabeth Taylor and Mickey Rooney. Willis Hall wrote another three scripts for us after that. This episode went out on 11 September 1980 and reached the top 20 in the television charts. This was definitely a triumph for us, especially as the episode had a few problems during production. Firstly, the original story was about greyhound racing rather than horse racing but, when it came to finding locations, the governing body for greyhound racing in Britain was far from impressed with the idea of cooperating with a story suggesting that there might be a dishonest side to the sport. The producers, therefore, rewrote the story around horse racing.

Filming was not without its share of mishaps. Liza Goddard was playing a jockey and, when she tried to make friends with one of the horses by offering it an apple, the horse nipped her finger and she had to go to hospital for an injection. What's more Dennis had a fight scene with a character brandishing a piece of wood but misjudged the distance and ended up with a bad gash in his arm that needed a hospital visit and stitches.

The second episode, 'Whose Wife is it Anyway' by Tony Hoare, was one that could probably not go out in the same form these days. The story was about Dennis having to mind the gay manager of an antique shop, and focused largely on issues of prejudice. What made it unusual by today's standards was that the gay theme was handled in what was then considered a humorous way, with homophobic expressions and slang terminology scattered liberally throughout. Today some of those expressions would be regarded as highly unacceptable if used in public and would attract numerous complaints if they were used in a television show. But in 1980 nobody seemed to care.

Although it was not originally intended as the last episode of the series, the one that went out the week before Christmas 1980, 'A Lot of Bull and a Pat on the Back' by Tony Hoare, ensured that we went out on a high. It was a hilarious episode in which Dennis and I are led to believe that we are repossessing a prize bull but, in reality, we are stealing it. When we discover we have stolen it, we decide to repossess it again and return it to its owner. There are some great scenes where we have to entice the animal into a trailer. Scenes like this cannot be scripted and rely on creating humour from the situation as it presents itself on the shoot. Dennis and I had a field day (literally). At one point we have to run across the mud-soaked field with the bull in close pursuit. Along the way I step into a giant unscripted cowpat. I call out to Terry and Dennis ad-libs,

'That's supposed to be lucky, innit?' The director liked the shot so much that he left it in the final cut.

We didn't usually ad-lib on *Minder*. The scripts were so good that we seldom needed to. But occasionally we would try a scene in rehearsal and realise that it might be slightly better if we did it another way. The trick was always to do it so that no one realised we had changed anything and the scriptwriters would think they had written it. And if one of us made a slip as we delivered a line, nine times out of ten the other would adjust his next line without anyone noticing. We learned early on that the best approach was not to lay claim to anything we said that was not in the script. Scriptwriters make their living writing words for other people to deliver and, naturally, get a bit edgy if actors start saying things that they did not write. We allowed it to become a team effort. If an ad-lib worked and everyone was happy with it, we were more than happy for the writers to believe they had written it. If it didn't work and the director called, 'Cut!' we could always do the scene again. When the television show *It'll Be Alright on the Night* started, they asked us to send in some out-takes from *Minder* and we had little to send them. Most of our dialogue slips were corrected as they happened and did not come across as problems.

We had a bit of unexpected excitement while we were doing the episode with the bull. We were at the production base one afternoon after shooting a scene on location in Hertfordshire when a carload of police pulled up outside. It seems that a security van had been held up and robbed no more than a mile away from where we had been shooting. Someone told the police that a film crew had been working there and the police came to satisfy themselves that our crew had not been planted there as a distraction. They interviewed everyone on the set and left, apparently satisfied that there were no real villains among us. The coincidence was that the episode was

172

written by Tony Hoare, who had gained some experience in that line of work in a previous career.

We did 13 episodes in that series and the ratings were generally fairly good but not good enough to guarantee another series. But it was clear that the show was reaching a wider audience.

There were a few spin-offs along the way. *I Could Be So Good For You*, the show's theme tune, which was sung by Dennis (and co-written by Gerard Kenny and Dennis's then wife Pat), reached number three in the British pop music charts in November 1980 and the top ten in the Australian and New Zealand charts. There was also a *Minder Annual* that year – a Christmas stocking filler to go alongside the *Dandy Annual*, the *Beano Annual* and all the other annuals that go on sale at the end of the year.

People were certainly taking notice of the show, and Leon Griffiths received a Writers' Guild award in 1980 for his work on it. Ironically, because of his poor health, he had not written any of the episodes in the second series but in the industry his name was inextricably linked to *Minder*. Without him, there would not have been a *Minder* at all. And though he may not have done any writing that year, he was fighting back from his health problems with a vengeance. He undertook a gruelling course of physiotherapy and speech therapy and came back to write another 10 episodes a couple of years later. The Writers' Guild award to Leon could well be what clinched Euston's decision to do a third series.

There was a year's break between the end of the second series and the start of the third. We stormed back in January 1982 with another Tony Hoare masterpiece, 'Dead Men Do Tell Tales', and went straight into the top 10 of the ratings and hovered around there for the rest of the 13 episodes. Twice we hit the number-four slot. We could sense the change of attitude among the audience. Taxi drivers started saying things like, 'How's 'er indoors?' or complaining that I didn't pay Terry enough money. There was one occasion when I was invited for lunch at Scotland Yard. The taxi driver asked me where I was going and I said 'Scotland Yard'. He said, 'No, come on, where do you really want to go?' He just couldn't believe that I would actually want to go there.

We had some marvellous guests in the third series, including rock star Suzy Quatro, Harry Fowler, Derek Fowlds, Avril Angers, Mike Reid, George Sewell, Max Wall, Alfie Bass, Michael Medwin, Richard Griffiths and Nigel Davenport to name a few. Many were established comedy actors and the show took on a new direction in which we put more emphasis on the humour. This seemed to be the way the audience wanted it – and this is what we gave them.

I think the first episode of series three, in which Derek Fowlds played an undertaker, was one of the best of all. He was so accustomed to the dynamics of that sort of show after *Yes, Minister* that his character came across brilliantly. And Tony Hoare's script was outstanding. He had already written five scripts in the first and second series and had discovered how to get the best from individual cast members with his writing.

Tony told a wonderful story about that episode when we did a commentary together in 2005 for the Australian release of the *Minder* DVD set. Harry Fowler was in the episode playing a Jewish undertaker. Tony told how he had a friend who kept pestering him to use his name for a character in an episode and he eventually agreed and gave his friend's name, Monty Wiseman, to the undertaker. When the episode went out, his friend sued the company because the Monty Wiseman in the episode was a villain and his friend claimed that it reflected badly on his character. This caused all sorts of problems for the company because they could not sell the episode overseas as it was the subject of ongoing litigation. The company finally settled with Tony's friend and made an out-of-court payment to him. Tony never found out whether that was his friend's original intention but he became more careful about using his friends' names after that. The episode 'Dead Men Do Tell Tales' was nominated for a BAFTA award the following year.

Towards the middle of the third series, we did an episode with Max Wall playing an elderly bank robber who has just been released from prison after a long sentence and who wants to track down the loot from the job that put him inside. Max was an interesting person to work with. He cut his teeth in the music halls of the 1930s and had a highly successful career as a stand-up comedian, where he could work according to his own timing. He also did some drama after that. I don't know how he got on then but, when he came on *Minder*, he had some difficulty keeping pace with the dialogue and missed quite a few of his cues and we had to do several retakes. I think it was simply because he had spent the majority of his professional life working at his own pace and just had difficulty adjusting to someone else's. But he was a wonderful guest to have on the show and it was lovely working with him.

Also in the cast of that episode was a tall, attractive actress with stunning red hair named Rula Lenska, who had no hesitation in telling anyone who would listen that she was a genuine Polish countess. She had made something of a name for herself in a 1976 Thames Television series called *Rock Follies* about three female pop singers. It was as a result of their meeting on the *Minder* episode that she and Dennis became what I think is known today as 'an item', despite the fact that they were both married to different people at the time.

The affair between Dennis and Rula soon became a huge tabloid scandal and caused the break-up of their existing marriages. But, as a true professional, Dennis did not allow the matter to affect his performance on the show, either before or after the ensuing publicity.

At the height of the affair, Rula was in and out of our Winnebago all the time. If Dennis was on set and I wasn't, she would be in there alone with me. If I was on set and Dennis wasn't, she would be in there alone with Dennis. Everyone on the show knew what was going on but these things happen in our business, just as they do in others, and we had a show to work on, with no time to focus on other people's personal affairs. Dennis and I were good friends and I had got to know his wife Pat Maynard fairly well. They were a lovely couple and up until then seemed to be highly supportive of each other.

Personally, I didn't approve of what was happening. I liked Pat very much and I felt that Dennis was getting himself into a lot of trouble. But it was his decision and none of my business. There turned out to be one member of the crew who didn't fully understand exactly what was going on. When the story finally hit the press, she came up to me and said, 'George, I'm so sorry, I thought it was you.'

I said, 'What do you mean?'

She replied, 'Having the affair. Every time I came into your Winnebago she was in there with you. I thought it was you.'

Then it clicked. Every time she came into the Winnebago when Rula was there alone with me, she would say, 'Oh, sorry,' and quickly leave.

Rula appeared in two more episodes of *Minder* after that, each time as a different character. There was an interesting scene towards the end of her third appearance on the show in an episode called 'The Last Video Show' in the seventh series. When we did the scene, Dennis was standing at the front desk of a police station talking to Michael Troughton, who played Detective Constable Melish, when

176

a tall red-haired woman looking remarkably like Rula and dressed in a police uniform walks past but says nothing. Michael says, 'Bye, Sandy.' Dennis was not expecting her to appear as it had no connection with the story and had not been rehearsed. He glances behind and looks taken aback but continues in character and delivers his next line. In fact, it was Dennis's birthday and the crew had conspired with Rula to go on to deliver him a singing telegram. I think that was the only time anything like that happened.

The third series ended in April 1982 and we were off the air for 20 months until Boxing Day 1983, when the show returned with a Christmas special containing clips from some of the earlier episodes spun around a Christmas theme. This acted as a prelude to a series of another 11 episodes beginning on 11 January 1984. In the meantime, I had the honour of receiving a nomination as Best Actor at the 1983 BAFTA awards ceremony for my work on *Minder* but lost out to Alec Guinness, who won with *Smiley's People*. George Taylor and Lloyd Shirley also received award nominations for *Minder* at the same event in the category Best Drama Series/Serial.

Again, the fourth series was extremely satisfying. Some episodes stood out particularly. The second, 'Rocky Eight and a Half', was by Leon Griffiths and involved a rigged boxing contest. This was the episode in which I got to deliver a priceless line that became synonymous with *Minder*. Actually, it wasn't priceless. It cost me £25.

My son Crispin is a scriptwriter. He dropped in one afternoon and said, 'I've just heard someone in a pub come out with a great Arthur Daley line.' He told me what it was and I liked it. I gave him £25 and said, 'Don't use it. Save that one for me.' I kept it for a couple of years and then ad-libbed it in the boxing episode when I was trying to instil some confidence in Terry and told him, 'The world's your lobster, my son.' The line got a great laugh and stayed in and immediately became a favourite with the audience. Leon Griffiths came up to me afterwards and said, 'That was one of the best lines I've ever written. I think I owe you £12.50.'

Crispin has become a talented scriptwriter over the years and has recently had a successful series on Sky called *Mad Dogs*. To be honest, I'm starting to wonder whether he really did overhear the lobster line in a pub or came up with it himself. But I don't want to spoil the magic of the line by asking him outright. And now I'm using it as the title for my book, I don't want to pay him any more money!

Arthur Daley's tendency to use malapropisms was a real joy and something I looked forward to when I received a new script. One that I particularly liked was, 'How would you have fared in the Blitz with bombs raining down from the Lufthansa?' Another was when Arthur 'saw a window of opportunity and jumped through it,' and when he 'felt like Rommel before the Battle of Waterloo'. These were pure gems from the scriptwriters.

They also made good use of catchphrases such as 'a nice little earner', 'a word in your shell-like' and 'stand on me, Terry'. Many of these were already in use, particularly around London, but *Minder* certainly gave them some added exposure.

Back to the fourth series, though, and another episode I especially liked was the third one in the series, 'Senior Citizen Caine' by Andrew Payne. In this one, veteran actor Lionel Jeffries (who was born two months after I was and appeared in one of the *St. Trinian's* films with me) played an eccentric widower who intended to enjoy his fortune while he was still around instead of passing it on to his family. Two weeks later 'Sorry Pal, Wrong Number', another episode by Leon, saw T. P. McKenna playing a professional conman who Arthur teams up with to sell horse-racing tips. Leon based the character on someone he knew who did the same thing. It had some great comedy when Dennis has to mind three telephone boxes so that I can use them to give out racing tips. That scene with the telephone boxes was such a splendid collaboration of writing, direction and casting that it was one of the funniest in the series. Leon actually wrote the episode with T. P. in mind for the conman. He even gave the character the name T. P. Mooney in the script. However, when T. P. arrived on set on the first day of shooting, flattered as he was, he and director Terry Green agreed to change the character's name to J. J. Mooney.

Two episodes in that series reached the number-two spot in the ratings. The series ended on 21 March 1984 on a roll and was bringing in a substantial amount of income to Thames Television from its overseas sales. In Germany, the show went out dubbed into German under the title *Der Aufpasser*, which can be translated as 'the guard' or 'the watchdog'. In Russia we were dubbed into Russian and we all seemed to speak the language flawlessly. In Hong Kong they kept the English voice track and showed the programme on the English-language channel but added Chinese subtitles. These were translated literally from the English wherever there was a literal translation, like 'philharmonic', but phonetically when there was not, like 'Vera'. This resulted in much of the show's slang being entirely meaningless to the handful of non-English speakers who happened to be watching on the Sunday lunchtimes when it went out.

Ours was not the only series bringing in money for the company. *Benny Hill* and *Rumpole of the Bailey* were among some of the others. As a result, Thames Television International received an award under the Queen's Awards for Export and Technology in 1984 for generating an export income of £18 million for its programmes the previous year. *Minder* was also honoured that year at the BAFTA television awards ceremony when Leon Griffiths received the 1984 writer's award for his television writing.

Boosting Thames Television's coffers a little more, we were back on air six months after the fourth series ended, with a fifth series of nine episodes. They saved the ninth episode and showed it on Boxing Day 1984.

Two months later, on 5 February 1985, Dennis and I received awards from the Variety Club of Great Britain as joint ITV personalities of the year for our performances as Terry McCann and Arthur Daley in *Minder*. This was a great honour for both of us. Around the same time, I received another Best Actor nomination for *Minder* at the 1985 BAFTA awards ceremony and George Taylor received one for Best Drama Series/Serial. We both lost out to *The Jewel in the Crown*.

Nine months after the fifth series ended, a sixth series of six episodes began on 4 September 1985. We had some brilliant scripts and the series was unashamedly played for laughs, except, perhaps, for the last episode, which ended with Terry walking out on Arthur after an argument.

During the production of this series we also fitted in a special episode, 'A Little Bit of Give and Take', that was never intended for broadcast on national television and has become much sought after in recent years by fans and collectors. The episode was made to discourage schoolchildren and young people from using illicit drugs and was distributed to schools and local health authorities as part of a health-education project initiated by the Department of Health and Social Security. Dennis, Glynn and I appeared in our *Minder* roles along with a group of teenagers. Many of the *Minder* production team were also involved in the project and it was immensely satisfying to know that our show was able to contribute to such a worthwhile purpose.

One episode in the sixth series, 'Arthur is Dead, Long Live Arthur' by Tony Hoare, was particularly good fun as I was playing alongside my wife Penny. Arthur was hiding out in a boarding house pretending to be a writer after faking his suicide to avoid paying a sizeable tax bill. Penny played the lonely widow who runs the boarding house and eventually sees through my disguise. I remember some highly amusing dialogue when I try to plan my funeral with an undertaker without revealing that the funeral is actually for me. There were also some worrying scenes on top of a building as I choose whether I would want to end it all by jumping.

The guest artist in the final episode of that series, 'Waiting for Goddard', was well-loved comedy actor Ronald Fraser, playing a straight role as an elderly recluse who comes into a fortune that Arthur wants to get his hands on. When Terry walks out on Arthur at the end of the episode after an argument, it certainly reinforced the impression that *Minder*'s days were over. George Taylor still received another BAFTA nomination for the show in 1986, although the prize went to *Edge of Darkness*.

We did a special two-hour Christmas feature film, *Minder on the Orient Express* by Andrew Payne, which went out on Christmas Day 1985. That was a particularly enjoyable experience, not least because we had four weeks to shoot it instead of the usual two. On top of that we had 10 days on location in Boulogne and an excellent cast including co-stars Honor Blackman, Adam Faith and Robert Beatty, plus all the regulars. There was also a delightful trip on the Orient Express, although, in reality, many of the scenes on board the train were shot on location at Twickenham Studios in carriage sets mounted on springs with studio staff on the edges jumping up and down.

The 'Waiting for Goddard' episode was the last one written by Leon Griffiths. I think poor Leon had become rather unhappy about the direction the show was taking. He had conceived it as a rough, tough and gritty crime show and, for various reasons, it had lost much of what he saw as central to the subject matter. It had lost most of its violence and womanising and was now focusing on comedy rather than crime. But at its peak in the sixth series, the show was attracting 17.5 million viewers – nearly double the audience at the peak of the first series.

There was no doubt that the show had changed a lot in the six years since it first appeared. One thing that Dennis and I agreed about early on was that we would not allow any swearing or bad language on the show. I was working on *The Pirates of Penzance* at the Theatre Royal in London at the time and there were always lots of fans at the stage door calling out things like 'Where's Terry?' and 'How's 'er indoors?' and I realised that many of them were children and youngsters. Dennis was working not far away at the Victoria Palace Theatre at the same time, doing *Windy City*, and he noticed the same thing. Although *Minder* always had the 9 p.m. timeslot when restrictions on adult content were relaxed, we both became aware as we left our respective theatres that there were a lot of young children waiting for autographs and telling us that *Minder* was their favourite show. That was why we made the decision that the swearing would have to go. The Independent Broadcasting Authority was thrilled to bits about it. But we had to be careful how we handled the matter with the company. We didn't want to give anyone the impression that we were making policy decisions. We were invited to lunch with the bigwigs of ITV on one occasion and that was when we told them we had deliberately cut out the swearing. As it turned out, they were delighted to hear it. Today, when *Minder* goes out as a repeat, even 'damn' gets bleeped out. But there were other changes on the way that changed the whole nature of the show.

Political correctness was beginning to show itself in society in the early 1980s and this slowly permeated into the show. In the first three series, Dennis's character was never slow to jump into bed with a pretty girl at the first opportunity. But the AIDS scare at the beginning of the 1980s put a stop to all this. There was a directive from the senior management of the company saying that it had to stop.

The early episodes also contained a lot of graphic violence. But Terry was a minder, and an occasional fight was a necessary part of his job, whether for the protection of his boss or whoever else he happened to be minding. Whenever we showed any sort of violent behaviour it was necessary for the story and was never gratuitous. If we showed a thug kicking someone who was unable to defend himself it was because that was what a thug would do, not because we wanted to glorify it. Even this, however, had to be drastically cut in the early 1980s when Mrs Mary Whitehouse and her supporters began to campaign against the depiction of violence on television.

The fight scenes, while we had them, were choreographed in meticulous detail. One that I recall took a lot of planning was in an episode called 'In' at the end of the third series. Dennis got involved in a fight on the platform of a London Transport bus and we had scenes in which people's heads were being forced over the side of the bus platform just inches above the road as the bus drove along the street. We relied a lot on stunt people to do scenes like this but it was often difficult to get Dennis to agree to let a stunt man do his stunts.

We did another episode at the Carlton Tower Hotel in their penthouse suite and they had a press lady looking after us to ensure that everything we needed was there for the asking. The hospitality was without equal. What I don't think she fully realised was that we were going to stage a fight there and make it look as if we were smashing up her suite. At the crucial time we had to carefully keep her busy somewhere else. Actually, she need not have worried. We moved their things out of the suite and into another room close by and replaced them with ours. We even replaced their doors with ours if we thought there was any chance that they would be damaged when we started to break things up. It was a wonderful sequence but I think she would have been rather worried if she knew exactly what we were planning to do.

When the sixth series ended in 1985, it definitely seemed that this was the last of *Minder*. The show was off the air, apart from repeats, for three years. Like everyone else on the show, I got on with my life and my career.

It was a pleasant surprise, therefore, when I got the call in 1988 to do another series. This was preceded by a 90-minute feature film, *An Officer and a Car Salesman*, written by Tony Hoare, which was broadcast on Boxing Day in 1988. The premise of the story was that Terry had just been released from an 18-month prison sentence after Arthur had stored stolen video players at Terry's flat without his knowledge and Terry now wants nothing to do with him. This was the final appearance of Patrick Malahide as Chisholm. His departure was explained by having the Chisholm character suspended from the police force as a result of his vendetta against Arthur and now working as a consultant for a private security company.

Tony Hoare, who wrote the Christmas special, was not at all happy with the way it was edited. He felt that bits had been arbitrarily cut out and 'they turned it into a kind of *Carry On* film'. He swore he would never write another episode of *Minder*. He did though. He wrote 4 episodes in the final series, including the 100th one and the last one of all.

The seventh series began on 2 January 1989, the week after the

Officer and a Car Salesman Christmas special. The series had some good stories but the ratings were not as high as in the previous one. Following Terry's latest spell in prison, the relationship between him and Arthur had reached a definite low and perhaps the audience was reacting to this. The last episode of that series went out on 6 February 1989. This was when Dennis chose to pull out. To this day I don't know exactly why, although he has said in interviews since then that he was unhappy with the fact that his role as a minder had become diluted and that too much comedy had taken over. At the time, he seemed to be tightly under the control of his new wife Rula Lenska and I wondered if she exerted some pressure but he has never told me personally what the reason was and I have never asked.

Nevertheless, *Minder* was still a major money-spinner for Thames Television. During the seven minutes of peak-time advertising in any one episode of *Minder* during that series, Thames Television earned £1.4 million. But after the seventh series ended, early in 1989, *Minder* was off the air for two and a half years. It was generally believed, once again, as much by me as by everyone else, that its days were finally over – until I got a call in 1991 inviting me to work on a new series. As usual, I asked them to check with Dennis first. The company called me back again and said he was working on a film somewhere and they couldn't locate him. I told them to keep looking and to let me know his reply when they found him. Eventually, they got back to me to say that Dennis didn't want to do it. I said, 'If Dennis isn't in it, neither am I.' As far as I was concerned, that was it: no Dennis, no George. Thames Television came back to me four days later saying they thought it would work with a new character playing the minder. I gave it some more thought and eventually told them I would do it, although I had serious doubts about whether it would work without Dennis.

Euston pulled out all the stops to keep the new series at the top of the ratings and set aside a budget of £7 million, which was a huge amount for a series at the time. But with potential customers for the series in 80 countries around the world, it made sound business sense.

The eighth series started transmission on 5 September 1991 with an episode entitled 'The Loneliness of the Long Distance Entrepreneur' written by David Yallop. Dennis's absence was explained by his having got married and gone to live in Australia. That was a nice gesture to the fans, who could relax in the knowledge that he had now settled down and was free from Arthur's manipulation. The new minder was Arthur's nephew, Ray Daley, the son of Arthur's brother Bert and sister-in-law Doreen. Ray Daley was played by a relative newcomer, 26-year-old Gary Webster, who was already known to viewers from his role as Graham in *EastEnders*.

But the show now had a completely different feel from before. I think there was a deliberate move by the company to bring the show into the 1990s rather than continue with a format that was already 12 years old. Naturally, the opening and closing credit sequences had to be changed. The theme tune remained the same (Dennis's *I Could Be So Good For You*) but this time they did it in a synthesised 1990s style without vocals. They brought in several new writers and significantly changed the dynamic between the two main characters. There was now a family connection holding Arthur and his minder together; it was no longer simply a relationship between Arthur and a paid employee. Ray supported Arthur as his uncle rather than his employer. There was less bickering between the two than there was with Terry. Ray stayed out of trouble unless it was absolutely necessary and Arthur put him in fewer high-risk situations than he had inflicted on Terry. Even the storylines had a 1990s feel to them, with abundant threads involving relations with Europe and the Common Market.

I think it was fairly adventurous of Euston to revive the series with Gary as the minder but it seemed to work well and I found it easy to adapt. However, I think this had a lot to do with the excellent script that David Yallop wrote for that first episode. It was definitely one of the biggest contributions to the smooth transition. David said at the time that, when he was asked to write that first episode, he felt that he 'was on a hiding to nothing'. He thought that the new character could not just be a mark II version of Terry – he needed to be 'a man of the nineties, more intelligent and cynical' and able to open up a new seam of humour as a result. In the end, David felt they were able to pull it off by reassembling a partnership and injecting new life in the process.

The episode opened with a wedding in the Daley family and continued as a spoof on *The Godfather*. The wedding was the closest the audience ever came to seeing 'er indoors. The camera panned across the back of her head while she was in the church congregation during the marriage ceremony. During the reception, Arthur meets up with his brother Bert (Ray's father) and some of his other male relatives and it is clear that they all hold Arthur in great esteem as a successful and legitimate businessman. Brother Bert introduces Ray to Arthur, trying to interest Arthur in taking him on as an assistant. It was clever scripting because, whereas the family thinks Arthur is amazing, which Arthur enjoys immensely, the audience knows him much better and can see that it will not work out the way the family is hoping.

I found myself perfectly at ease working with Gary. In fact, I think there was another element of déjà vu at play. When he joined the team, he was given his own trailer. After a few weeks, I found I was missing the freedom to discuss things with him without having to leave my own trailer and go next door to find him. I invited him to share my Winnebago, which was much bigger than I needed, and I don't think he had any hesitation in accepting. It worked out perfectly.

We did 3 series and a total of 22 episodes in the new format. The episodes were enjoyable and generally well received and we had some excellent co-stars. Many well-known actors and personalities were calling up to ask if they could have a part.

A few months after the eighth series started, dear old Leon Griffiths passed away following more strokes and a brain tumour. He died in 1992 aged 64.

One of the highlights of the new format for me was a trilogy comprising one episode in Britain and two in Australia, with Arthur and Ray travelling to Sydney to chase an inheritance from a distant ancestor of Arthur's. We made the two Australian episodes in collaboration with the Australian Broadcasting Corporation. We were out there filming when the first series with Gary was just starting in Australia so we did a fair amount of promotional work to introduce him.

I loved the time we spent in Sydney working on *Minder*. I was able to take Penny with me and we managed to do a bit of touring. From the time we boarded our Qantas flight in London, the Australians really took to us and made us welcome wherever we went. We knew that Australia had the biggest market for the show outside Britain but we had no idea just how popular it was. Even the word 'minder' had an official ring to it: the staff of the Prime Minister's office were referred to as the PM's minders. It was also rumoured that some sittings of the Australian parliament had to be rescheduled because members would mysteriously disappear whenever *Minder* was being shown on television. I suspect that this is apocryphal because Bob Hawke, the Prime Minister, is also reputed to have said in response to a request to reschedule a session, 'No. Do what I do – record it!'

The people in Sydney were very warm towards us and it was all thoroughly enjoyable. But then I had to leave Penny behind in Sydney and fly out to the outback with Gary to do some location work in Broken Hill. That was an entirely different experience. The people out there seemed to be unusually friendly and appeared to wave a lot more than the town-dwellers did. I assumed they were waving to me and, like an idiot, I started waving back at them. But then I realised they weren't waving at me at all. They were waving away those dreadful flies. They were terrible; they would go in your eyes, up your nose and around your lips and, when they landed on you, they would just want to hang on as if their life depended on it, like miniature mountaineers.

It happened that while we were in Sydney, Queen Elizabeth was also visiting. We were filming in Bridge Street at the time and we heard that Her Majesty would be passing by on the way from the airport. I insisted that we take a break from shooting until she had passed and told everyone on the set that they would need to raise their hats as she drove past. When I saw her car approaching, I ordered them all to raise their hats, which they did, and all the onlookers clapped wildly. I felt proud to be British. Gary was convinced that the Queen noticed us and broke into a smile.

We initially stayed at the luxurious Regent Hotel on the Sydney waterfront, where we did some of the shooting for the show, and then moved to a palatial serviced apartment close by with a spectacular view overlooking the harbour and the Opera House. Dennis Waterman was also in Sydney at the same time, touring Australia in Keith Waterhouse's play *Jeffrey Bernard is Unwell*. He was staying at a swish hotel practically next door. Penny happened to see him going into the lift with Rula as she walked past. Neither of us had any idea that the other one was there. I sent him a message to tell him we were there but our schedules were so tight that, even halfway round the world, we didn't get a chance to meet up. I was out on location all day and he was in the theatre in the evening. Dennis tells in his autobiography *ReMinder* how his marriage to Rula was in the final stages of its breakdown during this Australian trip, so perhaps he was just not in the mood for socialising, but it was a pity we could not get together.

Australia remains one of my favourite location trips. The Australians took us on a wonderful harbour tour over to Manly. Penny had her birthday while we were there and Gary Webster had his birthday the previous day. We had a celebration at a delightful seafood restaurant on the beach. I remember that they served the meal in paper, the way they used to in the old fish-and-chip shops that I frequented in London as a boy.

It was a huge learning experience for us. I had no idea there would be camels roaming around in the desert. Apparently, the early British colonists introduced them. They thought that if they had deserts over there, they would need a few camels, so they packed some up and shipped them over. All the camels in the desert today are descended from those early imports. I was also amazed by the natural wildlife. There were insects bigger than any I had ever seen before.

We were out one day doing a car scene when another car just appeared from nowhere and crashed into us. It seems that an enormous spider had dropped into the driver's lap while she was driving and caused her to panic and lose control of the car. Apparently, this sort of spider looks for warm places to sleep at night. The locals assumed that this particular one nodded off behind the sunshade on the driver's side of the car the previous night and fell off when the driver flipped the sunshade down while she was driving the next morning. Fortunately, nobody was hurt, although I'm not too sure what happened to the spider.

The worst part of the trip was when I got back from the location shoot in Broken Hill and found that Penny had got into some difficulty while she was out swimming. The production company had generously found her a lovely 1920s house on the beach where she could stay with an actress friend from way back while I was in Broken Hill. Penny's friend originally went over to Australia on an assignment from the BBC and loved it so much that she and her husband stayed there. Penny used to be a strong swimmer but one day while she was staying at the beach house she went for a swim by herself and got caught in the current and had a terrible struggle getting back to the beach. When she managed to get back, she said to her friend, 'Gosh, that was tough,' and her friend said, 'Oh, darling, I wondered why you were messing about like that!' It was actually poor Penny trying not to drown! In all seriousness, I would caution anyone who goes swimming around the Australian coast and is not familiar with the area to treat the waters with great respect. The currents there can be deadly.

To make matters worse, when they both drove back afterwards in the car that the production team had provided, there was the most frightful fuss because the police recognised the car and thought they had stolen it. They had nothing on them to prove that they hadn't. It nearly ended in terrible tears. But Penny still looks back on our Australian trip with great affection. We were both treated beautifully.

The 100th episode of *Minder* went out on 20 January 1994 with a story called 'All Things Brighton Beautiful' by Tony Hoare in the tenth and final series. This was the third series in the new format with Gary. (It was actually the 101st episode but the company chose to ignore an early Christmas compilation in the tally.) The company threw a huge anniversary party to celebrate. Sadly, one important face that was missing was Dennis's. When the press heard that he was not there, they started to ask why and I remember reading in *The Times* a few days later that an unnamed organiser had told them that Dennis was not invited because 'it would have been just too embarrassing'. I never understood that. Why on earth should it have been embarrassing? It was not as if Dennis left on bad terms with anyone, at least not to my knowledge. And he *was* the minder for nearly three-quarters of the show's life. Whether or not he would have chosen to attend if he had been invited is another matter but I do feel that a bit of corporate recognition for his contribution would not have gone amiss.

The plot of the Brighton episode was totally implausible but it was still an amusing story, with Andrew Sachs as the guest. His character arranges to be delivered to Arthur's lock-up in a wooden crate to avoid a skinhead he has paid to kill him in the mistaken belief that he has a terminal illness and cannot stand the suspense of waiting to die. Apart from the opening and closing credits, which were played over contextual video, this was classic *Minder* from the pen of Tony Hoare and was well received by the audience. I particularly liked the way they did the closing credits over footage of Arthur in the congregation at a Salvation Army hostel singing *Onward Christian Soldiers* with brass-band accompaniment.

The final episode of all, 'The Long Good Thursday' by Tony Hoare, aired on 10 March 1994. The company had wisely decided, because of new circumstances, that it was a good time to bring the show to a close. I did a commentary on this episode a few years ago with Tony Hoare for the Australian release of the *Minder* DVD set by a company called Madman Entertainment. What I didn't know until we did the commentary was that, when Tony was asked to write the script, he wasn't told it was to be the final episode of the show ever. He was told that the company needed an episode that would end the series on the right note. It just turned out that the ending he wrote was appropriate for the end of the show. It ends with Arthur, Ray and Dave being bundled into a police van on the way to the nick on suspicion of harbouring an escaped criminal. Ironically, they were all innocent, the escapee being a psychopath who had broken into Arthur's lock-up and held the others hostage. Purely by chance, the last episode became a mirror of the first episode in that it was written around a siege, the difference being that in the first episode Arthur was on the outside of the siege and in the last he was part of it. Tony, apparently, had met a few psychopaths in his time and had formed the impression that, in general, they 'are really quite nice guys – until they start to do things'. There was another touch of irony because it was one of the few times we had to do a retake. I had to grab hold of the window bars inside the police van as they drove us away and, as I did so, they came off in my hands. They were made of rubber!

The following week, in the same timeslot, I appeared as myself but wearing Arthur Daley's overcoat and trilby hat and talked directly to the camera about my choice of favourite episode. To tell the truth, with one possible exception, I don't think there was a single episode that I'm not proud of or happy about. For want of something to choose, I chose the first episode, 'Gunfight at the O.K. Laundrette'. As a sign of how times had changed over a period of nearly 15 years, the episode needed some edits before it was deemed suitable for retransmission. Racist language (when I asked Dennis how he could get himself captured by 'dopey spades'), a close-up shot of a stripper's breasts and a blasphemous expression all had to be removed in the name of political correctness.

If I am honest, I have to say that I was sorry when it all came to an end. *Minder* gave me the opportunity to work with hundreds of artists, technicians and support staff, all of the highest calibre, and we were privileged to work with material from more than 30 of the profession's highest-rated scriptwriters. The scripts were so crisp and well written that they were usually easy to learn.

Over the course of the show, I got into a routine for learning the lines that I found worked well. The production schedules were always tight. Except for the two Christmas specials, we would always have two weeks to finish shooting an episode. We would receive the script on a Friday afternoon and start filming the following Monday. Every morning I would drive to the production base and a driver would take me to the day's location. Over the weekend I would record all the dialogue for that episode on an audiocassette tape and play the day's dialogue in the car on the way to the base. On the way home in the evening and again the following morning, I would play the following day's dialogue. This way I was usually pretty familiar with the lines by the time I arrived on location.

One of my favourite lines was right at the beginning of the series. I said to Dennis, 'I swear on my sainted mother's grave.' Dennis replies, 'Now, normally, this would be OK for me, Arthur, but I happen to know that your old mum is alive and well and living in Frinton!' That one line was written so beautifully. It has a wonderful flow to it and a certain reality that makes you imagine someone saying it in real life and it says so much about Arthur's attitude to common decency. He did have a well-developed, if somewhat unconventional, sense of values though. Towards the end of the run he expressed the view that drinking mineral water in the Winchester Club was 'like visiting St Peter's and not banging off a couple of Hail Marys'.

Another episode had a vaguely church-centred theme, with the talented and highly amusing James Booth playing a character named Godfrey. This gave me the opportunity to answer a telephone and say, 'Oh, hello, God.' Those three words, along with Glynn Edwards' reaction and the skilful editing, were what good television comedy is all about. In yet another episode, I was able to say goodbye to a Swedish character with a polite 'smorgasbord'. With scripts like that it was not like work at all but sheer pleasure to deliver the lines.

I think they made a big mistake with one episode though. That script was unusually difficult to learn; somehow, it just did not have a good flow to it. All the scripts had a date of writing on the back page and, when I checked this one, I saw that it had been written about three years earlier. I think the management probably read through it when it first arrived, had doubts about it and left it in a drawer somewhere for a rainy day. The end result of scripts like those is often disappointing, partly, I suppose, because you are prejudiced against them from the beginning.

One thing that was lovely about *Minder* was the amount of support and cooperation we received from the community while we were making the shows. We did an episode in the seventh series featuring Billy Connolly that involved a house on the outskirts of Heathrow airport. The location presented a few problems because we needed to avoid starting a take and then having to abandon it when an aircraft flew overhead. The traffic control people at the airport could not have been more helpful. They would phone and tell us how many minutes we had before the next plane flew over. But there was one scene that needed a plane to fly overhead at a critical point in the dialogue. The controllers would phone and tell us exactly how many seconds we had until the next plane was immediately overhead.

The public were also generally helpful and understanding. Often, while we were filming in the street, we would have to stop the traffic, which doubtless caused inconvenience and disruption to people's lives. But when they found out we were doing *Minder*, they would usually say, 'Oh well, that's all right then.' I lost count of how many times I saw cars driving into the back of the car in front while the driver was peering out to catch a glimpse of what was going on. It used to happen under our noses. There was nothing we could do to prevent it happening and I always felt terribly sorry for the people involved.

The episode I mentioned with Billy Connolly was great fun. When we arrived at the location, we were all shocked by the amount of noise there was from the planes overhead. The house actually had a landing light in the back garden. Billy, in his thick Scottish accent, said to nobody in particular, 'Who the f*** would live here?' A man sitting nearby pointed to the lady next to him and said, 'Actually, we do.' Some people may have been a little fazed by the slight gaffe but not Billy; he just got into conversation with the man and his wife and they chatted like old friends.

It is divisive to single out individuals for particular credit for their contribution to *Minder* but it would be remiss of me not to mention Dennis Waterman and Gary Webster. They were the minders and they made the show what it was. No matter how good the scripts or how crisp the direction, there would not have been a show without them. They were wonderful. In addition, I have to mention Glynn Edwards, Patrick Malahide, Michael Povey, Nick Day and Peter Childs (who was taken away from us much too early in his life with leukaemia). They were all firm favourites with the audience and made major contributions to the show's success.

What saddened me particularly were the circumstances in which the series was brought to an end. It had nothing to do with the popularity of the show, its ratings, or whether or not it was outdated (I personally think it could have lasted at least another series). When Euston Films announced in October 1993 that the tenth series (which began the following January) would be the last, it was explained as being because it was becoming 'increasingly difficult to think of original stories and ideas' and that 'it is now harder to get absolutely top-class scripts'. That may have been correct but the primary reason was that Thames Television had lost its franchise as an Independent Television provider for the London area. They could have continued to make the programme but there was no guarantee that the next franchise holder, or any other franchise holder in the country, would buy it.

A few weeks after the final episode went out, I appeared on the cover of the prestigious weekly journal *The Economist* as an unmistakable Arthur Daley with watches lined up for sale hanging inside my overcoat (in the style of the spivs of the 1950s) as the face of British entrepreneurship. We didn't set out to use the watches theme – that idea came from the photographer. He did a superb job that completely brought out the character.

I think it is fair to say that, after its shaky start, *Minder* surprised most people with the success it eventually achieved. Without a doubt, this success had a lot to do with the era in which the series appeared. We came in before Margaret Thatcher became Prime Minister and we outstayed her by four years.

The Thatcher years contributed much more to *Minder*'s longevity than many people realise. They were times when greed was running high. The country was already unhappy about Value Added Tax (VAT) but, when her government came into office and introduced additional taxes, people began to feel that enough was enough. When Arthur Daley came along and tried to shortcut the system and rake in something he wasn't entitled to, he was seen as something of a folk hero, despite the fact that he usually failed.

I think people generally seem to admire others who try to put one over on authority, like not paying VAT or Income Tax, and they like to see someone getting away with it. Not that Arthur ever did, of course; he wasn't successful at all. And then when he followed Mrs Thatcher's call to go into the Common Market, he was out in front again, firmly believing that he was doing his entrepreneurial bit – and continuing to get it completely wrong.

It used to be worrying sometimes when I got letters from young children saying that Arthur Daley was just like their dad. I wouldn't wish that on any of them. In my opinion, he was a rather unlikeable person. In fact, not to mince words, I think he was a dreadful character. Although he lived on the edge of criminality, I don't think he was a petty criminal or a villain in the way a policeman might use the term but he was definitely a rogue. He was actually written as a loveable rogue but, personally, I am not so sure about the 'loveable' part. I just can't understand how he could have become so popular. He behaved terribly to people who got in the way of his making a quick quid – and still the audience loved him. But I certainly earned a few sovs out of him over the years, so I should be the last person to complain. Over the years I've played hundreds of different parts but, without a doubt, Arthur Daley has to be my favourite one. You can't play a part like that for 15 years and have it not be your favourite.

I'm sure that on some of the nights *Minder* went out there was a bit of thunder and lightning over my house, a few tiles would fall off the roof and Alastair's voice could be heard booming from above, 'This is not what I trained you for!' He never saw the show but his wife Naomi did and she enjoyed it very much. And, seriously, I think Alastair would have loved it as well.

What was so wonderful about working on the show was the enthusiasm and commitment of the casts and crew: a camera operator who came from behind his camera after a take with a smile on his face and a twinkle in his eye. This told us that what we were trying for had worked. If you had a prop with a mind of its own, a prop man would always be there to sort it out for you. And all the actors were happy to run lines with you without a groan.

The location manager Ron Holtzer was responsible for me becoming a regular Jaguar driver. I had never driven a Jag until the series started in 1979. My first car was a Fiat two-seater. From there I moved up to a Hillman and then on to Fords. I had a Consul, a Zodiac and then a Capri. For the first six years of *Minder* I would drive to wherever we were shooting in my Capri (not the one Dennis drove in the show), change into my Arthur costume and then start driving his Jag.

In 1985, at the end of the sixth series, I was sitting in Arthur's Jaguar chatting to Ron Holtzer and mentioned to him that I was thinking about buying a new car. My Capri had suffered a few bumps and bruises and was not exactly a family car. He said, 'Why don't you put in a bid for this one?' meaning the *Minder* Jag, which was leased from Jaguar, and I said, 'OK.' The rest is history. He contacted Jaguar and they said they would give it a thorough overhaul and would let me have it for a reasonable price.

A couple of days later I had a phone call from the *TV Times* saying that they wanted to give the car as a prize in a competition. I said, 'Well, I'm sorry but I want it.' They called me back the following day and said, 'If we arrange a brand new Jag at a good discount, would you let us have the other one?' I jumped at the chance and accepted the offer straight away. The *TV Times* ran the competition the week the final episode of Series 6 went out in October 1985 and I went to pick out the winning entry a couple of weeks later. I've had brand new Jags ever since. I've had two Sovereigns, a Daimler and an XK8. I loved the XK8. You could drive as far as you like and never get backache. It was slightly shorter than all the others were and was the first one I was able to get into my garage! I tried an S-type once but I was a cigar smoker at the time and the ashtray was too small. I think I'm on my eighth at the moment. It's an X type, which I like a lot, as it is another one that fits nicely into my garage.

Funnily enough, Leon Griffiths wrote the Jaguar into the original script of *Minder*. He said it was the only car that the people Arthur Daley admired would aspire to.

One event that gave me enormous pleasure was in June 2002 when I was invited to draw the winning ticket in a raffle of the Daimler I used to drive in *Minder*. Apparently, the person who won the car in the *TV Times* competition back in 1985 sold it to one of her relatives, a gentleman in Alderbury, just outside Salisbury. He drove it until 2002 and then donated it to Salisbury Hospice Care Trust for fundraising purposes in memory of his wife, who had died of cancer. He wrote to me to ask if I would draw the winning raffle ticket. The raffle raised £9,000 for the charity and I was delighted to be part of such a worthy event. By coincidence, the event was held in the courtyard of the Red Lion Hotel in Salisbury, which was where I stayed nearly 60 years earlier with Alastair Sim and Leslie Banks when we were touring in *Cottage to Let*. What made it even more special was that when they contacted the person with the winning ticket, he said, 'I don't want it, raffle it again,' so they auctioned it on eBay. The winner of the eBay auction was an ardent *Minder* fan who had the car thoroughly overhauled and now drives it around its new home in Nottingham. Even hard-hearted Arthur Daley would have been proud of that story.

In the years following the end of the show I was approached a few times asking if I was interested in recreating the *Minder* concept but I always said no. The show was successful because of the way things were at the time it was made. I never really believed it would work as well without Thatcherism. This, I think, was borne out by the audience reaction to the new series of *Minder* that ran in 2009.

Lex Shrapnel, who played the minder in the 2009 series, is a good actor and seemed far superior to Shane Richie, who played one of Arthur Daley's relatives. But, without intending any disrespect to the cast or anyone else involved in the project, I was not surprised that the critics were generally unsupportive. As an actor, I am always sorry when people put a lot of effort into a project that is poorly received but I have to make it clear that I did not see much of the new show, so I cannot comment much on its content. I did try hard to watch it but I felt that there was just no substance to it and no chemistry between the two actors. I eventually had to give up.

I strongly believe that it was a big mistake to make a new series under the *Minder* name. I think it was inevitable that the audience would draw comparisons with the original *Minder*. The original belongs to a different era when politics were different, society was different and attitudes were different. Perhaps if they had made it under another name the reaction might have been different. One of the things that troubled Dennis and me was that they were allowed to call it *Minder* at all but we later discovered that Leon Griffith's widow had given permission. After the series went out, she sent us both a note saying, 'Oh dear. We live and learn.' I think her meaning was pretty clear.

Another thing that irked me (and it was reported in the press at the time) was that neither Dennis nor I were invited to give any input into the project – until it was time to promote it and then Channel Five asked us to help them. Audiences mainly remember *Minder* as Dennis and me. How could we possibly help them promote something using the *Minder* name that we were not involved in and had no knowledge of? Of course, celebrities promote things they have no connection with all the time for advertising purposes and the public understand that the celebrities do it because they are being paid for it, not necessarily because they believe in the product. In the case of the new *Minder*, it would have been dishonest for us to endorse something with which we had a historical connection but about which we knew nothing. We both gave them a resounding, 'No!'

CHAPTER 12

THE EIGHTIES

By the start of the 1980s domestic and parenting duties had become major parts of our day-to-day lives. Tara was ten and Toby eight. Penny had selflessly put her acting career on hold to be the principal parent. She was the one who dealt with schooling matters and taking the kids to the seaside for a few days while I was off on location or on a play tour somewhere. In fact, the only big family holiday we had together was when Penny and I went to Hong Kong in 1978 to do *Something's Afoot* and we took the children with us.

Tara had already become an exact copy of her mother. She looked like Penny, talked like Penny, behaved like Penny and had all of Penny's qualities of generosity, kindness and concern for other people. Toby had become a clone of me in every respect.

Penny and I had strong principles about the children's secondary education and we wanted them to have a 'normal' life without undue privilege. With this as the goal, we sent them, initially, to the local comprehensive school. It happened that *Minder* was just becoming popular at the time and we were worried, wrongly as it turned out, that this might result in some sort of celebrity status for them, which we were hoping to avoid. We soon discovered that the reverse was true. The other kids would say things like, 'Why are you here at a comprehensive school? You can afford to go to a proper school. Why don't you go to a private school?' Tara particularly suffered some bullying over it. Toby seemed to rise above it. At least, we think he did, although he probably wouldn't have told us even if it were a problem for him.

The turning point for Toby came when the teachers went on strike and started a three-day week. He got terribly upset about it and said, 'If this goes on, I'm not going to get good O-level results. I'd really like to go to another school.'

I said, 'Well, it won't be a public school because I don't approve of them.' He replied, 'But it's not your life, is it?' It was a reasonable response and hard to argue with, so we applied for a place for him at a public school as a result. The headmaster went through his academic record and told him, 'This is all very good but you don't seem to do a lot of things with other people.' He was just like his father. But the headmaster went on to give him an opportunity that could change his life forever. The headmaster said, 'Well, Toby, you're obviously not a yobbo. I think we'll be able to offer you a place here.' Toby replied with a casual, 'I'll think about it.' Thankfully, he accepted and just took off. He did wonderfully there. It was Reading Blue Coat School in Sonning-on-Thames, Berkshire.

At one point, he had worked so hard and did so well at school that I said to him, 'Your mother and I would like to give you a present of some sort. Is there anything special you would like?'

We thought he'd say something like, 'Well, I like this book very much.' He didn't need to think. He said, 'I'd really like to go to the Austrian Grand Prix.'

That answer threw me a bit but by then he had a holiday job in Henley at a place called The Share Shop. So I said, 'Well, have a good look at the shares and, if there is one you think is going to go up, I'll buy it for you and maybe you'll make enough money out of it to go to the Austrian Grand Prix.' The shares went through the roof and he went to the Grand Prix.

In April 1982, a few weeks after the third series of *Minder* ended, I was back on television in *The Bounder*, a sitcom from Yorkshire Television written by Eric Chappell and produced and directed by Vernon Lawrence. I played an estate agent named Trevor Mountjoy whose wife Mary (played by Rosalind Ayres) has allowed her brother Howard Booth (played by Peter Bowles) to move in with them when he is released from a two-year prison sentence for fraud. We did 14 episodes spread over 2 series. In many respects, my role of Trevor in *The Bounder* was something of a reversal of my role in *Minder*. I was the one who was put upon all the time and Peter Bowles was the one who took all the liberties.

Also in 1982, I did something entirely different for Yorkshire Television. I narrated a series of children's stories based on the adventures of a character named Heggerty Haggerty, whose name was used as the title of the series. These were lovely stories written by Elizabeth Lindsay.

In May 1982 I started a nine-month run as Major-General Stanley in the Broadway musical version of Gilbert and Sullivan's *The Pirates of Penzance* at the Theatre Royal, Drury Lane in London. Wilford Leach was the director. This was a real song-and-dance show and I was absolutely petrified.

I'd done a few musical things over the years but I'm not a

musician by any means and I wasn't that familiar with how the music rehearsals work. When I did the first music rehearsal for *Pirates*, I was given a time to go and work privately with William Elliott, the musical director, at the piano. I went in at the appointed time and he said, 'OK, George, after four.'

I said, 'No problem,' and started to walk out.

Bill said, 'Where are you going?'

I replied, 'Don't worry. I'll just go upstairs and have a cup of tea and I'll see you later.'

'Why?'

'You just told me to come back after four.'

'No, George,' he said, 'I meant that I'll count up to four and then you start singing.'

Afterwards, he came onto the next song: 'Two, three, four.' I didn't do anything. He said, 'Where are you? Why didn't you come in?'

I said, 'There was no "one".'

I did get the hang of it in the end. But later on, when we were rehearsing with the band, I said to Bill, 'I'll need a lot of help here. I don't know when to come in.'

He said, 'Look, don't worry. When I do that with my hand, it's the time for you to come in.' And then I discovered that, for my second song in the second act, I had to come in around the outside of the orchestra pit with my back to the conductor. I said, 'I can't see you. How will I know when it's time to come in?'

He thought about it for a while and came up with the solution: 'I'll put some "pings" in.' So every time I heard this ping I knew it was time to come in and I eventually got it right (most of the time). The ping is probably still there. Whenever they do the show now, they probably hear these pings and say, 'What the hell is this here for?' Gilbert and Sullivan are probably turning in their graves.

I had another phrase towards the end of the show that I just could not get right. And every time I screwed it up in rehearsals, the band fell about laughing. All I had to sing was, 'Away with her and take her to the guard,' but, try as I might, I just couldn't get it right. And then somebody said, 'Look, you have to get it right because your line is the cue for the leading lady to come in and if you mess it up, she'll miss her cue.' That started to put real pressure on me and I began to get worried.

I said, 'Well, I'm really sorry but there's nothing I can do about it because I just can't tell whether I've got it right or not. The only way I know that I've missed it is when the band start peeing themselves laughing.' I can't remember how we resolved it but I'm sure we did because we had a highly successful run. Pamela Stephenson took to the singing much more easily in her role as a delightful Mabel than I did in mine. Annie Ross also did a sterling job as the nursemaid. Tim Curry was a highly energetic and dashing Pirate King.

On the opening night, the theatre was packed and, as I stood waiting for my cue, I thought, 'What on earth am I doing here? I can't sing and I can't dance and I'm hopeless at coming in on cue. Why am I here?' And then I heard my cue and had to go on through a small door at the back of the stage. As I went through I hit my head on the side of the door. I can only assume that I got through that first night fuelled by concussion because everything was fine. I loved it – and the show ran for nine months after that.

Still on the lookout for something different, I played in a 23-minute promotional piece in 1983 entitled *Perishing Solicitors*, which had been commissioned by the Law Society to improve the public image of the solicitor. I played someone with a remarkably similar character to Arthur Daley. In fact, I think he could well have been Arthur's distant cousin. He was someone we have all met somewhere or another in our lives – the archetypal bar-room lawyer who spends his time criticising the legal profession and giving out gratuitous legal advice, which usually turns out to be wrong (and expensive) for anyone who follows it. There was a wonderfully amusing script by Denis Norden that included such gems as, 'That lot could find eight loopholes in the Ten Commandments.'

In the middle of 1984, my family had a frightening experience that made us realise just how vulnerable we all are and sadly reflected the way attitudes and social behaviour were declining at the time. Penny, who was then in her forties, and Toby, who was thirteen, were shopping in Oxford Street when suddenly and without warning a man lunged forward at Penny brandishing a knife, knocked her to the ground, ripped off the gold necklace she was wearing and attempted to run off. Penny was on the ground with blood all over her face from a gash on her forehead and Toby chased off after the assailant. He was joined by a public-spirited passer-by, a Mr Evans, who later managed to identify the attacker at a police identity parade. The attacker outran Toby and managed to jump on a bus. But someone on the bus saw what was happening and pointed to a wastepaper basket into which the attacker had thrown something. It turned out that there was a knife in the wastepaper basket. You can't begin to imagine what might have happened if the knife had made contact with Penny in the attack.

Penny rang me to tell me what had happened and told me she was at the Middlesex Hospital in London. It is chilling beyond belief to suddenly receive information like this about a member of your family and it certainly brings about a re-evaluation of one's value systems. The attacker received a three-year prison sentence and the judge praised Toby and Mr Evans for their bravery. The necklace was never recovered. The experience affected all the family. Penny soon recovered from the physical wounds but suffered from panic attacks for a long time afterwards.

Comrade Dad was an eight-part satirical comedy series I did for BBC Television in 1984 and 1985 written by Ian Davidson and Peter Vincent. It took a tongue-in-cheek look at what could happen if the UK were to be invaded by the Soviet Union and turned into a communist state. The pilot episode was broadcast in December 1984 and the next seven parts were shown in January and February 1986.

The series was set in 1999 in Londongrad, the capital of Communist Britain, which came about in a bloodless coup that the story told us occurred on 27 June 1989. In the pilot episode, the Russians cleverly take over by tricking Britain into believing it is about to be hit by a barrage of missiles and then blocking off the entrances to the safety shelters where the Royal family and government take refuge. I played a character called Reg Dudgeon, a working-class Londoner, and the series tells the story of how he and his family adapt to the new circumstances. Initially, Reg quite enjoys the new lifestyle but his enjoyment begins to pale when he discovers the excesses that are available to members of 'the party'.

I enjoyed doing the show and I thought Ian Davidson and Peter Vincent did a brilliant job in turning what was essentially a depressing scenario into a comedy that gave the audience something to think about outside the humour. Unfortunately, I couldn't see where it was likely to lead in another series. I think the company wanted to do more but it seemed to me that we had done everything we could with it. One joke I did enjoy was the idea that, if you are planning to invade England, you should do it on a Saturday afternoon because half the population will be out watching football.

When production of the fifth series of *Minder* was drawing to a close in 1984 the BBC offered me the role of Sir Giles Lynchwood in Malcolm Bradbury's six-part television adaptation of Tom Sharpe's comic novel *Blott on the Landscape*, which was broadcast between 6 February and 13 March 1985. Sir Giles was a rich and powerful Conservative MP who is married to a titled landowner, Lady Maud Lynchwood (played by Geraldine James) with whom he now lives in her huge and crumbling ancestral manor house along with their handyman, Blott (played by David Suchet). More than anything else, Lady Maud wants an heir to continue the family name but her marriage to Sir Giles has never been consummated as his preferred sexual outlet comes from bondage and flagellation, which she wants nothing to do with. Sir Giles receives it instead from the middle-aged and somewhat absent-minded Mrs Forthby (played by Julia McKenzie) when he goes into London on parliamentary business requiring him to stay overnight. Such is the extent of her absent-mindedness that Mrs Forthby often leaves Sir Giles tied to the bed while she pops out to the theatre or to dine with her friends. Giles has little time for Lady Maud or the manor house and comes up with a plan to have a motorway built across the grounds so he can get his hands on the compulsory purchase settlement and hopefully divorce Maud.

I knew the book. It was a riotous, bawdy story. But I thought, 'This is the BBC. It won't be that salacious.' How wrong could I have been! It was all there! In the first episode I found myself gagged and strapped naked to a bed while Julia McKenzie (who in another life was Agatha Christie's sedate Miss Marple) cheerfully thrashes me with a horsewhip. I had to be completely naked for that scene. When the press got hold of the story, someone asked me what Julia thought about it. I told them, 'Well, unless she has a penchant for soft herring roes, I don't think it bothered her at all.'

In another episode, I was supposed to have climbed a tree in the

210

grounds of the manor house while trying to avoid Blott's shotgun. I think I'd lost nearly all my clothes. The crew hoisted me up in a cherry picker before the take and I had to sit there on a branch waiting for the action. I had to look down and discover there was a lion at the bottom of the tree. As they always do, the director said, 'Don't worry, George, you'll be perfectly safe. The wardens are around.' But at that moment, I felt something licking my face and turned round to discover it was a giraffe. I've never been so frightened in my life. One of the crew shouted out, 'I hope you haven't got a yellow handbag, George, because they love bananas!'

We did the location work for the manor house and safari park at the magnificent castellated house in Stanage Park, Ludlow, close to the border between England and Wales at Powys. Before we did the series, I didn't know there was a stately home at Ludlow. When I discovered that we were going to do a lot of shooting there, I went along like a gawking tourist to have a look at it. My first impression was a wonderful notice that said, 'We regret that the toilets are temporarily out of use. Would visitors please use the litter bins.' I thought, 'I'm going to enjoy working here.' And I did. It was tremendous fun and it was an excellent series. Roger Bamford was the director.

After that I went back on stage for a while to recover as I often did after a hectic film or television shoot. I played in a lovely comedy entitled *First Sunday in Every Month* at the Nuffield Theatre in Southampton in 1985. The play was later retitled *A Month of Sundays* and I opened in it at the Duchess Theatre in London in 1986. This was the first production at the Duchess after Stoll Moss Theatres Ltd acquired the freehold of the theatre. The play was written by Bob Larbey, who had a collection of successful television comedies to his credit with fellow writer John Esmonde, such as *Please Sir!* and *The Good Life*. Although it was primarily a comedy, there was an element of pathos in the story. It was set in a rest home for seniors. My character, Cooper, put himself there at his own expense because he couldn't bear living alone and he knows that he would give everyone a hard time if he lived at home with his family. When he gets to the rest home, he and his newfound friend Aylott (played by Geoffrey Bayldon) realise that they don't enjoy the stilted and condescending visits from their families every month on the first Sunday and discover that they can best be handled if they are treated with humour. At a deeper level both Cooper and his friend, already in their seventies and becoming increasingly aware of their forgetfulness and repetitiveness, are dreading the possibility that they might become like 'the zombies', their fellow residents who are in an advanced stage of hopeless senility. This was a gentle and sensitive comedy about a serious subject that probably left many of the audience taking a long and hard look at themselves and the people around them as they left the theatre. The show won the *London Evening Standard* award for best comedy of 1986.

Coincidentally, I did a television play for the BBC that year called *Day to Remember* that went out a few days before Christmas. I played a man named Wally who is suffering from dementia following a stroke some years previously and the play is about the effect it has on his family. The subject matter was handled in a humorous but sensitive way that brought out the horror of this condition to a 1986 audience that was considerably less informed about it than we are today. Writer Jack Rosenthal based the story on his personal experience with his father-in-law. Rosemary Leach played my wife, who is desperately wishing for a Christmas miracle.

In 1985 I was invited to appear in a television advertising campaign for the Olympus Trip camera with fashion photographer David Bailey, who appeared as himself. I played a nerd with a collection of camera devices around my neck.

above: 'Genuine Scotch Whisky, made in Japan' – with Dennis and Glynn in *Minder* episode 'Senior Citizen Caine' transmitted in January 1984.   © *Fremantle Media Enterprises*

below: 'Would I do a thing like that, Terry?' With Dennis and Glynn on set of *Minder* 1982.   © *DC Thompson. Used with kind permission*

Above: Here is the partial crew of *Minder* in 1984. Back Row (from left): Leon Griffiths – Creator, George Taylor – Producer, Frances Heasman – Story Editor, Ian Toynton – Assoc Prod, Tony Hoare and Andrew Payne – writers. Front Row (from left): Dennis Waterman, Verity Lambert – Exec Prod, Johnny Goodman – Exec in charge of production, and, of course, me.

© *Fremantle Media Enterpris*

Below: With *Minder* director, and later producer, Ian Toynton, on location waiting for something to happen.

© *Fremantle Media Enterpris*

Above: With Dennis on location for a *Minder* shoot, definitely in agreement with each other.

© *Fremantle Media Enterprises*

Below: Outside the famous front door.

© *Fremantle Media Enterprises*

Above: Arriving at the BAFTA awards ceremony on 5 March 1985 with Penny. I was nominated for the Best Actor award but lost out to Alec Guinness. © *Getty Image*

Below: At the Variety Club of Great Britain Awards Ceremony with Penny and Dennis on 5 February 1985. Dennis and I were voted 'Joint ITV Personalities of the Year' for our work on *Minder*. © *Getty Image*

Above: Pictured with (from left) Toby, Penny and Tara attending the opening night of *A Piece of my Mind* at the Apollo Theatre in London, 1987.

© *Getty Images*

Below Left: In costume with Penny in *Mrs Cole's Music Hall* at the Beck Theatre in Hayes, 1986. Penny was the producer.

© *Mike Hollist/Associated Newspapers/Rex Features*

Below Right: Lulu and I in a photocall for the musical production *Peter Pan* at the Cambridge Theatre in London, 1987.

© *Chris Barham/Associated Newspapers/Rex Features*

Above: Sharing a behind the scenes joke with Dennis and a cue card during production of Dennis's final *Minder* episode 'The Wrong Goodbye', transmitted February 1989.

© *Fremantle Media Enterprises*

Below: With director Roy Ward Baker and Richard Briers behind the scenes of 'An Officer and a Car Salesman' in 1988.

© *Fremantle Media Enterprises*

bove Left: Me posing with my OBE.   © *Solo Syndication*

bove Right and Below: Taking a curtain call after Richard Harris's comedy *Party Piece*
1 tour in Eastbourne in 2004.   © Jonathan Gibbs

'Thank you Ma'am for a nice little earner'

Above: With Penny in the grounds of Buckingham Palace, having just received my OBE

© *Solo Syndicati*

Below: Bill Caldwell's view

© *Bill Caldwell/Express Syndicati*

When I first arrived at the studio, David was already there. We introduced ourselves and he said, 'This your first commercial then, George?'

I said, 'No, I did one a few years ago.'

'D'ya enjoy doing it?'

'Well, the commercial was fine but I didn't like the director that much.'

'Who was it?' So I told him.

He replied, 'Well, don't look now but there's the director.' And it was the same one!

David was great fun to be with but his language was unbelievable – he never stopped swearing. The swearing was continuous but it didn't seem to bother anyone. There was a shot where he was supposed to load his camera with film. He said, 'I don't know about f***ing cameras. I've got a gofer to do that. Let George do it. I'm not doing it.'

Then someone from wardrobe came on and said, 'Are you ready for wardrobe, Mr Bailey?' I can't print his reply!

He was wonderful to work with but he just didn't want to do the lines and he kept giving them to me. But the point is that, with a commercial, it's not many pages and it lasts only a minute so, if you end up giving someone else this line here and that action there, you end up doing nothing. You're just there for the face. But it was tremendous fun. And it must have been effective because they asked us back two years later for another campaign to launch the Olympus Compact AF-10 camera. I managed to pick up a Best Actor award for it in the 1989 Golden Break Awards presented by the advertising industry.

I did a few more commercials for Olympus with David after that. The basic theme was always the same: David had an Olympus camera and got the shot, I was the nerd with lots of equipment and

I missed it. The wonderful thing about them was the outstanding scripting that conveyed the important product details in a way that was humorous and entertaining. My character in the commercials never knew immediately that he was talking to David Bailey and, when he realises it, he delivers an amusing line. In one it was, 'David Bailey? Stone me, I've got all your records.' In another it was, 'David Bailey? I thought he only done weddings.' And when he thought he recognised David it was, 'Stone me, it's you! Of course. You still with the Tremeloes?' They always came across beautifully.

Around the same time in 1985 that I was asked to do the Olympus campaign, my agent had a request for me to feature in a campaign promoting the Leeds Permanent Building Society. They were excellent, highly amusing (and highly lucrative) ads in which I featured as a character very much like Arthur Daley but not quite. The ads immediately became very popular with the audience. But it was not long before other building societies started to complain to the Independent Broadcasting Authority (IBA), the regulators of Independent Television, that the commercials were contravening the IBA's Code of Advertising Practice on the grounds that I seemed to be appearing in the role of Arthur Daley.

The IBA wrote to my agent and said something to the effect that, 'George Cole must not do the Leeds advert because you can't use an actor to advertise something on television in a character role that is on independent television at the time.' I sent a message back saying, 'That character is definitely not Arthur Daley. He would not be seen dead in that sheepskin coat and flat cap.' They were still not too happy about it and said, 'Well, you are using Arthur Daley's voice.' I replied, 'I'm really sorry but it's not Arthur Daley's voice. It's my voice and it's the only one I've got.' After that, we received a nice letter from the IBA saying that they accepted that the Leeds man was not Arthur Daley but a distant relative of his.

The campaign extended into the 1990s, during which time we did some interesting and creative stories in the time available. I think they were successful because of the excellent scripts. We did two one-minute spots and two thirty-second spots each year and it took about a week's work a year to complete them – for a lot of money in return. I laughed all the way to the building society! The curious thing was that long before I started the campaign I had invested money in the Leeds Permanent Building Society. But I don't think they gave me a better interest rate because of the campaign.

Still in the long break between the sixth and seventh series of *Minder*, I was back on stage in the West End in 1987 in Peter Nichols' new comedy *A Piece of My Mind* at the Apollo Theatre. This was Peter's first stage play in five years after he became disillusioned with writing for the theatre and started to write for television instead. I read the play and took a liking to it and invited him down for dinner. It so happened that it snowed heavily during dinner and he ended up staying the night. In a way, I suppose it was rather like *The Man Who Came to Dinner*.

We took the play on tour to places such as Richmond, Brighton and Bath (all within driving distance of home!) and then went into the Apollo in London. This was my first time back at the Apollo since I did *Flare Path* there more than 40 years earlier. It was also my first real tour since I did *The Philanthropist* back in 1971. I found it all quite different. And it was amazing how many people complained that they came expecting to see an Arthur Daley character but found a slightly grumpy old playwright suffering from writer's block. My character, Ted Forrest, a thinly veiled autobiographical representation of Peter Nichols, once had a promising future ahead of him as a playwright but has now been overtaken in popularity by a rival. In the absence of inspiration for original material to regain his reputation, Ted resorts to basing his characters on his family and other people and events in his life. Many of his creations could easily be identified with real-life personalities in the theatrical world. To add to the theatrical theme, there was no real division between the players and the audience. Director Justin Greene had characters appearing from behind the audience and actors addressing the audience directly, making them an integral part of the proceedings. Anna Carteret played my amazingly tolerant wife.

I personally thought this to be a brilliant return to stage writing for Peter Nichols, especially as it was the sort of play that can only be done properly on the stage. The critics were generally positive about it but, as sometimes happens inexplicably – and to everybody's disappointment – the play did not last very long in the West End.

Later that year, 1987, I was back in song-and-dance mode performing in the dual roles of Mr Darling and Captain Hook in a musical version of *Peter Pan* at the Cambridge Theatre in London. This was another theatre that had been taken over and refurbished by Stoll Moss Theatres, and *Peter Pan* was the first performance at the theatre since it was renovated. It was lovely to see the theatre back as it was 40 years before. Pop singer Lulu played the part of Peter Pan and was a major attraction. This was not the traditional British version of the story but an American version that had been performed here only once before. I have to admit that I enjoyed it immensely. The show ran over the Christmas season and well into the New Year and played to packed houses every night. It wasn't strictly speaking a pantomime but it did have lots of audience participation.

At one point, while I was Captain Hook, I had to take a teddy bear away from the little boy Michael but, because I had a hook where my hand ought to be, the boy had to push the teddy into the hook. One night he did this and the teddy fell onto the floor. I couldn't pick it up again because of the hook so I trod on it instead and said, 'Tread on a teddy tonight!' The kids went absolutely wild. I think if there had not been an orchestra pit in the way, they would have climbed up on the stage to get at me.

Natural Causes was a black comedy I appeared in from Yorkshire Television written by Eric Chappell and directed by Vernon Lawrence that was first shown in September 1988. I played a representative of a company called Exodus that provides assisted 'suicides' for one's loved ones when they are no longer required.

I believe the idea for the play came from an organisation called Exit that helped people who genuinely wanted to end their lives to do so in a dignified way when they had such things as a terminal disease, unbearable pain, the inability to fend for themselves and the like. When I first saw the script for the stage play, I thought, 'This is a bit black. I can't see much opportunity for humour there.' But as I worked my way through I thought it was hilarious and I accepted immediately. I had a wonderful time working on it with Prunella Scales, Benjamin Whitrow and Leslie Ash in the cast. I ended up performing it on stage at the Theatre Royal, Windsor in 1992 with Penny, my wife.

My character was called Vincent Vincent – both his first and second names are Vincent – 'and neither', he hastens to add. He explains that nobody in his profession uses their real name; 'Would you?' he asks.

The story begins when I arrive at a mansion prepared to send its owner, Walter Bryce (Benjamin Whitrow), into the hereafter. However, after a preliminary chat with him (and after pouring poison into his sherry), I realise that it is his wife Celia (Prunella Scales) who he intends to finish off. He considers it perfectly justified as she has been depressed for years and he has a drawer full of her suicide notes to prove it. Vincent, however, soon realises that it is not out of concern for his wife that he wants to dispose of her. He is having an affair with his secretary Angie (Leslie Ash).

When I finally meet Celia, I am delighted to find that she is prepared to go through with her exit, provided her husband exits with her, as they go everywhere together. This would be my first double suicide and the prospect excites me enormously.

There followed the most delightful farce in which poisoned sherry glasses are switched and emptied as one by one the participants have second and third thoughts about whether they want to go through with the pact.

Eric Chappell provided some wonderful dialogue, like this exchange between me and Prunella after her husband believes he has taken poison then discovers he has not:

'How is Mr Bryce?'

'Well, he seems to have stopped twitching. I'm just going to take him a hot water bottle.'

'What about the young lady?'

'No, I think he'll have to make do with a hot water bottle from now on.'

Lines such as 'What's your poison?' when I invite Walter Bryce to drink a toast after agreeing on the details of his wife's exit keep the comedy running high throughout. And when Walter starts to get nervy before drinking his poisoned drink, I make a point of letting him know that the cigarette I offer to calm him down is a low-tar one. There are many ways the story could go and the ending was not obvious until the closing minutes.

One of the more unusual parts I played during the 1980s was the voice-over for a mouse named Vernon in a children's animated series called *Tube Mice* around the time that *Minder* was enjoying its biggest success. The series was created by Sara and Simon Bor and covered the adventures of four mice who lived at Oxford Circus Tube station in London. My character was something of a wheeler-dealer. He dressed like a teddy boy and behaved remarkably like Arthur Daley, with whom he also shared similarities in his greed and underhandedness.

Another of the mice, voiced by Dennis Waterman, was Vernon's associate named Toaster. He dressed like a punk, was a little slow on the uptake, but loved his food, which often upset any plans that Vernon might have made.

They were delightful creations. They lived in their own cohesive society with leaders and followers and used the Tube to travel around London to wherever their adventures took them. They recycled junk left behind on trains by humans and had strict moral codes. The two other main characters were a female Rastafarian mouse named Bubble, who was voiced by Sheila Hyde, and an upper-class type named Squeak, voiced by Rupert Farley. We did 26 episodes that were first transmitted on ITV between 5 September and 18 October 1988. It was a wonderful series to work on.

CHAPTER 13

THE NINETIES

As the 1980s rolled into the 1990s I was a few months away from my 65th birthday, a time when most people start to think about slowing down. But for me the work just kept coming in and I couldn't have been happier. The children were now 18 and 20 and pretty much independent. Toby had spent a gap year in New Zealand and was now studying at the University of Bristol and Tara was doing a Business English course at Henley Technical College.

Minder was out of production at the time. The last episode with Dennis went out in February 1989 and there was currently no talk of a new series. Coincidentally, I did a made-for-television film in 1990 called *Life After Life* in which Gary Webster had a small part as a removal man. A year later he was playing my nephew in a new series of *Minder*. *Life After Life* was written by Jonathan Lynn and was about a 70-year-old man who is pushed off to live in a retirement home for everybody's comfort and convenience except his own. The film was shown on 30 December 1990.

By the end of summer 1990 the wheels had already started turning on a new series of *Minder*, using a new character to take over Dennis's old role. I had been told that the company had shortlisted four possible actors for the part but I had no idea who they were. Gary, however, had been tipped off that he would be playing the part while we were working on *Life After Life* but had been sworn to secrecy by Thames Television pending an official announcement to be made a few days after he was told. Somehow, the way things often happen with the British media, the *Daily Mail* released the news the day before the official announcement was due to be made. The first I knew was when I saw the *Daily Mail* article. I was absolutely furious about it. I was supposed to be the star of the new series but the *Daily Mail* apparently knew more about what was going on than I did. This was not something that Gary had any control over and he cannot be criticised in any way over it but I have to say that it took me a day or two to calm down.

The first series of *Minder* with Gary Webster began transmission in September 1991 and the last episode of all went out in March 1994. I did 35 episodes with Gary spread over three series. We had 2 weeks to shoot each episode, so that is already 70 weeks of shooting. On top of that, we needed to spend extra time on the two episodes we made in Australia. They took a month each instead of the usual two weeks, so *Minder* kept us continuously busy from the middle of 1991 to the end of 1993.

1991 was a good year all round for me. The Leeds Permanent Building Society started a new series of attention-grabbing television ads on 9 September in which I featured once again as a character who looked a bit like Arthur Daley – but not quite.

Just before Christmas that year I received some unexpectedly pleasing news. Gary Webster and I were shooting a photo for the cover of the Christmas edition of *TV Times*. We were both wearing

Santa Claus outfits and I was wearing my Arthur Daley trilby hat instead of a Santa hat. One of the staff called out to me that I had a phone call in the office. I said, 'There can't be. Only my agent knows I'm here and she wouldn't be calling me,' but the person was insistent that the call was for me. I said, 'All right but I can't walk through the building dressed like this. Tell them to leave a message and I'll call back.' The assistant came back soon after and said, 'It's the Prime Minister's office and they want to speak to you now.' I thought someone was playing a joke but I answered the call and they told me I had been nominated to become an Officer of the Most Excellent Order of the British Empire (OBE) and asked if I would be prepared to accept it. I was over the moon about it. The award was announced in the New Year's Honours List on 1 January 1992 and I went to Buckingham Palace for the investiture by the Queen at a ceremony in March. The Queen asked if I was still doing the television show and said she did not see much of me because she was so busy. I mentioned the incident in Sydney when she drove past and I told all the crew to raise their hats to her. She smiled and thanked me but said she was too busy to notice at the time.

I have to say that it was a great honour to receive recognition in the form of an official award although, until it happened, I tended not to approve of such things. I do now though! I think I felt that it was more appropriate for people in other professions to have their work recognised, such as people who make important medical and scientific discoveries that benefit humankind and people who do similar things. We actors get paid well for something we like to do but a lot of people in other walks of life make a difference in the world and are not recognised.

I took Penny and our children Tara and Toby to the Palace with me. I felt absolutely wonderful about it. All of the cars had to be searched for security reasons as they drove into the Palace and we happened to have two pots of curry in the car that Penny had brought to deliver to someone. The police were extremely interested in them!

It was a marvellous feeling to be there holding the OBE medal, which I treasure greatly. But as I said at the time, 'If it was Arthur, he'd probably flog it.' It was actually the second time I had been to Buckingham Palace. I had the honour to visit a few years earlier when Her Majesty invited me to a luncheon party in October 1987 at which Princess Margaret and some other guests were present. I sat next to Princess Margaret and she was an absolutely charming lunch companion.

My first major television work in the 1990s apart from *Minder* was *Root Into Europe*, which was a comedy drama based on the character from William Donaldson's book *The Henry Root Letters*. William Donaldson and Mark Chapman wrote five episodes that were produced by Aspect Film and Television for Central Television. We started shooting in the summer of 1991 and the series was first broadcast in May and June 1992. I played Henry Root, a committed and self-centred Anglophile who barges his way around Europe pointing out all that is good in England and all that's bad everywhere else. Pat Heywood played his long-suffering wife Muriel. I never really liked the character Henry Root. He was a right-wing bigot, a terrible bore and a pushy know-all. But the scripts were written in a way that made him come across as funny.

The series was partly scripted and partly improvised so we had a fair amount of flexibility in what we covered and how we presented things. What I didn't know at the time was that the director, Mark Chapman, had only ever made documentaries previously and was not accustomed to the jargon of drama. He was a total gentleman who could never bring himself to say 'Action!' He'd say, 'In your own time, please.' And when he should have said 'Cut!' he would say, 'Right, what are we doing next?' It took some time for the crew to get used to his directorial style.

Strangely enough, the whole style of *Root Into Europe* was that of a documentary; the way that this terrible bigot interacted with the people he encountered on a holiday trip. In typical documentary fashion, they had lined up various people and situations in all the locations. Before we started they told me that all the people they had found could speak English but were not actors. In fact, their abilities in English were mostly rather limited.

There was one sequence where Mark had arranged for the police to take us out on a drug bust. The police were happy to do it and provided cars and all sorts of support. They took us on three genuine drug busts and I, as Henry Root, actually made some arrests and handcuffed a pimp, which made it to the show. After they finished shooting, they released the pimp and let him go. Then the senior officer said, 'Why don't we take you to the Bois de Boulogne to see the girls?' But what nobody told me was that they were not girls at all but were Brazilian seamen in drag! Not knowing they were men, I felt a little uncomfortable about the rough way the police were treating them. The men, in turn, didn't know that I was not a policeman and the real policeman let me go and ask for their permits and identification papers, which was extremely frightening because they were all enormous.

There was a lovely sequence where Henry Root went into a motorway restaurant, ordered a meal and then went back to get knives and forks or something. When I got back to the table, my meal had gone. It turned out that I'd put it on the wrong table and a Frenchman had started eating it. This was not in the script but I immediately saw the comic potential of the situation. Henry Root became implacable about it and walked out. On the way out, there was a woman with a tiny dog. Henry saw the dog and kicked it

225

right up in the air. In the scene they replaced the real dog with a toy one but it was a clever scene and it worked out so nicely for one that had not been scripted.

Henry Root was an absolutely terrible person. He was an opinionated know-all who loved his country and hated anything foreign, I think to the extent that he was almost a neo-fascist – a totally objectionable character but one who made excellent television.

Also making excellent television but rather less radical, *My Good Friend* was a sensitive and amusing situation-comedy series written by Bob Larbey that was commissioned from independent producer Hartswood Films for Anglia Television. It consisted of two seven-part series, one shown in 1995 and the other in 1996. I played Peter Banks, a lonely old man living with his daughter and her husband. Thoroughly bored with his life, Peter strikes up a friendship with Harry (played by Richard Pearson), who is in similar circumstances to his own, and they later meet a young single mother played by Minnie Driver with whom they find they are able to mutually fulfil each other's lives.

The storylines also touched gently on other problems affecting the elderly. In the final episode Joan Sims' character, the lodger, starts to develop memory loss, which leads her to believe that she lives in the house next door. When she does manage to find the right house, she ends up in the wrong bed. But there are happy endings all round: Joan moves into a residential care home for seniors and my daughter-in-law discovers she is pregnant, which gives me something to look forward to in the future.

The series was produced by Beryl Vertue, the owner of Hartswood, and was the first major project to be directly commissioned from the company. I very much liked Bob Larbey's style of writing. He was able to write about old people in a way that was not patronising or full of sentimentality and, as far as my character was concerned, with a hint of dry humour that I was able to make full use of. What was particularly nice was that, when the series finished, we received many letters from viewers, a number of them relatively young, saying how much they appreciated the series because it made them aware of problems they did not know existed.

Immediately after we finished the second series of *My Good Friend* I added to the catalogue of roles I played over the years and became a hairdresser in 1996. This was for a seven-part series for Anglia Television entitled *An Independent Man*, written by David Yallop and produced by WitzEnd Productions. I played a hairdresser named Freddie Patterson who stands as a Tory councillor for the local council to prevent two of his salons and his favourite restaurant from being redeveloped. When he is unexpectedly elected, he announces that he will be an Independent. My wife Penny appeared in two episodes as Mrs Bamford, who is secretly in love with Freddie and makes frequent visits to his salon in the hope of seeing him. To bring out the character to the fullest, the director felt that I needed a thicker head of hair than I was currently blessed with to make me look a little younger. The make-up people managed to fix up a tonsorial masterpiece for me crafted by Sean Connery's toupee maker.

David Yallop had previously written several excellent scripts for *Minder*, including one with a similar theme about a local council. In the *Minder* episode Arthur stands as a local councillor when his car lot becomes the subject of a compulsory purchase order by the local council. The idea for *An Independent Man* grew from this. Much to our disappointment, however, the audience did not seem to warm to the series and it did poorly in the viewer ratings.

Among my stage work around that time I did a summer play tour in 1995 with Eric Chappell's comedy mystery *Theft*. I played at the

Theatre Royal, Windsor, the Richmond Theatre and the Theatre Royal, Bath, portraying a character similar in many respects to Arthur Daley. I was honoured that Eric Chappell had specially written the comedy with me in mind. My first appearance in the play is when two couples arrive home from a night out and find me hiding in a cupboard after burgling the place. I then start uncovering things about the two couples they would prefer not to be made public. This was another production in which Penny appeared with me.

The following year, in October 1996, I appeared as the corrupt judge Mr Justice Squeezum in a stage production of the comedy *Lock Up Your Daughters* at the Chichester Festival Theatre. Driving to and from Chichester was just about manageable to do the show every day. Bernard Miles adapted the story from Henry Fielding's 1730 farce *Rape Upon Rape*, which he came across while looking for a show to open at the new Mermaid Theatre in 1959. Set in 18th-century London, *Lock Up Your Daughters* tells of a naïve young woman who sets out to elope with her lover but along the way accuses another character of rape. Her maid, meanwhile, accuses the woman's lover of rape, and I have to try the cases in my somewhat distorted judicial capacity. Squeezum's lecherous wife, played by Sheila Hancock, adds to the general confusion. It was a great British comedy.

The 1959 version was produced as a musical with songs composed by Lionel Bart and music by Laurie Johnson and was originally booked for a six-week run but lasted a year. The songs were deleted from our version at Chichester. Also deleted was much of the non-politically correct material that remained from the 1959 version and its revival ten years later. Sheila Hancock refused outright to perform some of the original sexist material. But I think that the director Stephen Rayne did a splendid job in balancing

1990s sensitivities with Henry Fielding's 18th-century intentions. Importantly, I think Stephen managed to minimise the inference that we were making light of rape. That was never the intention anyway, although some people perceived it that way. But as I said at the time, 'You can't go to a show called *Lock Up Your Daughters* and come away offended, can you? You must know what you're going to.'

Still trying to do at least one quality play a year, I appeared in Stephen Churchett's play *Heritage* at the Hampstead Theatre in 1997 and later at the Theatre Royal, Bath, playing a proud Chelsea pensioner named Harry who, at 75 years old, was just two or three years older than I was at the time. Harry holds on to his old-fashioned value systems and struggles to adjust to the times. But the times bring with them the prospect of the Royal Hospital in Chelsea being redeveloped into a conference centre, his son in a gay relationship and his daughter on the verge of a marital breakdown. The whole theme of the play was the value of relationships: mine with my son, my son's with his partner, my daughter's with her husband, and mine with my past and how it all related to the future. I liked the play a lot and I felt that the cast gelled very well but overall I found it was rather sad. Tim Pigott-Smith and Gwen Taylor played Harry's son and daughter.

Back on television, *Dad* was a BBC One sitcom written by Andrew Marshall and produced by Marcus Mortimer that ran over two series in 1997 and 1999, each consisting of six thirty-minute episodes, plus a Christmas special that went out in December 1999. I played Brian Hook, a slightly irritating and eccentric pensioner with annoying habits, such as bringing home junk from the breaker's yard in case it comes in useful and leaving incomplete and rambling messages on his son's answer machine. He didn't mean to be eccentric and irritating and was actually quite well meaning. He just does things that to him seem natural and reasonable, completely unaware that they drive his son crazy. He lives alone after his wife has died and occupies his time happily pottering around in his workshop, making and mending things and ensuring that the house is in smooth running order.

Kevin McNally played his son Alan, who had distanced himself from his father over the years because of his annoying personality and the incessant gratuitous advice he insists on giving, but he is trying to get closer to him now his father has had heart surgery. Alan, who is already having difficulty relating to his 18-year-old son Vincent (played by Toby Ross-Bryant), tries hard to keep the lines of communication open between himself, his father and his son, while Julia Hills, who played Alan's wife Beryl, tries hard to run the house. All the episode titles contained the word 'dad' in the form of a pun, such as 'Dadmestic' and 'Dadcipline'.

Kevin McNally was no stranger to television comedy, having been in a successful comedy series in 1993 called *Full Stretch* about a limousine hire company. I knew Kevin fairly well as he had worked as a scriptwriter for nine episodes of *Minder* under the name Kevin Sperring in collaboration with Bernard Dempsey. Together they produced some of our best scripts. Kevin had also performed in a *Minder* episode in which Arthur Daley was suspected of bumping off 'er indoors, so we gelled quickly when we worked together on *Dad*.

What was rather unusual about this show was that I was asked to go and meet the people at the BBC for a chat before I was offered the part. During the meeting Andrew Marshall told me how he came up with the idea for *Dad* based on the generational problems he had with his own father. He told me some of his ideas for the show and then they asked if I would be prepared to do a reading for them if I chose to do the show. It did seem a little strange for them to ask if I was interested in the part and then ask me to do a reading.

Normally, it is done the other way round. Perhaps they just wanted to see if I knew how to act. I'd only been doing it for 50-odd years but I went along with it because I really liked the part.

Andrew Marshall did a similar show for the BBC before this one entitled *2point4 Children*. Julia Hills, who played my daughter-in-law Beryl in *Dad*, had a major part in *2point4 Children* and the BBC was initially reluctant to cast her in this one because they felt that it might confuse the audience. They relented only when she made a personal plea to have an audition because she liked the part so much.

The first episode was transmitted in September 1997. This was originally intended as a pilot but it was later decided that it would make a good first episode. We spent the first week of production doing all the exterior shots for the whole series and then worked on one episode a week in the studio. We recorded each episode in front of an audience on Saturday evenings. Interestingly, it brought home to me just how much stress there is in working in front of a studio audience for a television show. John Thaw once said he preferred to do an opening night of Shakespeare at Stratford rather than a live situation comedy for television in front of a studio audience. As actors, we are accustomed to doing comedy in front of a live audience in the theatre all the time and we can read an audience relatively easily and gauge how to deliver lines to get the best effect. Theatre audiences are often different from one night to the next in how they react to a particular line and we adjust accordingly. In television, we are not only delivering comic lines, we are thinking about camera angles and matters of timing that just do not exist in the theatre. Adjusting to a television environment can be highly stressful for actors brought up in the theatre.

Writer Andrew Marshall credits Alfred Hitchcock as one of his major inspirations and the opening two minutes or so of the first episode of *Dad* have a definite Hitchcock feel about them in the build-up to my character's first appearance. They even play the music from *Vertigo* in the background to add to the atmosphere. There is a similar Hitchcock feel in an episode in the second series when I am working as a night watchman in a model village when they play the music from *Psycho* in the background.

I particularly liked the scripts for *Dad*. They were paced much faster than many of the other British situation comedies around at that time and allowed the laughs to come from creative dialogue rather than relying constantly on visual gags. At the same time, they were not over-written to the extent that they would force a laugh when it was not required.

But the show was not all humour. There were also some genuinely touching moments, particularly when one of the characters begins to reminisce about the happy times we have all spent together in the past. In one episode the tears started to well up while we are watching some old home movies, and again in another episode when I get taken into hospital.

One piece of trivia from the first series is that an unusual star emerged from it that no one expected. The blue Ford Anglia car we used in the series went on to achieve a modicum of fame in the *Harry Potter* films!

The second series began transmission in January 1999. I have to say that I was a little disappointed when the BBC announced that they would not be doing a third series. I think the concept could easily have sustained another series and both Kevin McNally and I had new ideas we would like to have explored. I also feel that we did not make enough use of Toby Ross-Bryant, who played my grandson. There were a lot of interesting directions that the relationship could have taken. But I thoroughly enjoyed the two series we did and it was a pleasure to work with such a talented team.

In 1995, I started work at Pinewood Studios on the American-funded film *Mary Reilly*. It was produced by TriStar Pictures, directed by Stephen Frears, and starred Julia Roberts and John Malkovich. This was a dark horror story set in the household of Dr Jekyll and his mysterious counterpart Mr Hyde (both played by John Malkovich) in which one of the housemaids (played by Julia) falls in love with Dr Jekyll. I played the role of Mr Poole, the butler and head of domestic staff in the household who guards his territory with extraordinary possessiveness. Michael Gambon played Mary's drunken, brutal father. It was a gruesome, gory film that was given an R certificate in America and was restricted to cinema audiences over the age of 15 in the UK.

My character, Mr Poole, reminded me of Sir Winston Churchill's description of Clement Attlee. Churchill said, or is said to have said, that Attlee was like a pianist in a brothel who has no idea what is going on upstairs. I liked my part in it and I enjoyed working with Stephen Frears. Julia was also lovely to work with. I was a little taken aback when she told me she had seen *Minder* and knew what 'a nice little earner' was. She was certainly much easier to get along with than John Malkovich.

The one thing I did find strange was that the cast were at each other's throats for much of the time. They just didn't seem to get on with each other. It got to the stage where one person wasn't speaking to another person and that person wasn't speaking to someone else. It was absolutely dreadful. Stephen said to me after one of the uprisings, 'My heart lifts up when I come in and see you sitting in the chair doing *The Times* crossword because then I know that everything is right with the world after all.' One of the crew said to me, 'You should have been here last week, George. No one was speaking to anyone!'

We finished shooting towards the end of 1995 and the film was released in Britain the following year. Apart from the studio work at Pinewood, we did some location work in Scotland. Unfortunately, it was not the critical success we had all hoped for.

Coincidentally, my next film was also a ghost story. But unlike *Mary Reilly*, *The Ghost of Greville Lodge* was intended for the whole family. The story was adapted from the novel *Down Came a Blackbird* by Nicholas Wilde and involved a teenager (played by Jon Newman) who has lived in children's homes all his life and is surprised to receive an invitation to stay with a great-uncle for a holiday in his country manor Greville Lodge. While exploring the manor, the boy discovers that the house holds many secrets and believes that they might help explain his uncle's rather solemn nature. If he can uncover those secrets, he might be able to bring some joy back into his uncle's life. During his search he finds himself transported back to Christmas 1939. I played the great-uncle and Prunella Scales played my housekeeper Sarah, who is linked to a sad incident in the Lodge's past. We started shooting in 1999 and the film was released in October 2000. I found it a genuinely heart-warming Christmas story. Niall Johnson produced and directed. Incidentally, the film was made by Renown Pictures, which 50 years earlier produced the Christmas classic *Scrooge* in which I appeared with Alastair Sim. I don't know if it was a deliberate decision by the company to celebrate the 50th anniversary of *Scrooge* with another supernatural Christmas film but, as far as I was concerned, I could not have asked for a more fitting celebration.

In the midst of all the film, television and stage work I did in the 1990s, I never stopped looking out for interesting radio projects. I have always enjoyed working on the radio since my 15-year grounding on *A Life of Bliss*. Radio has a completely different feel to the other three media.

Acting is all about immersing yourself in another person's character and persuading the audience to believe that you are that character. In front of a camera you have make-up, costumes, lighting, scenery and body language to help in the transformation. In radio you just have your voice and, perhaps, a few sound effects. This creates a very different challenge to the actor to make the character come alive in the listener's imagination. I enjoy that challenge immensely.

In 1995 I made a welcome return to radio when the BBC commissioned Rewind Productions to produce 17 episodes and 2 Christmas specials of Emlyn Harris's *The Sexton's Tales*, in which I played the sexton of Highgate cemetery in London. The stories were absolutely fascinating true-life accounts of the lives of some of the people buried in Highgate cemetery, such as writer George Eliot, inventor Michael Faraday, socialist Karl Marx and comedian Max Wall. Warren Mitchell, Ian Lavender, Alistair Cooke and the show's writer Emlyn Harris were among the guests who appeared in the show.

Emlyn Harris came up with the idea for the series while working as a volunteer tour guide taking groups of visitors around the cemetery, when he felt that the notes he had been given needed some livening up. He began to research the lives of some of the occupants of the graves and found that they made entertaining reading.

They were all lovely stories but I particularly remember the last one of all. It was a special ghostly Christmas edition broadcast just before midnight on Christmas Eve 1997 and it told the story of Henry Payne, who in Victorian times was known as the 'Clown Prince of Pantomime'. My character, the gravedigger, was taken back in time by Henry Payne's ghost to the birth of the Christmas pantomime. Roy Hudd, who has been in more pantomimes than I can count, played the ghost. It was enormous fun.

Also in 1995 I did a radio version with Louise Lombard of the 1949 Ealing comedy *Passport to Pimlico* in which I played Arthur

Pemberton, the role originally played by Stanley Holloway, who discovers an old parchment proving that Pimlico actually belongs to Burgundy. This had particular relevance to post-war Britain because it meant that the area known as Pimlico in London was no longer subject to wartime rationing restrictions. The story was broadcast on BBC Radio 4 in January 1996.

I continued to slip into the recording studio after that whenever I could. Among the other radio plays I did was a five-part series in 2002 for BBC Radio 4 playing Agatha Christies's amateur detective Mr Satterthwaite. I like Agatha Christie's writing style. You can do a lot with it when you read it aloud.

To round off the decade I was the subject of the biographical series *The Best of British* in an episode that aired on 23 December 1999 in which I talked about many of the things I have been talking about in this book. To mark the end of the millennium, I subscribed to an offer in *The Times* of a hogshead of Aberlour single malt Scotch whisky that would reach you in time for the celebration. I think it came to something like 34 cases, which I sent to some of my good friends, including Dennis and Christopher Fry. I got a lovely letter from Christopher saying his neighbour couldn't believe it was *12* bottles. The neighbour said, 'Shall I go and get a corkscrew?' to which Christopher replied, 'No, go and get a screwdriver so we can open the case!' It was great fun. My garage was like some sort of bonded warehouse. And buying 34 cases at the same time made it much cheaper than if you bought them from the off-licence. I don't know exactly how that worked out but I found it a huge attraction.

CHAPTER 14

THE 21ST CENTURY

When an actor reaches my time of life, the number of possible characters one could be asked to play tends to become rather more limited than previously. It is fairly easy for the make-up people to make a young actor look old, but it is much harder to make an old actor look convincingly young. Inevitably, as I started to find in the 1990s, we usually end up playing seniors. But I enjoy playing senior roles. It is always comforting to accept a part knowing that there is not much likelihood of being asked to fall into a filthy river – or even a clean swimming pool. And even if the script calls for it, there would always be a stunt person on hand to do it. I am still being offered projects to work on and I can pick and choose the ones that interest me. Meanwhile, I have plenty of time to catch up on all the books I have planned to read and to work on *The Times* crossword every day. If I'm not doing that or pottering around the garden, there is a good chance I'll be spoiling our Newfoundland dog Lincoln.

We had a lovely pair of Newfoundlands at the beginning of the millennium named Boris and Nola. When we first had them, we had recently installed an automatic gate on the property so we didn't have to get out of the car to open and close the gate in the pouring rain. Unfortunately, Newfoundlands are an extremely intelligent breed and it didn't take them long to work out that the gate opened and closed very slowly and gave them plenty of time to do a runner whenever they heard the gate start to open. Many was the time they would rush out without our knowledge and take a stroll down the lane to the local pub and wait to be brought back by the landlord. But when the police received a report one day that there were two black bears running around the Oxfordshire countryside, we realised that more stringent security was necessary.

Around the property, just under the ground, we installed a perimeter wire that emits some sort of radio signal. The dogs then needed to wear a small receiver on their collars and, if they went too close to the gate, the receiver would make a growling sound that was supposed to scare them away. If that failed and they strayed any closer, they would get a slight electric shock, which I am assured only annoys them rather than hurts them. I sometimes wonder if the radio receiver should be tuned to a particular radio station I know. The music they play would keep anyone away from the gate.

Newfoundlands are huge dogs and are prone to developing various canine diseases quite early in life. Sadly, we lost one over Christmas 2002 and the other the following year. It was a tremendous loss to us. Much as we loved Newfoundlands, we decided we had reached a time in our lives when we should get a smaller dog and so we went along to the animal adoption centre to see what they had available. We came home with another Newfoundland! Lincoln.

The Times crossword was something that was introduced to me by Alastair and Naomi. They used to do it every evening when I lived with them and I always felt terribly left out. Then one day I managed to solve a clue that they couldn't get. It was something like 'not there, somewhere else' in five letters. I immediately said 'alibi' and then I was hooked. Since then I've spent hundreds of happy and contented hours turning carthorses into orchestras and 'that great charmer' into Margaret Thatcher. I even managed to teach Dennis Waterman how to do *The Times* crossword. I always say that, in return, he taught me how to swear in public. He doesn't seem to mind me telling people that.

While I was in Australia working on *Minder*, I did *The Times* crossword every day in one of the local newspapers and started to find that I was getting through them much faster than I ever did back at home. Then it suddenly dawned on me that the newspaper was using crosswords that I had done at home months ago!

Another leisure pursuit that has kept me occupied over the years has been horse racing. And I can't resist the temptation to use the old joke that at my age it is hard enough trying to keep up with them let alone race them!

I've had a couple of horses at different times but I eventually felt that it was time to give them up. At one stage I had a share in a horse called Talented Ting. I think my share was a leg. The reason I think this is because, as soon as I got my share, the horse didn't seem to understand that he was still allowed to use all four when he ran. But it did eventually improve. I had a hurdler that won five races and still didn't pay for its keep. That was when I felt I'd had enough. The best moment for me was when we had Lester Piggott riding in one of the races. The horse won and, when he got off the horse, he said something to the trainer that I found unintelligible because of his strong accent. I said to the trainer, 'What did he say?'

The trainer replied, 'It'll win again.' And sure enough, the following week, with a different jockey, the horse won again.

I think the trick is that, if you have a moderate horse that wins occasionally, you should sell it and buy another one. The mistake I made was to hang onto it. But it was always a nice day out for the family going to the races together when your horse is running. When I gave up, my son Toby started having horses and whenever they are running, he takes our grandson along to watch. They have a lovely time together. I get my pleasure these days from watching the races on television on Saturday afternoons.

I've also enjoyed doing what I can for various charities over the years. Back in the early 1970s I got involved in launching the unrelated bone-marrow donor registry in Bristol along with actress Pauline Collins. I think it was when she was becoming popular as the cheeky maid Sarah in *Upstairs, Downstairs*. Someone rang my agent and asked whether I would be prepared to do it. I didn't know anything about it when they first asked me and they explained that it was a register to which you could sign up and, if your blood type matched that of a patient with leukaemia, you could donate some of your bone marrow and help save the patient's life. It sounded a very worthwhile cause and I immediately said, 'Why not?'

It was an impressive launch. They took us by helicopter from Battersea helipad to Leavesden in Hertfordshire and then flew us on to Bristol in a small passenger plane. It was all terribly exciting.

I also did some work for what is now known as the Royal National Institute of Blind People, helping them with some audiobooks. This was another situation where someone just contacted my agent and asked if I would record a book for them. I ended up doing three: *Straight Up*, which was Arthur Daley's biography, *Arthur Daley's Guide to Doing It Right* by Leon

Griffiths and Tom Sharpe's book *Blott on the Landscape*, which I did previously as a BBC Television series.

In 1990 I appeared in a television commercial promoting organ donation after death, which is something I feel passionate about. My commercial set out to encourage people who wish to donate their organs after death to carry a donor card indicating their wish to do so. It must be a dreadfully harrowing experience for relatives of someone who has just died unexpectedly to be approached by hospital staff asking for consent to remove organs from their loved one so they can be transplanted to someone else. That one small donor card can make the experience so much easier for everyone involved.

Also in 1990 I took part in a 'Find a Family' campaign run by Independent Television aimed at finding families for children seeking adoption. Every day for 14 days a different celebrity with experience of adoption told the story of a particular child in need of adoption. I have a special interest in adoption because of my background. My long-time friend Dora Bryan, with whom I have worked many times in my career, also had a special interest in adoption because she and her husband had adopted two children three decades previously. One of them, a four-week-old boy, developed a debilitating and painful disease in his teens. Dora was also a key person in the ITV campaign and explained how the love between her and her son seemed to grow as a result of his illness. As I said in the programme, 'It just doesn't seem right for any child to be denied a normal home. It doesn't matter that you're placed in a working-class home where money doesn't come easily. It's the love that counts.' I sincerely hope that our contributions to the campaign had a successful outcome.

One of the joys the 21st century has brought to Penny and me has been the chance to see our two children develop into adulthood.

After a childhood seeing their parents earning their living as professional actors, neither of the children showed any inclination to follow in our footsteps. They went in two widely different directions but both have done extremely well in their careers and we are very proud of them.

After Tara graduated from Henley College she worked in television as a comedy researcher for a few years and enjoyed it immensely but then thought she might try her hand in the theatre in the wardrobe department. She started as a dresser on *Mamma Mia!* just after the show opened in the West End, worked her way up to wardrobe mistress and on to costume supervisor in the West End and went on tour with many of the productions. She loved what she was doing but after ten years thought it was time to look for a new challenge.

Over Christmas 2009 I happened to mention that my ideal present would be a black-and-white mint liquorice sweet dipped in chocolate. That was the challenge she was looking for. Tara immediately set about getting the basic equipment needed to create one. From there she progressed to making chocolates and created a range of handmade truffles that she began selling successfully. She received various awards from the catering industry and became involved with the wedding and event industry, providing personalised, handmade chocolates.

This all went well until Easter 2011 when there was a terrible heatwave that caused three months' worth of handmade chocolates to disintegrate in the heat. Undeterred, she had the idea of buying an old 1970s ice-cream van, renovating it and promoting it as a private-hire vintage ice-cream van that she could take to weddings and events.

She then turned herself into an expert on vehicle renovations and mobile freezers. After that there was no stopping her. She called the resulting ice-cream van 'Daisy' and developed her into a vibrant business. Now she takes Daisy to weddings, parties, events and festivals in the summer, stocked with luxury ice cream and old-fashioned sweets and, in the winter, stocked with hot chocolate and seasonal ice cream. She is now taking bookings for up to two years ahead.

Toby went into the banking business after he graduated from Bristol and it was not long after joining his first bank that he met a delightful colleague, Sally, whom he later married. While he was with his first bank he had some sort of job appraisal and came out of it with flying colours. But then they said, 'You do have one problem though. You are too nice.' Whether they really did see it as a problem or were just letting him know that it had been noticed we don't know but it was something we were happy to hear about. Today he is a successful executive in a well-known commercial bank.

Toby and Sally now have three lovely children: Harry, Amelia and Thomas. When Harry was around five, he asked Toby, 'What is it like when you go to work? What do you do? What happens there?'

Toby answered, 'Well, we all meet and talk about what we're going to do that day. It's a bit like your assembly. You have assembly at school, don't you?' Harry said that he did.

'And what did you talk about today in assembly?' asked Toby.

'Cheeses,' replied Harry.

'What sort of cheeses?'

'Cheeses Christ,' came the reply.

Professionally, one of the first things I did in the new millennium was a darkly amusing two-part supernatural thriller for BBC Television called *The Sleeper*. It was adapted by Gwyneth Hughes from a novel by Gillian White. Anna Massey and I played a pair of senior citizens named Lillian and George who live a boring life in an old people's home in Devon with too much time on our hands and not enough to do to fill it – until we start investigating the disappearance of Lillian's friend Cath, which involves us in séances, storms and farmyard manure. My character was a widower who has taken a fancy to Lillian and follows her around diligently. Eileen Atkins played the rather unendearing character who runs the old folks' home.

The story is set over the Christmas period and the film was first shown in two parts on Boxing Day and the following day in 2000. We started shooting around the end of March that year and whenever we turned our backs, another spring flower would sneak out. The crew had to keep going around covering them up to maintain the harsh December feel we needed.

The pairing between Anna and I had an unexpectedly nostalgic element. My previous connection with her was back in 1943 when I took her for a haircut when she was 5 years old and I was about 17. I was touring in Terence Rattigan's play *Flare Path* at the time and Anna's mother Adrianne Allen was also in the cast. For reasons that are now beyond me I was lumbered with the job of taking Anna and her brother Daniel (who also became a well-known actor) into Newcastle for a haircut. Anna sent me a postcard afterwards to thank me for taking her and I happened to find it just before the initial read-through for *The Sleeper* and I took it with me. It definitely broke the ice.

Much of the film was shot on Dartmoor in Devon, close to the prison, and at night the mist swirls in and makes the place feel totally inhospitable. Not only that but, although there was unseasonal rain at the time, the director needed more and brought in rain machines and hail-making machines. It was not one of the most comfortable locations I had worked in but not as bad as being on Southend Pier in the middle of the night in the middle of winter, as I was in a *Minder* episode. But in one scene, cast member Elizabeth Spriggs, a mere youngster of 72 years at the time (playing Lillian's friend Cath), had to wade through a slurry pit up to her neck in the middle of a bitterly cold night with a genuine blizzard raging above her head. They used fake slurry, so that was one consolation, but I don't think it would have been very pleasant for her. Apart from being spared the slurry pit, what appealed to me about the show was that it achieved a good mixture of comedy and the spooky stuff, which is often a difficult combination. I think it made good Christmas entertainment and also prodded a social conscience with its underlying theme about the loss of dignity that some seniors experience when they go to live in retirement homes.

Many people in the business say that the most difficult actors to work with are children and animals. I did a delightful 90-minute family film for BBC Television's 2001 Christmas season entitled *Station Jim* in which I found myself working with both and it was a tremendous experience. I played Mr Pope, the stationmaster at a rural English railway station in Victorian times who is about to retire and is looking for a successor. One of his porters, Bob (played by Charlie Creed-Miles), who is vying for the job, has a newfound love interest who teaches at the local orphanage, which is in danger of closing because of funding problems. When Bob discovers in the station a stray Jack Russell terrier (the 'Station Jim' of the title), he finds that the dog is able to perform tricks. He realises he can make money for the orphanage by charging the public to see the dog perform. We know, because we saw the beginning of the film, but Bob does not, that the dog ran away from a travelling circus to avoid a bullet from its trainer and jumped from a bridge onto a passing train. Now, with some experience of guns and bullets, the dog eventually foils an assassination attempt on Queen Victoria (played by Prunella Scales), who is passing through the station on the royal train, and the Queen agrees to become the patron of the orphanage and prevent its closure. We started filming late in 2000 and the film was shown over Christmas the following year.

Mark Wallington wrote the screenplay following a visit to the Railway Museum in York with his children. John Roberts was the director. We did all the railway scenes on location at the Bluebell Railway in East Sussex, which is a wonderful heritage project that allows visitors to ride on steam trains and generally experience what travel was like in the steam era.

We shot part of the film at a time when a large part of the country was experiencing terrible floods. When you see the finished product, you would have no idea how bad the conditions were at the time. The rain was blanketing down and you could barely see anything. I think it all goes to show how talented the technicians are back in the studio. We actors are privileged to have people like that making us look good.

I did a run of television dramas by Tony Grounds over the next few years: *Bodily Harm* in 2002, *Family Business* in 2004 and *A Class Apart* and *The Dinner Party* in 2007. Tony had already written extensively for television and had a number of plays, episodes and series to his credit.

The first of his plays I appeared in was *Bodily Harm*, a two-part mini-series directed by Joe Wright that was first shown on Channel Four in 2002. Timothy Spall played a successful businessman in a close-knit three-generation suburban family who suffers a mental breakdown when, in a short space of time, he loses his job, discovers that his wife is cheating on him and learns that his father is dying. I played the dying father, re-evaluating my relationship with my son before I leave the world. It is hard to imagine that there would be much humour in the midst of all that but Tony managed

246

to find some, albeit a little on the black side. His script was excellent and the series was well received by the critics.

Two years later, I was in the second episode of the BBC One family drama series *Family Business*, produced by Tiger Aspect and transmitted in February 2004. The family business of the title is a building and renovation business run by a character played by Jamie Foreman, who is now well known in *EastEnders*. I died in my sleep in that episode and had to hold my breath for several seconds, which caused my pacemaker some serious consternation. This was another series about a family falling apart but treated in a humorous way. The show is definitely not connected with the one on American television with a similar name, which is about the pornography business!

A Class Apart, directed by Nick Hurran and produced by Paloma Films, was a one-off comedy drama transmitted on BBC One in March 2007. This was a very different sort of comedy to the previous two. The film tells the story of a working-class single mother (played by Jessie Wallace) with an 11-year-old son who is something of a handful, having only me, his grandfather, as a somewhat inappropriate male role model. Furious when her application to get the boy into a local private school is rejected, she chains herself to the school gates in protest. The headmaster (played by Nathaniel Parker) eventually gives the boy a place – but only in a *Pygmalion* sort of way because he has entered into a bet with his deputy that he can transform the boy into a charming young man. Tony Grounds had an acting role in this one. It was a rather sentimental story but good fun all the same – and it did manage to make a gentle social comment about the British educational system and draw attention to the difference between the haves and have-nots.

The Dinner Party, first shown on BBC One in September 2007, was another one-off drama from Tony Grounds. The BBC called it a 'black comedy'. An ex-orphanage boy who made a fortune in the City (played by Rupert Graves) and his wife (played by Elizabeth Berrington) hold a dinner party for two other couples, which gradually goes downhill as perceptions of their hierarchical status in society start to come into play. I played George, the ageing father of one of the dinner guests, who has been forced to sell his house and live with his son and daughter-in-law so they can afford to live in a more upmarket area. Tony Grounds directed this one in addition to writing it. Like his other plays, there was a definite social message behind the comedy.

In 2007 I had the pleasure of working with Dennis Waterman again in an episode entitled 'Powerhouse' in his successful *New Tricks* series, which at that stage was in its fourth series. As I write this, the show is scheduled to start its tenth series in autumn 2013. In 'Powerhouse' I played a successful businessman, Sir Edward Chambers, who had a dubious diplomatic past in Kenya during the communist uprising in the 1950s. Back in Britain, his identification evidence was a crucial factor in sending a man to the gallows for murder. The three ageing policemen have to determine whether the wrong man was executed.

As I mentioned earlier, Dennis and I are complete opposites: Dennis loves pubs, I hate them; Dennis loves football, I hate football; Dennis loves to be with a crowd, I hate crowds. But he is a genuinely entertaining companion to be with and to work with. When I went to do that episode of *New Tricks*, I realised that he had taken all the qualities that I remembered from *Minder* to his new show. And everyone there adored him. He kept them amused all the time and it seemed to have a calming effect on the set. He's usually an amusing person but he also has a sensitive and caring side when he realises an actor is not feeling comfortable.

There came a time while we were doing *Minder* when we had both become relatively well known and a few actors were a little intimidated about working with us. Dennis would be the first to notice and say to me, 'So and so is looking a bit uncomfortable. Let's have a word with him.' And he would invite him into the Winnebago and we would try to put him at ease. I think we only ever had one actor who had to be replaced. The pour soul was getting so tongue-tied and nervous and unable to get a line right that we had to get someone else in.

I have been fortunate with my health over the years, although I had a bit of a hiccup at the beginning of 2002. I was just about to start a run at the Richmond Theatre of the comedy *Party Piece* by Richard Harris, playing a grumpy old man who can't get along with his neighbours. Penny was away and I was at home by myself and I went outside to get a few logs for the fire. Because I was on my own I didn't want to use the garden tractor to bring them in and used a wheelbarrow instead. After about 50 yards I got a bit puffed and had to stop for a few minutes to catch my breath. After a short rest I tried again but soon found myself huffing and puffing again. I thought, 'This isn't me; I'm fitter than that.' Then I did something totally out of character: I rang the doctor's surgery and asked to see someone. They made an appointment for me that afternoon. My GP did an ECG to check my heart and asked me to wait in the waiting room. A few minutes later he called me back in and said, 'I've just faxed your ECG to the John Radcliffe Hospital in Oxford and they want you in immediately.' He went on, 'You can't drive home. I've sent for an ambulance!'

'Hang on,' I said, 'I'm not going anywhere tonight. I have to get my wife back. Tell them I'll come in first thing tomorrow,' which I did.

It seems that one of my heart valves had packed up. The funny thing is that I rang Penny to ask her to collect me but, before I could say anything, she said, 'I'm talking to Tara on the mobile! I'll ring you back.'

I went in the next day, which was a Tuesday, and they operated on the Saturday. They put in a valve from a pig's heart and fitted me with a pacemaker.

The children brought in some cassettes to keep me entertained while I was there. One of the tapes was of Tommy Cooper and it had a highly appropriate joke on it.

'I was fitted with a pig's heart valve yesterday.'

'Is it OK?'

'Yes, but you get a bit of crackling around the ears from time to time!'

Tara brought in a cassette tape of Jasper Carrott, which we listened to and enjoyed before I had my surgery. All the way through, Jasper kept mentioning Birmingham City Football Club, of which he is a dedicated supporter. I had my surgery and was in the intensive-care unit afterwards, recovering from the anaesthetic. Penny had popped out for a cup of tea and Tara was sitting with me. As I started to come round I saw I was connected to all sorts of equipment with tubes, wires and who knows what else and I started to get angry about what they had done to me. I started pulling wires and things off and said to Tara, 'Your mother has gone off to find somewhere nice to eat. Let's go and join her.' Tara fled and found a nurse, who said she would give me some morphine to keep the pain down and I immediately fell into a deep sleep.

The next thing I knew, someone was asking me to join Birmingham City Football Club to take over the running of the club. I said, 'I don't know anything about football,' so I contacted Dennis Waterman to help me out. I can't repeat what he said when he heard which team it was. Then, suddenly, some paparazzi arrived and I said, 'Look, there's something wrong here. I'm wearing a hospital gown. I don't look anything like a football manager, do I?' And then some of the players turned up. It was one of the most vivid dreams I've ever had. Since then I've learned that lots of people have vivid dreams while they are sedated with morphine but, for me, everything seemed totally real. I'm still waiting for the official contract with Birmingham City FC to arrive in the mail.

The heart problem came as a complete shock as I hadn't been feeling unwell in the slightest. But three weeks later I was cutting the grass. Two weeks after that I was doing an episode of something.

It all happened so quickly that there was no time to worry or even to think about how close to death I might have been.

I have the highest respect for the cardiac team at the John Radcliffe Hospital in Oxford. They did a wonderful job on me and I probably would not be here now if it were not for their skill and dedication. They were good-humoured as well. I remember before the surgery the surgeon saying, 'Well, while we've got the bonnet open, we might as well do a full service. Let's put in a pacemaker as well.'

Since then, I have attached my name to some of the fundraising for the British Heart Foundation. I'm still alive today and it's the least I can do to show my appreciation.

The worst part was that I was told I had to quit smoking. I have always loved a good cigar and smoked at least 4 a day for more than 40 years but I had no choice in the matter. The doctors said that, if I continued smoking, the problem would soon come back. I stopped there and then and haven't had a cigar since. I don't think that willpower came into it at all. I think it was pure fear of what would happen if I continued.

At least I was still allowed the occasional tipple of a good single-malt whisky. I never drink before a show or, in most cases, after one, probably because I like to drive home afterwards, so I don't go into a pub particularly often. But there was one amusing incident when I did go into a pub. I had been living where I am now for close to 20 years and, while I was driving home one night with Penny, she said, 'I need some eggs. Let's call into the pub near our house and buy some.' I have to explain that we live in the country and we had seen a sign outside the pub saying 'Fresh eggs for sale'. We went in and bought the eggs and thought we ought to have a drink while we were there. We got talking to the barman and he eventually said, 'So are you thinking of moving down here?' 'I've lived here for over 20 years,' I said, 'I've just never been in this pub!'

In July 2004, just to prove that I wouldn't allow a small thing like heart surgery to let people down, I did a tour with Richard Harris's play *Party Piece* – the tour I was just about to start when the heart problem cropped up. We started at the Windsor Theatre. It could not have been a better return to the stage. I love working at the Windsor Theatre and *Party Piece* is a really lovely play and extremely funny. The play is set in two adjoining gardens. I played this terrible old man who can't get on with anybody and worries too much about his bowels. When his upmarket neighbour and his wife next door invite some guests to a housewarming barbecue, the old man proudly protects the privacy he holds dear and his right to keep a broken-down motorbike in his garden.

The welcome I received from the audience when I first went on stage was touching beyond description – and expectation. I just cannot describe the feeling when I made my first entry and the audience gave me a standing ovation. It was a welcome that was so full of love and support that I found it quite emotional. And I still had a show to perform ahead of me! I could not have been happier to be back. I even had the use of a Zimmer frame, which, I hasten to add, was there for the character's benefit and not for mine!

After that I carried on as normal, doing the occasional television episode here and there. They included the last episode of *Marple*, *Diamond Geezer* (in which I played a retired getaway car driver), *Midsomer Murders* and two episodes of *Heartbeat*. Working with Penny has always been fun and I only agreed to do the first *Heartbeat* episode if she could have a part as well. The producers agreed and cast me as a petty criminal who moves into a retirement home of which Penny is the matron. On that basis, I was happy to drive the 250 miles up to Yorkshire to do the episode. I did another episode two years later as the same character, who had escaped from prison and returned to engage in a little more petty burglary.

I had a strange reunion while I was doing the *Marple* episode (called 'Nemesis'). One of the cast, former *Coronation Street* regular Johnny Briggs, and I last worked together 60 years earlier while we were making the film *The Kite*. Johnny had an uncredited part in the 1948 film as a young boy flying a kite on the common. There can't be that many professions where 2 people can find themselves working together in 2 separate projects 60 years apart with no common projects in the interim. Acting sometimes presents the most unusual situations.

CHAPTER 15

LOOKING BACK

As I write this, I am looking forward to my 88th birthday and I feel like any other 40-year-old. I am having a wonderful life. I have a lovely wife and a loving family and I am enjoying every moment of my life.

I've had the good fortune to work in more roles than I can remember. I was over at Elstree Studios not too long ago and the crew started talking about the actual number of roles I've had. The assistant director said, 'Google will know,' and he disappeared to look me up. He came back a few minutes later with a wad of printouts. One of the crew looked at it and said, 'Bloody hell, George. That's not a CV – it's a bleeding novel!' I've never kept my own chronological record of all the work I've done and I always have to rely on memory. But even I was a little taken aback by what Google came up with.

The last work I did was an audiobook of a tragedy called *Giant's*

Bread by Mary Westmacott, who in reality was Agatha Christie writing under a pseudonym. She wrote six novels under that name because she wanted to be considered more of a serious writer than just a writer of detective stories. It took 5 days to tape 570 pages.

My last television work was an episode of *Midsomer Murders* called 'Shot at Dawn'. This was about a long-standing feud between two families dating back to the First World War when a member of one of the families was shot at dawn by a firing squad that included a member of the other family. I found myself having to sing *The Galloping Major* and the old French army song *Mademoiselle from Armentières*, which often used to get a good bashing at night while I was working in the RAF bars during my National Service. The episode went out on New Year's Day 2008 and contained rather more humour than usual in *Midsomer Murders*. Donald Sinden and I were the feuding old soldiers, both now in wheelchairs, and the feuding had reached the stage where we got involved in a dreadful fight using French bread as weapons. I hope the fight came across as spontaneous but, in fact, we choreographed it in great detail – and got through a lot of French bread in the process! Sadly, as often happens in the Midsomer district, one of us did not survive the entire episode and left it with a bullet in his head. John Nettles had the job of finding out who put the bullet there and why.

Apart from my family, there is another person who has worked wonders helping me to get the most out of my life. She is my wonderful agent Joy Jameson.

In this profession, we rely heavily on our agents. Those actors who think they can go it alone without an agent are usually not that successful. Theatrical agents don't, as many people believe, just find work and then take a percentage of the pay. Managing the work is an ongoing process involving such things as relations with the employers, billing (in the sense of how one's ranking in the cast is portrayed), publicity and keeping tabs on residuals such as repeat fees. Some of the work you get yourself anyway and it's just a question of asking the agent to handle it. In my case, it wasn't an agent who found *Minder*, it was *Minder* that found me.

Half a century ago I had an agent called Christopher Mann but I heard about another agent who was just setting up and I felt that it would be a good time to make a change. The new agent was working in an agency with a man who was managing Elizabeth Taylor and Richard Burton among his clients. He eventually began to feel that they needed his full-time attention, so his partner took over the rest of the agency. Joy Jameson was that partner and she has remained my agent for well over 50 years ever since. She is one of the loveliest ladies around and is someone for whom I feel the utmost trust and respect for her judgement. She has done an amazing job for me over all these years.

One of Joy's most endearing charms is that she will never say one word if a hundred will do. She will telephone and, as soon as you pick up the phone, she will start talking; it is often several minutes before she stops. On one occasion she phoned me at home and started speaking and then, for some reason, the line went dead. I waited for a while to see if she would call back and, when she didn't, I rang her office and said to her secretary, 'Hello, this is George. Could I speak to Joy, please?' The secretary sounded a little confused. She said, 'But you're already speaking to her.' Dear Joy was so tied up in whatever she was telling me that she didn't even realise that I wasn't on the other end of the line.

Many years ago, Joy phoned and my son Toby took the call. Toby's voice sounds much like mine and it is hard to tell us apart on the phone. As always, as soon as Joy heard the voice she was away. Toby tried to interrupt and tell her that she was not speaking to me but he couldn't stop her. She was talking about how much I was going to get for a particular show. Toby politely waited for the flow of words to slow down and, when they did, he said, 'Could you just hold on a second? I'll go and get Dad.' When I finished the call, Toby said, 'Dad, I think we need to have a talk about my allowance.'

Joy is still in the business but does a lot of work from home these days, although she keeps an office and an assistant in London. She still has several clients on her books but most of them are fairly advanced in years. One of her favourite lines is, 'I hope we don't have a flu epidemic this winter because, if we do, I could lose half my clients.'

Looking back, it was definitely *Minder* that brought me the biggest financial rewards of my career but I think *A Man of Our Times* was the point when I felt that I had definitely made it in the business. For some reason, I felt that this was the high spot of my life. But I suppose I probably thought the same thing when I got the play *Cottage to Let* in 1940. And it was the same with *A Life of Bliss*. That show lasted 15 years on radio, so at that stage I must have felt that I'd made it. I suppose you never know whether something is the real high point of your life until you take your last breath. Perhaps something will happen tomorrow and I'll say, 'Well, now I really have made it in the business.' Who knows?

But what does 'made it' actually mean? Does it mean making a lot of money? Being well known? Or just knowing that you've done the best possible job with something and you've got the best possible result from it? I think that, even now, I'm still learning what it takes to be an actor. I love to watch all the old DVDs of my films and reruns of my television shows. It isn't out of vanity or nostalgia. I just watch myself and think, 'How could I have done that better?'

Some actors think that all that is necessary to be an actor is to learn the lines and that once you know them, you are there. It isn't like that at all. You have to be able to listen to what the other actors are saying and reply to them with words or actions that are appropriate to what the other actor has just said and done. You have to respond with behaviour or body language that looks natural and not as if you know what the other actor is about to say and are waiting for him to say it. If you don't do that, you are not acting, you are just saying your lines.

Another thing I have learned to live with over the years is the insecurity of acting. You never know when the next script will come through the door. That insecurity is something all actors feel at one time or another in their careers. But I think it only becomes a problem when the interval between one job and the next starts to become too long. I had one period of eleven months without work and then I got four days' work in Michael Powell's film *Gone to Earth*. That was the longest break I ever had but I don't think it ever occurred to me to look for another job, so I suppose I wasn't too worried about it and I managed to get through.

At the other end of the scale, there are times when success in the acting profession puts some pressure on one's family life that one would prefer not to be there. At the height of *Minder*'s success it became almost impossible to do the sort of family things that other people take for granted, like going on a shopping trip. We soon learned that we had to keep moving. We couldn't go window-shopping, for example. If we did, person after person would stand in front of you and tell you in great detail what they thought of the most recent episode. It was when you stood still that you were in trouble. Also, it was a bit claustrophobic sometimes when I went to the theatre with Penny to see a show as members of the audience. We would go to the bar during the interval and people would stand up and stare at us as if we were a couple of zoo animals. But what you certainly don't want is to be driving along the motorway at 70 miles an hour and have someone drive up alongside, wind down the passenger window and yell out, 'Hello, Arthur, how's 'er indoors?' That's one of the consequences of success that is hard to adjust to. These occasions aside, I love the fans and the knowledge that somehow one's performance has touched them so much that they feel that they know you (or more likely your character) personally. Sometimes, though, the reverse is true.

At the beginning of summer 1982 *Minder* had just finished its third series and had started to become something of an institution. During the break between the third and fourth series, I had just opened in *The Pirates of Penzance* at the Theatre Royal in London playing Major-General Stanley. I was driving into London one day to do the show and the traffic, as usual, was fairly heavy and was just crawling along. Suddenly, two policemen on motorcycles drove past and waved me over. I thought, 'What's all this about? I certainly wasn't speeding.' I pulled over and one of the officers got off his bike and slowly walked back to my car. The passers-by started calling out things like 'Oh dear, Arthur. They've really got you now.' And 'Bang to rights now, eh, Arthur?' The policeman walked up to the window and slowly took off his gloves, pushed his goggles up onto his helmet and said, 'If I give you the address of my station, could you send me a signed photo for my girlfriend?' I was livid. It is terribly unnerving when you get stopped like that and you know you were not doing anything wrong. I can't print what I said to him. I think he realised he had taken a bit of a liberty. He said, 'Where are you going?' I told him and he said, 'Come on, follow us, we'll take you there.' But I politely declined. That was one of the occasions when being recognised had a completely undesirable outcome. There was another occasion when it totally backfired.

While I was doing *Minder* I did a bit of work visiting various care homes for the elderly, dressed as Arthur Daley. The residents usually seemed to enjoy it. I went to one and they were all sitting in a circle and were happy to see me and seemed to be having a lot of fun. But just inside an alcove, sitting by herself, was an old lady who seemed to want nothing to do with it. I pointed her out to the lady who was showing me around and she said, 'You must come over and meet her.' She said to the old lady, 'You know who this is, don't you, Gladys?'

'No.' said Gladys.

'Look at the hat and the coat. *Minder?*'

'No.'

'It's George Cole!'

'Who?'

'George Cole, you know! Arthur Daley!'

'No, never 'eard of 'im.'

I thought I'd better stop it there. I said to Gladys, 'Why are you sitting out here? Why aren't you in there with all the others?'

She said, 'They're all barmy in there, every bloody one of 'em.'

So I swiftly retreated to the safety of the circle.

This was something I was able to smile about. But sadly there are times when the association with your character works in a way you wish it hadn't. I used to get terribly upset in *Minder* when people took an episode so seriously that they thought I genuinely did have a lock-up full of garden gnomes and wanted to know if they could buy one. It was extremely worrying.

I once got a terrible letter when the scriptwriter mentioned a particular illness in a script and I used the line on the show. I thought it was something he'd made up, but it wasn't. It was a real illness and I got this troubling letter saying I shouldn't be so light-hearted about it and that it's a horrible disease. I had to write back apologising and saying that I had no idea it was a real illness and that I honestly believed it was something that had been invented for the script.

Another time there was an episode where Dennis began to get fed up with repossessing cars and it was upsetting him to see people who couldn't get to work anymore because he'd taken back their car for the owner. Arthur Daley said something like, 'What are you talking about? Look around you. All the pensioners have got a Mercedes now.' I received a terribly distressing letter complaining about it and including the writer's pension book. All I could do was slip some money in the book and write back with an apology. It was extremely upsetting.

All things considered, apart from the health hiccup I mentioned earlier, I have been blessed with a good life and good health. I have been able to work hard and have been rewarded with a successful career through which I have been privileged to give pleasure to millions of people around the world and to work with some of the nicest people in the world. I know that my natural parents and my adoptive parents would have been immensely proud of what I have managed to achieve.

But when you work with hundreds of people over the years, there will always be one or two about whom you look back and think, 'I wish they hadn't done that.' There are not many I can think of in my career. But one was a talented and well-known actor who was appearing in a *Minder* episode. While he was on the set he came over and introduced a friend and asked to have a photograph taken with Dennis, his friend and me. We were always pleased to do that and we took the photograph. A couple of years later Dennis and I both received letters from the tax office asking why we hadn't declared income of £500 each for the sale of our images. It turned out that the actor had claimed that he had paid £500 to each of us for having his photograph taken with us and was claiming tax relief on it as part of his professional expenses. Of course, we both replied that it never happened like that and we had not received any payment. We heard no more about it but it left a bad taste behind that one of our own profession should do such a thing. The actor concerned is no longer with us, so it would be unfair to mention his name, but both Dennis and I feel that he stretched the friendship too far over that.

There were other people who seemed genuinely eccentric. I was working with one well-known actor doing a television episode somewhere in the Midlands when he realised he was wearing the wrong socks. They weren't odd; they were simply not the ones he wanted to wear. He immediately got on the phone to his wife in London and asked her to drive up to wherever it was we were shooting to deliver the right pair. Why he couldn't just ask the wardrobe people to deal with it or get a runner to go and buy a pair at the local shops I'll never know. There's one thing of which I'm perfectly sure: his socks didn't appear in anything we were shooting that day. But that is actors for you!

There is one thing, perhaps, that has made me slightly different from many other members of my profession over the years. I keep myself to myself and I hate doing interviews. Dennis is not keen on doing interviews either. I think this has led many of my colleagues to suggest that I am a shy person. I think I should try to quash that idea right now. How can you be shy when you are on a stage in front of a thousand people, the central part of their thoughts and their collective emotions? You cause them to laugh or to shed tears or to re-evaluate their opinions. There is no way a shy person could do that. I would say I am a 'private' person. I do my job and then I go back home to live my own private life the same way that a train driver or a postman does when he finishes his shift.

I've been an actor for more than 70 years and, by now, I have become quite fed up with the sound of my own voice telling the same old stories about 70-year-old events in interviews. I did a radio interview with Michael Parkinson not too long ago and I thought it went reasonably well. When it was finished and we were off air, Parky said, 'The trouble with you, George, is that you just don't like talking about yourself.' I was a bit offended by it at the time. I thought, 'Who is he to tell me what the trouble with me is if I didn't ask him?' But he did have a valid point. I am not my favourite subject of conversation. I do value my privacy. But I also hope this book helps to clarify some of the things people would like to know about me. I have certainly enjoyed sharing them.

People often ask if I have any plans to retire. I've never had a specific plan for my career; I've taken it pretty much as it came. There have been many high spots and, thankfully, only a few low spots. I don't think I could ever formally retire from it. I don't think I could face the reality of finally stopping work – I think I'd go barmy. Even if I did retire, I probably wouldn't tell anyone. To be honest, I don't want to stop at all. I'm still enjoying every second of it. There hasn't been that much work over the last couple of years but I'm still happy. It's just that I refuse to say I have retired. I haven't. I'll be back on stage or in front of the cameras as soon as the right script comes along.

I think at this point I'd like to go back to the subject of adoption. I know that many people who discover they are adopted become highly troubled by the fact and obsessed about their natural parents and what things might have been like if they had not been adopted. I was certainly curious about it when I first discovered the fact when I was 13, but I was able to spend the next 70 and more years looking to the future and not worrying about what I couldn't change. This is what I would strongly recommend to anyone for whom being adopted is causing discomfort. But if this doesn't work, there are lots of professional people out there who can help you get through it. When I do think about it myself, which does not happen often, I always remember my delightful adoptive parents who loved me as their son and, given their circumstances, could not have treated me better.

As Arthur Daley might have said, the world really was my lobster. It still is and there is plenty more I want to get out of it. Among other things, over the years I've been to war, to prison, crucified, beheaded and tied naked to a bed and horsewhipped, all in the name of entertainment. What more could a little cockney boy in pre-war Tooting have asked for?

If things had been different, I might still have been delivering sausages.

FILMOGRAPHY

Films produced primarily for television are not included in this list and are listed in Table I. For each entry below, the first title given, the date of release (in parentheses) and distributors refer to the film's release in the UK. All other details are obtained from credits listed in the UK theatrical release of the film. The cast names refer to the first four or five actors named in the opening credits. GC, of course, refers to George Cole. Release dates are as listed on the Internet Movie Database (IMDb).

Cottage to Let (1941)
US title: *Bombsight Stolen*
Presented by Eros Films Ltd. and Gaumont British Picture Corporation. Produced by Edward Black. Directed by Anthony Asquith. Screenplay by Anatole de Grunwald and J. O. C. Orton adapted from the play by Geoffrey Kerr. Production company: Gainsborough Pictures. Distributed by General Film Distributors.

Cast: Leslie Banks, Alastair Sim, John Mills, Jeanne de Casalis, Carla Lehmann. GC character: Ronald.

Those Kids from Town (1942)
US title: not known, probably not released in the US
Produced by Richard Vernon. Directed by Lance Comfort. Screenplay by Adrian Alington based on his novel *These Our Strangers*. Production company: British National Films. Distributed by Anglo-American Film Corporation. Cast: Shirley Lenner, Jeanne de Casalis, Percy Marmot, D. J. Williams. GC character: Charlie.

Fiddling Fuel (1943)
US title: not known, unlikely to have been released in the US
Produced by the Ministry of Information. Screenplay by Roger MacDougall. Production company: General Production Division. Distributed by the Ministry of Information. Cast: Alastair Sim, George Cole. GC character: Schoolboy.

The Demi-Paradise (20 December 1943, uncredited)
US title: *Adventure for Two*
Written and produced by Anatole de Grunwald. Directed by Anthony Asquith. Production company: The Rank Organisation and Two Cities Films. Distributed by General Film Distributors. Cast: Laurence Olivier, Penelope Ward, Marjorie Fielding, Margaret Rutherford. GC character: Percy.

Henry V (22 November 1944)
US title: same
Produced and directed by Laurence Olivier based on the play *Henry V* by William Shakespeare. Production company: Two Cities Films.

Distributed by Eagle-Lion Distributors Ltd. Cast: Laurence Olivier, Robert Newton, Leslie Banks. GC character: Boy.

Journey Together (1 October 1945)
US title: same
Directed by John Boulting. Screenplay by John Boulting based on a story by Terence Rattigan. Production company: Royal Air Force Film Production Unit. Distributed by RKO Radio Pictures. Cast: Richard Attenborough, Jack Watling, David Tomlinson, Edward G. Robinson. GC character: Curly, Lancaster Crew.

My Brother's Keeper (9 August 1948)
US title: same
Presented by J. Arthur Rank. Produced by Antony Darnborough. Directed by Alfred Roome. Screenplay by Frank Harvey Jr after a story by Maurice Wiltshire. Production company: Gainsborough Pictures. Distributed by General Film Distributors Ltd. Cast: Jack Warner, Jane Hylton, David Tomlinson, Bill Owen, George Cole. GC character: Willie Stannard.

The Kite (26 October 1948 – a segment in a four-part anthology of stories by W. Somerset Maugham under the collective title *Quartet*)
US title: same
Presented by J. Arthur Rank. Produced by Antony Darnborough. *The Kite* story directed by Arthur Crabtree. Screenplay by R. C. Sherriff based on the story *The Kite* by W. Somerset Maugham. Production company: Gainsborough Pictures. Distributed by General Film Distributors Ltd. Cast: Hermione Baddeley, Mervyn Johns, Susan Shaw, George Cole. GC character: Herbert Sunbury.

The Spider and the Fly (1 December 1949)
US title: same

Presented by J. Arthur Rank. Produced by Aubrey Baring. Directed by Robert Hamer. Screenplay by Robert Westerby from his original story. Production company: 'A Setton-Baring "Mayflower" Production'. Distribution: A Universal-International Release. Cast: Eric Portman, Guy Rolfe, Nadia Gray. GC character: Marc.

Morning Departure (21 February 1950)
US title: *Operation Disaster*
Presented by the J. Arthur Rank Organisation. Produced by Jay Lewis. Directed by Roy Baker. Screenplay by W. E. C. Fairchild based on the stage play *Morning Departure* by Kenneth Woollard. Production company: Jay Lewis Independent Productions. Distributed by General Film Distributors. Cast: John Mills, Richard Attenborough, Nigel Patrick, James Hayter. GC character: E. R. A. Marks.

The Happiest Days of Your Life (8 March 1950 – uncredited)
US title: same
Produced by Sidney Gilliat and Frank Launder. Directed by Frank Launder. Screenplay by Frank Launder and John Dighton from the play by John Dighton. Production company: Individual Pictures. Distributed by British Lion Film Corporation. Cast: Alastair Sim, Margaret Rutherford, Guy Middleton, Joyce Grenfell. GC character: Junior assistant caretaker.

Gone to Earth (6 November 1950)
US title: *The Wild Heart* (after re-editing of the original version)
Presented by Alexander Korda and David O. Selznick. Produced, directed and written by Michael Powell and Emeric Pressburger adapted from the novel by Mary Webb. Production company: London Film Productions. Distributed by British Lion Film

Corporation Ltd. Cast: Jennifer Jones, David Farrar, Cyril Cusack. GC character: Cousin Albert.

Flesh and Blood (6 March 1951)
US title: not known if released in the US
Presented by London Films. Produced by Anatole de Grunwald. Directed by Anthony Kimmins. Screenplay adapted by Anatole de Grunwald from the play *A Sleeping Clergyman* by James Bridie. Production company: De Grunwald Productions. Distributed by British Lion Film Corporation Ltd. Cast: Richard Todd, Glynis Johns, Joan Greenwood, Andre Morell. GC character: John Hannah.

Laughter in Paradise (13 June 1951)
US title: same
Produced and directed by Mario Zampi. Screenplay by Jack Davies and Michael Pertwee. Production company: Mario Zampi Productions. Distributed by Associated British-Pathé. Cast: Alastair Sim, Fay Compton, George Cole, Guy Middleton. GC character: Herbert Russell.

Lady Godiva Rides Again (25 October 1951)
US title: *Bikini Baby*
Produced by Sidney Gilliat and Frank Launder. Directed by Frank Launder. Screenplay by Frank Launder and Val Valentine. Produced in association with and distributed by British Lion Film Corporation. Cast: Dennis Price, John McCallum, Stanley Holloway, and introducing Pauline Stroud, with Diana Dors, George Cole. GC character: Johnny.

Scrooge (31 October 1951)
US title: *A Christmas Carol*
Presented by George Minter. Produced and directed by Brian Desmond-Hurst. Screenplay by Noel Langley adapted from *A Christmas Carol* by Charles Dickens. Production company: George Minter Productions (uncredited). Distributed by Renown Pictures Corporation Ltd. Cast: Alastair Sim, Kathleen Harrison, Mervyn Johns, Hermione Baddeley, Michael Hordern, George Cole, (by special arrangement) Jack Warner. GC character: Young Ebenezer Scrooge.

The Happy Family (31 March 1952)
US title: *Mr. Lord Says No*
Produced by Sydney Box and William MacQuitty. Directed by Muriel Box. Screenplay by Muriel and Sydney Box based on the play *The Happy Family* by Michael Clayton Hutton. Production company: London Independent Producers. Distributed by Apex Film Distributors. Cast: Stanley Holloway, Kathleen Harrison, Naunton Wayne, Dandy Nichols, George Cole. GC character: Cyril.

Who Goes There! (10 June 1952)
US title: *The Passionate Sentry*
Produced and directed by Anthony Kimmins. Screenplay by John Dighton based on his 1951 play of the same name. Production company: British Lion Film Corporation. Distributed by British Lion Film Corporation. Cast: Nigel Patrick, Valerie Hobson, Peggy Cummins, George Cole. GC character: Arthur Crisp.

Top Secret (19 November 1952)
US title: *Mr. Potts Goes to Moscow*
Presented by Associated British Picture Corporation Ltd. Produced

and directed by Mario Zampi. Screenplay and original story by Jack Davies and Michael Pertwee. Production company: Mario Zampi Productions. Distributed by Associated British Film Distributors: Cast: Oskar Homolka, Nadia Gray, George Cole. GC character: George Potts.

Folly to Be Wise (19 January 1953 – uncredited)
US title: same
Produced by Sidney Gilliat. Directed by Frank Launder. Screenplay by Frank Launder and John Dighton based on the play *It Depends What You Mean* by James Bridie. Production company: British Lion Film Corporation. Distributed by British Lion Film Corporation. Cast: Alastair Sim, Roland Culver, Elizabeth Allan, Martita Hunt, Colin Gordon. GC character: Soldier in audience.

Will Any Gentleman...? (25 August 1953)
US title: same
Presented by Associated British Picture Corporation Ltd. Produced by Hamilton G. Inglis. Directed by Michael Anderson. Screenplay by Vernon Sylvaine from his play *Will Any Gentleman?* Production company: Associated British Picture Corporation Ltd. Distributed by Associated British-Pathé. Cast: George Cole, Veronica Hurst, Jon Pertwee, James Hayter, Heather Thatcher. GC character: Henry Sterling.

The Intruder (19 October 1953)
US title: same
Presented by British Lion Film Corporation. Produced by Ivan Foxwell. Directed by Guy Hamilton. Screenplay by Robin Maugham, John Hunter, and (additional scenes) Anthony Squire based on the novel *Line on Ginger* by Robin Maugham. Production

company: Ivan Foxwell Productions. Distributed by British Lion Film Corporation. Cast: Jack Hawkins, George Cole, Dennis Price, Michael Medwin. GC character: John Summers.

The Clue of the Missing Ape (November 1953)
US title: not known if released in the US
Presented by the Gaumont Specialised Film Unit. Produced by Frank Wells. Directed by James Hill. Screenplay by James Hill based on an idea by Donald Carter and Frank Wells with original treatment by Gilbert and Margaret Hackforth-Jones. Production company: Children's Film Foundation. Distributed by British Lion. Cast: George Cole, Patrick Boxill, William Patrick, Nati Banda, Roy Savage. GC character: Gobo.

Our Girl Friday (1 December 1953)
US title: *The Adventures of Sadie*
Presented and produced by George Minter. Directed by Noel Langley. Screenplay by Noel Langley based on the book *The Cautious Amorist* by Norman Lindsay. Production company: 'A Langley-Minter Production' (George Minter Productions). Distributed by Renown Pictures Productions Ltd. Cast: Joan Collins, George Cole, Kenneth More, Robertson Hare. GC character: Carrol.

Happy Ever After (29 June 1954)
US title: *Tonight's the Night*
Presented by Associated British Picture Corporation Ltd. Produced and directed by Mario Zampi. Story and screenplay by Jack Davies and Michael Pertwee, with additional dialogue by L. A. G. Strong. Production company: Mario Zampi Productions. Distributed by Allied Artists Pictures Corporation. Cast: David

Niven, Yvonne De Carlo, Barry Fitzgerald and guest artist George Cole. GC character: Terence.

The Belles of St. Trinian's (28 September 1954)
US title: same
Presented and produced by Sidney Gilliat and Frank Launder. Directed by Frank Launder. Screenplay by Frank Launder, Sidney Gilliat and Val Valentine. Production company: British Lion Film Corporation. Distributed by British Lion Film Corporation. Cast: Alastair Sim, Joyce Grenfell, George Cole, Hermione Baddeley. GC character: Flash Harry.

An Inspector Calls (16 March 1954 – uncredited)
US title: same
Produced by A. D. Peters. Directed by Guy Hamilton. Screenplay by Desmond Davis based on the play by J. B. Priestley. Production company: Watergate Productions Ltd. Distributed by British Lion Film Corporation. Cast: Alastair Sim, with (from end credits) Olga Lindo, Arthur Young, Brian Worth. GC character: Tram conductor.

Where There's a Will (March 1955)
US title: not known if released in the US
Produced by George Maynard. Directed by Vernon Sewell. Screenplay by R. F. Delderfield, adapted from his play. Distributed by Eros Films. Cast: Kathleen Harrison, George Cole, Leslie Dwyer. GC character: Fred Slater.

A Prize of Gold (17 February 1955)
US title: same
Produced by Irving Allen and Albert R. Broccoli. Directed by Mark Robson. Screenplay by Robert Buckner and John Paxton from the

novel *A Prize of Gold* by Max Catto. Production company: Warwick Film Productions. Distributed by Columbia Pictures Corporation. Cast: Richard Widmark, Mai Zetterling, Nigel Patrick, George Cole. GC character: Sergeant Roger Morris.

The Constant Husband (16 May 1955)
US title: *Marriage a la Mode*
Presented by London Films. Produced by Frank Launder and Sidney Gilliat. Directed by Sidney Gilliat. Screenplay by Sidney Gilliat and Val Valentine. Production company: London Film Productions. Distributed by British Lion Film Corporation Ltd. Cast: Rex Harrison, Margaret Leighton, Kay Kendall, Cecil Parker. GC character: Luigi Sopranelli.

The Adventures of Quentin Durward (1 March 1956)
US titles: *Quentin Durward* and *Sir Walter Scott's Quentin Durward*
Produced by Pandro S. Berman. Directed by Richard Thorpe. Screenplay by Robert Ardrey, adapted by George Froeschel from the novel *Quentin Durward* by Sir Walter Scott. Production company: Metro Goldwyn Mayer. Distributed by Metro Goldwyn Mayer. Cast: Robert Taylor, Kay Kendall, Robert Morley, George Cole. GC character: Hayraddin.

It's a Wonderful World (28 August 1956)
US title: same
Presented and produced by George Minter. Directed by Val Guest. Screenplay and original story by Val Guest. Production company: George Minter Productions. Distributed by Renown Pictures Corporation. Cast: Terence Morgan, George Cole, Kathleen Harrison, introducing Mylene Nicole. GC character: Ken Millar.

The Green Man (18 September 1956)
US title: same
Produced by Sidney Gilliat and Frank Launder. Directed by Robert Day. Screenplay by Sidney Gilliat and Frank Launder based on their play *Meet a Body*. Production company: Grenadier Films Ltd. Distributed by British Lion Film Corporation. Cast: Alastair Sim, George Cole, Terry-Thomas, Jill Adams. GC character: William Blake.

The Weapon (September 1956)
US title: same
Presented by Irving H. Levin. Produced by Hal E. Chester. Directed by Val Guest. Screenplay by Fred Freiberger based on an original story by Hal E. Chester and Fred Freiberger. Production company: 'A Republic Production'. Distributed by Eros Films. Cast: Steve Cochran, Lizabeth Scott, Herbert Marshall, Nicole Maurey. GC character: Joshua Henry.

Blue Murder at St. Trinian's (December 1957)
US title: same
Presented and produced by Sidney Gilliat and Frank Launder. Directed by Frank Launder. Screenplay by Frank Launder, Val Valentine and Sidney Gilliat. Production company: John Harvel Productions Ltd. Distributed by British Lion Film Corporation. Cast: Terry-Thomas, George Cole, Joyce Grenfell, Alastair Sim. GC character: Flash Harry.

Too Many Crooks (8 March 1959)
US title: same
Produced and directed by Mario Zampi. Screenplay by Michael Pertwee based on a story by Christiane Rochefort and Jean Nery. Production company: Mario Zampi Productions. Distributed by

Rank Film Distributors Ltd. Cast: Terry-Thomas, George Cole, Brenda de Banzie, Bernard Bresslaw. GC character: Fingers.

The Bridal Path (5 August 1959)
US title: same
Produced by Sidney Gilliat and Frank Launder. Directed by Frank Launder. Screenplay by Frank Launder and Geoffrey Willans from the novel by Nigel Tranter. Production company: Vale Film Productions in association with British Lion Films Ltd. Distributed by British Lion Film Corporation. Cast: Bill Travers, George Cole, Bernadette O'Farrell, Duncan Macrae. GC character: Police Sergeant Bruce.

Don't Panic Chaps (November 1959)
US title: not known if released in the US
Produced by Teddy Baird. Directed by George Pollock. Screenplay by Jack Davies adapted from an original radio play by Ronald Holroyd and Michael Corston. Production company: Hammer Film Productions and Association of Cinema Technicians. Distributed by Columbia Pictures Corporation. Cast: Dennis Price, George Cole, Thorley Walters, Nadja Regin, Harry Fowler. GC character: Finch.

The Pure Hell of St. Trinian's (December 1960)
US title: same
Presented and produced by Sidney Gilliat and Frank Launder. Directed by Frank Launder. Screenplay by Frank Launder, Val Valentine and Sidney Gilliat. Production company: British Lion Film Corporation. Distributed by British Lion Film Corporation. Cast: Cecil Parker, George Cole, Joyce Grenfell, Eric Barker. GC character: Flash Harry.

Cleopatra (31 July 1963)

US title: same

Produced by Walter Wanger. Directed by Joseph L. Mankiewicz. Screenplay by Joseph L. Mankiewicz, Ranald MacDougall and Sidney Buchman based on the book *The Life and Times of Cleopatra* by C. M. Franzero. Production company: Twentieth Century Fox Film Corporation. Distributed by Twentieth Century Fox Film Corporation. Cast: Elizabeth Taylor, Richard Burton, Rex Harrison, Pamela Brown, George Cole. GC character: Flavius.

Dr. Syn, Alias the Scarecrow (6 December 1963)

US title: *'Disneyland': The Scarecrow of Romney Marsh*

Presented and produced by Walt Disney. Directed by James Neilson. Screenplay by Robert Westerby based on *Christopher Syn* by Russell Thorndike and William Buchanan. Production company: Walt Disney Productions. Distributed by the Walt Disney Company. Cast: Patrick McGoohan, George Cole, Tony Britton, Michael Hordern, Geoffrey Keen. GC character: Mr Mipps/Hellspite.

One Way Pendulum (August 1964)

US title: same

Presented by Woodfall Film Presentations Ltd. Produced by Michael Deeley. Directed by Peter Yates. Screenplay by N. F. Simpson based on his stage play of the same name. Production company: Woodfall Films. Distributed by United Artists. Cast: Eric Sykes, George Cole, Julia Foster, Jonathan Miller, (guest star) Peggy Mount. GC character: Defence counsel/friend.

The Legend of Young Dick Turpin (1964)

US title: *'Disneyland': The Legend of Young Dick Turpin*

Presented and produced by Walt Disney. Directed by James Neilson. Screenplay by Robert Westerby. Production company: Walt Disney Productions. Distributed by Buena Vista International Inc. Cast: David Weston, Bernard Lee, George Cole, Maurice Denham. GC character: William Evans.

The Great St. Trinian's Train Robbery (4 April 1966)
US title: not known if released in the US
Presented by Frank Launder and Sidney Gilliat. Produced by Leslie Gilliat. Directed by Frank Launder and Sidney Gilliat. Screenplay by Frank Launder and Ivor Herbert based on an original story by Frank Launder, Sidney Gilliat and Leslie Gilliat. Production company: British Lion Film Corporation. Distributed by British Lion Film Corporation. Cast: Frankie Howerd, Dora Bryan, George Cole, Reg Varney. GC character: Flash Harry.

The Green Shoes (1968)
US title: not known if released in the US
Presented by Isleworth Productions. Produced by Ralph Solomons. Directed by Ian Brims. Screenplay by Ivor Jay. Production company: Isleworth Productions. Distributed by Paramount British Pictures. Cast: George Cole, Donald Webster, Tom Macaulay, Fred Davis. GC character: Braine.

The Vampire Lovers (4 October 1970)
US title: same
Produced by Harry Fine and Michael Style. Directed by Roy Ward Baker. Screenplay by Tudor Gates based on the story *Carmilla* by J. Sheridan Le Fanu, adapted by Harry Fine, Tudor Gates and Michael Style. Production company: American International Pictures and Hammer Film Productions. Distributed by MGM-EMI. Cast: Ingrid

Pitt, George Cole, Kate O'Mara, Peter Cushing. GC character: Roger Morton.

Fright (November 1971)
US titles: *Girl in the Dark* and (reissue title) *I'm Alone and I'm Scared*
Produced by Harry Fine and Michael Style. Directed by Peter Collinson. Screenplay by Tudor Gates. Production company: Fantale Films Ltd. Distributed by British Lion Film Corporation. Cast: Susan George, Honor Blackman, Ian Bannen, John Gregson, George Cole, Dennis Waterman. GC character: Jim.

Take Me High (1973)
US title: not known if released in the US
Produced by Kenneth Harper. Directed by David Askey. Story and screenplay by Christopher Penfold based on an original idea by Kenneth Harper. Production company: Balladeer Ltd. Distributed by Anglo-EMI Distributors Ltd. Cast: Cliff Richard, Debbie Watling, Hugh Griffith, George Cole. GC character: Bert Jackson.

The Blue Bird (US 1976. UK release date unknown)
US title: same
Produced by Paul Maslansky. Directed by George Cukor. Screenplay by Hugh Whitemore, Alfred Hayes and Aleksei Kapler based on the play *L'Oiseau Bleu* by Maurice Maeterlinck. Production company: Lenfilm. Distributed by Twentieth Century-Fox Film Corporation. Cast: Elizabeth Taylor, Jane Fonda, Ava Gardner, Cicely Tyson, Robert Morley. GC character: Tylo the Dog.

Perishing Solicitors (1983)
US title: probably not released outside UK
Directed by Charles Crichton. Screenplay by Denis Norden. Production company: Video Arts. Distributed by Video Arts (for the Law Society). Cast: George Cole, Maureen Lipman, Patsy Rowlands, Judy Cornwell. GC character: Mr Martin.

Mary Reilly (26 April 1996)
US title: same
Produced by Ned Tanen, Nancy Graham Tanen and Norma Heyman. Directed by Stephen Frears. Screenplay by Christopher Hampton based on the novel by Valerie Martin. Production company: TriStar Pictures. Distributed by TriStar Pictures. Cast: Julia Roberts, John Malkovich, George Cole, Michael Gambon. GC character: Mr Poole.

TABLE I

CHRONOLOGICAL LIST OF PRINCIPAL TELEVISION PERFORMANCES

Year	Programme or series title	Episode title or programme type	No. of series/ episodes	Character
1948	Dr Angelus	play		Dr Johnson
1950	Mr Gillie	play		Tom Donnelly
1955	A Phoenix Too Frequent	play		Tegeus-Chromis
1956	ITV Play of the Week	The Anatomist		Walter Anderson
1957	Suspicion	Rainy Day		George Willis
1959	Armchair Theatre	Wedding Day		

1960 –61	A Life of Bliss		2 series 20 episodes	David Bliss
1962	ATV Drama '62	The Pinedus Affair		
1963	Comedy Play-house	Nicked at the Bottle		Mossy Marcus
1964	Gideon's Way	The Firebug		Mr Bishop
1966	30-Minute Theatre	The Caramel Crisis		Caramel
1966	Comedy Play-house	The End of the Tunnel		Charles
1966	The Informer	Its an Unfair World, Baxter		Baxter
1966	Blackmail	The Sound of Distant Guns		
1967	A Man of Our Times		1 series 13 episodes	Max Osborne
1967	ITV Play of the Week	That Old Black Magic		Frank Cockburn
1967	Half Hour Story	Friends		Cyril
1967	Half Hour Story	The Gentleman Caller		Mr Hicks
1968	The Sex Game	Cold Game Pie		
1968	30-Minute Theatre	Of Public Concern		

TABLE I

1968	The Root of All Evil?	Of Course We Trust You Arnold		Syd
1969	Out of the Unknown	The Last Lonely Man		James Hale
1969	The Root of All Evil?	A Bit of a Holiday		Gordon Maple
1969	ITV Playhouse	Murder: Return to Yesterday		David
1969	ITV Saturday Night Theatre	The Comic		Tod
1969	The Gold Robbers	The Big Spender		Barry Porter
1969 –71	Jackanory		2 series 6 episodes	Storyteller
1970	Armchair Theatre	A Room in Town		Edwin (Ted) Nugent
1970	Play for Today	The Right Prospectus		Mr Newbold
1970	Menace	Killing Time		Douglas Willett
1971	The Ten Commandments	A Bit of Family Feeling		Peter
1971	UFO	Flight Path		Paul Roper
1971	Shadows of Fear	Return of Favours		Gordon Marsh
1972	Madigan	The London Beat		Policeman

1972	Six Faces	Commonwealth of Malignants		Arthur Drew
1973	Away from It All	Such A Small Word		Peter
1974	Dial M for Murder	Should Anyone Answer		Pearce
1974	Village Hall	Friendly Encounter		Ernest Groves
1974	Affairs of the Heart	Grace		Mr Prodmore
1975	Quiller	Safe Conduct		Mays
1975	Lloyd George Knew My Father	TV movie		Hubert Boothroyd MP
1976	The Sweeney	Tomorrow Man		Dennis Longfield
1977 –79	Don't Forget to Write!		2 series 12 episodes	Gordon Maple
1978	Saturday Drama	Losing Her		Harry
1978	The Good Life	When I'm 65		Bank Manager
1978	The Voyage of Charles Darwin		1 series 7 episodes	Josiah Wedgwood
1978	Return of the Saint	The Armageddon Alternative		Fred
1979 –94	Minder		10 series 108 episodes*	Arthur Daley

TABLE I

1979	ITV Playhouse	Getting In On Concorde		Willie
1982	The Bounder		2 series 14 episodes	Trevor Mountjoy
1984 –86	Comrade Dad		1 series 8 episodes	Reg Dudgeon
1985	Blott on the Landscape		1 series 6 episodes	Sir Giles Lynchwood
1985	Minder on the Orient Express	TV movie		Arthur Daley
1986	Day to Remember	play		Wally
1988	Natural Causes	TV movie		Vincent
1988	Tube Mice		1 series 26 episodes	Vernon the Mouse
1988	An Officer and a Car Salesman	TV movie		Arthur Daley
1990	Life After Life	TV movie		Eric Burt
1992	Root Into Europe		1 series 5 episodes	Henry Root
1995 –96	My Good Friend		2 series 14 episodes	Peter Banks
1996	An Independent Man		1 series 7 episodes	Freddie Patterson

(Opposite page) *2 of the 108 are listed individually in this table as TV movies

287

1997 –99	Dad		2 series 13 episodes	Brian Hook
1999	Best of British	bio-documentary		Self
2000	The Sleeper	TV movie		George
2000	The Ghost of Greville Lodge	TV movie		Great Uncle James
2001	Station Jim	TV movie		Station-master Pope
2002	Bodily Harm	episode		Sidney
2004	Family Business	episode		Pat Williams
2005	Heartbeat	Mastermind		Albert Hallows
2007	Marple	Nemesis		Mr Raeburn
2007	Diamond Geezer	A Royal Affair		Gerald
2007	New Tricks	Powerhouse		Sir Edward Chambers
2007	A Class Apart	TV movie		George
2007	The Dinner Party	TV movie		George
2008	Heartbeat	England Expects		Albert Hallows
2008	Midsomer Murders	Shot at Dawn		Lionel Hicks

TABLE II

CHRONOLOGICAL LIST OF PRINCIPAL STAGE PERFORMANCES

Year	Theatre	Play	Character
1939	Grand Theatre, Blackpool/Tour	The White Horse Inn	goat boy
1940	Coliseum, London	The White Horse Inn	goat boy
1940	Wyndham's Theatre, London	Cottage to Let	Ronald
1940	Prince of Wales Theatre, Birmingham	Cottage to Let	Ronald
1940–41	Tour	Cottage to Let	Ronald
1942	Tour	Old Master	
1942–43	New Theatre, London	Goodnight Children	Percy King
1942	Apollo Theatre, London	Flare Path	Percy

1943	Playhouse Theatre, London	Mr Bolfry	Cohen
1947	Tour	Dr Angelus	Dr Johnson
1947	Phoenix Theatre, London	Dr Angelus	Dr Johnson
1948	Westminster Theatre, London	The Anatomist	Walter Anderson
1950	Garrick Theatre, London	Mr Gillie	Tom Donnelly
1951	Lyric Theatre, Hammersmith	Thor, with Angels	Hoel
1951	Lyric Theatre, Hammersmith	A Phoenix Too Frequent	Tegeus-Chromis
1952	Citizens Theatre, Glasgow	The Anatomist	Walter Anderson
1952	Royal Princess Theatre, Glasgow	The Blaikie Charivari	Joe Mascara
1955	Duchess Theatre, London	Misery Me!	Adam
1956	Aldwych Theatre, London	Mr Bolfry	Cohen
1958	Strand Theatre, London	The Brass Butterfly	Phanocles
1960	Theatre Royal Bath/Tour	The Bargain	Morgan
1961	St Martin's Theatre, London	The Bargain	Morgan

TABLE II

1962	Royal Court Theatre, London	The Sponge Room	Leslie Edwards
1962	Royal Court Theatre, London	Squat Betty	Stanley Mintey
1963	Tour	Meet Me On the Fence	Toby Pilgrim
1963	Tour	The Yes Yes Yes Man	Toby Pilgrim
1964	New Arts Theatre, London	Hedda Gabler	George Tesman
1964	St. Martin's Theatre, London	Hedda Gabler	George Tesman
1964	Garrick Theatre, London	Too True to be Good	Sergeant Fielding
1965	Strand Theatre, London	Too True to be Good	Sergeant Fielding
1965	St. Martin's Theatre, London	A Public Mischief	Mark
1966	New Arts Theatre, London	The Waiting Game	Toby Pilgrim
1967	Royal Court Theatre, London	The Three Sisters	Andrei Prozorov (Andrey)
1968	Hampstead Theatre	Doubtful Haunts	Ballad / Butler
1969	Tour	The Passionate Husband	Dr Peter Estriss
1969	Thorndike Theatre, Leatherhead	There Was an Old Woman	Mr Mortymer/ Mr Pollard

1970	New Theatre, Bromley	The Man Most Likely To	Victor Cadwallader
1971	Mayfair Theatre, London/Tour	The Philanthropist	Philip
1973	Hampstead Theatre	Country Life	Richard
1974–75	New London Theatre	Déjà Revue	
1976	Yvonne Arnaud Theatre, Guildford	Motive	Andrew Creed
1976	Savoy Theatre, London	Banana Ridge	Willoughby Pink
1977	Yvonne Arnaud Theatre, Guildford	The Case of the Oily Levantine	Inspector Fathom
1978	Hilton Hotel, Hong Kong	Something's Afoot	Janitor
1979	Open Space Theatre, London	Brimstone and Treacle	Mr Bates
1980	Greenwich Theatre	Liberty Hall	Skinner
1982	Theatre Royal Drury Lane, London	The Pirates of Penzance	Major General Stanley
1985	Nuffield Theatre, Southampton	First Sunday in Every Month	Cooper
1986	Duchess Theatre, London	A Month of Sundays	Cooper
1987	Apollo Theatre, London	A Piece of my Mind	Ted Forrest

TABLE II

1987	Cambridge Theatre, London	Peter Pan	Mr Darling/ Captain Hook
1989	Yvonne Arnaud Theatre, Guildford	The Bread-Winner	
1992	Theatre Royal, Windsor	Natural Causes	Vincent
1995	Theatre Royal, Windsor/Richmond Theatre/Theatre Royal, Bath	Theft	Spriggs
1996	Chichester Festival Theatre	Lock Up Your Daughters	Justice Squeezum
1997	Hampstead Theatre	Heritage	Harry
1997–98	Theatre Royal, Bath	Heritage	Harry
2004–05	Theatre Royal, Windsor/Tour	Party Piece	Mr Hinson

BIBLIOGRAPHY

Books mentioned in the main text.

Ableman, Paul & Leon Griffiths (1991) *Straight Up: The autobiography of Arthur Daley*. Heinemann, London. (Audiobook read by George Cole.)

Collins, Joan (1996) *Second Act*. Boxtree, London.

Griffiths, Leon (1985) *Arthur Daley's Guide to Doing It Right!* Fontana, London. (Audiobook read by George Cole.)

Hawkins, Brian (2002) *The Phenomenon That Was Minder*. Chameleon Press, Hong Kong.

Lindsay, Norman (1960) *The Cautious Amorist*. World Distributors, London.

More, Kenneth (1979) *More or Less*. Coronet Books, London.

Root, Henry (1980) *The Henry Root Letters* (William Donaldson writing as Henry Root). Weidenfeld and Nicolson, London.

Sharpe, Tom (1975) *Blott on the Landscape*. Secker and Warburg, London. (Audiobook read by George Cole.)

Sim, Naomi (1987) *Dance and skylark: Fifty years with Alastair Sim*. Bloomsbury, London.

Terry-Thomas with Terry Daum (1990) *Terry-Thomas Tells Tales*. Robson Books, London.

Waterman, Dennis with Jill Arlon (2000) *ReMinder*. Hutchinson, London.

Westmacott, Mary (1997) *Giant's Bread* (Agatha Christie writing as Mary Westmacott). HarperCollins, London. (Audiobook read by George Cole.)

INDEX

For the purposes of this index, episodes are regarded as individual stories within a series in which the same character or characters appear in each story. Episode names are placed in quotation marks.

In a series in which the stories are generally unrelated and involve different characters, for example *Play of the Week*, the story names are italicised.

Names of characters played by George Cole are followed by (GC char). Other character names are followed by (char).

'A' or 'The' at the beginning of a title name are relocated to the end of the title name and follow a comma.

NB: The Index does not include characters, artists or performances that are mentioned in the Filmography, Table I or Table II but not mentioned in the main text.